Modern Popular Theatre

Theatre and Performance Practices

General Editors: Graham Ley and Jane Milling

Published

Christopher Baugh	*Theatre, Performance and Technology (2nd edn)*
Greg Giesekam	*Staging the Screen*
Deirdre Heddon	*Autobiography and Performance*
Deirdre Heddon and Jane Milling	*Devising Performance (Revised Edition)*
Helen Nicholson	*Applied Drama (2nd edn)*
Jason Price	*Modern Popular Theatre*
Cathy Turner and Synne K. Behrndt	*Dramaturgy and Performance*
Michael Wilson	*Storytelling and Theatre*
Philip B. Zarrilli, Jerri Daboo and Rebecca Loukes	*Acting*

Forthcoming

Mark Evans	*Performance, Movement and the Body*
Kerrie Schaefer	*Communities, Performance and Practice*

Theatre and Performance Practices Series
Series Standing Order
ISBN 978–1–4039–8735–8 hardcover
ISBN 978–1–4039–8736–5 paperback
(outside North America only)

You can receive future titles in this series as they are published by placing a standing order. Please contact your bookseller or, in the case of difficulty, write to us at the address below with your name and address, the title of the series and the ISBN quoted above.

Customer Services Department, Macmillan Distribution Ltd, Houndmills, Basingstoke, Hampshire, RG21 6XS, UK

Modern Popular Theatre

Jason Price

 palgrave

First published 2016 by
PALGRAVE

Palgrave in the UK is an imprint of Macmillan Publishers Limited,
registered in England, company number 785998, of 4 Crinan Street,
London, N1 9XW.

Palgrave Macmillan in the US is a division of St Martin's Press LLC,
175 Fifth Avenue, New York, NY 10010.

Palgrave is a global imprint of the above companies and is represented
throughout the world.

Palgrave® and Macmillan® are registered trademarks in the United States,
the United Kingdom, Europe and other countries.

ISBN 978–0–230–36894–1 hardback
ISBN 978–0–230–36895–8 paperback

This book is printed on paper suitable for recycling and made from fully
managed and sustained forest sources. Logging, pulping and manufacturing
processes are expected to conform to the environmental regulations of the
country of origin.

A catalogue record for this book is available from the British Library.

A catalog record for this book is available from the Library of Congress.

Printed in China

Contents

Acknowledgements

This book is the result of the support, advice and generosity of many people and organizations. I would like to start by thanking the Series Editors, Graham Ley and Jane Milling, for approaching me about a book on popular theatre and for their consistent encouragement and feedback throughout the writing process. I am especially grateful for Graham's comments on drafts of each chapter and for his help in resolving issues relating to structure late in the process. Thanks also go to the reviewers for their helpful feedback on the draft manuscript, and to the team at Palgrave for their patience. Any errors or faults in logic that remain within the book are completely my own doing. I take full responsibility for all of the book's shortcomings.

I would also like to extend my thanks to the theatre-makers and companies who appear in this study. I am grateful for your time and the generous access you gave me to your work and ideas. Thanks also to the School of English at the University of Sussex who provided me with a term of research leave and regular funding to complete this project. I have also been supported by my drama colleagues at Sussex, Sara Jane Bailes, David Barnett and William McEvoy, and by my Head of School, Tom Healy. I am grateful to you all for your advice, feedback and words of encouragement throughout this process.

Enormous thanks also go to my close friends, family and former teachers whose continued support makes lengthy projects like this more bearable. Mary Fleischer, Kathleen Rabensburg Laundy, Graham Ley, the late Tal Lostrocco, Christopher McCullough, Diana McGarr, Fred and Sheila Pankratz, Jim Rambo and Cindy SoRelle: it is because of your belief in me as teachers that I have landed where I have, and I am thankful every day that I had the opportunity to learn from you. Finally, I would like to thank my mom and dad, my brother Jamie and my partner Thomas. You may not have always understood what I was writing about, but you listened, encouraged and loved me anyway. I could not have managed to do this without you.

General Editors' Preface

This series sets out to explore key performance practices encountered in modern and contemporary theatre. Talking to students and scholars in seminar rooms and studios, and to practitioners in rehearsal, it became clear that there were widely used modes of practice that had received very little critical and analytical attention. In response, we offer these critical, research-based studies which draw on international fieldwork to produce fresh insight into a range of performance processes. Authors, who are specialists in their fields, have set each mode of practice in its social, political and aesthetic context. The series charts both a history of the development of modes of performance process and an assessment of their significance in contemporary culture.

Each volume is accessibly written, and gives a clear and pithy analysis of the historical and cultural development of a mode of practice. As well as offering readers a sense of the breadth of the field, the authors have also given key examples and performance illustrations. In different ways each book in the series asks readers to look again at processes and practices of theatre-making that seem obvious and self-evident, and to examine why and how they have developed as they have, and what their ideological content is. Ultimately the series aims to ask, what are the choices and responsibilities facing performance-makers today?

Graham Ley and Jane Milling

1 Introduction

What is Popular Theatre?

For many readers, the title *Modern Popular Theatre* likely conjures images of specific theatre productions, such as long-running commercial musical hits *Phantom of the Opera* or *Wicked*. This particular interpretation equates popular with audience viewing figures or longevity, making popular theatre an extension of popular culture like Hollywood movies or pop music. For something to be labelled popular, according to those 'criteria', it would have to be watched by a large number of people and be widely recognizable. While it is tempting to add 'financially successful' to these generic criteria, recent entertainment technologies like YouTube have shown us that this may not be the case. The comic antics of a house cat captured on a smartphone can now, through the Internet, be as widely viewed and subsequently recognizable as other forms of popular media, without significant expense to or financial gain for the house cat or her owner. Popularity is more connected to exposure than manufacture. It is about being widely consumed, shared and recognized. In theatrical terms, it could be argued that a commercial musical stands a greater chance of satisfying this than other forms of contemporary performance.

However, the definition of the field of popular theatre is not as straightforward as this. This is due largely to the slipperiness of the term popular and variations in how it can be applied to discussions about the theatre. For instance, the *Oxford English Dictionary* (OED) lists around a dozen definitions for the word popular. As an adjective, it could be used to delineate 'the people', a general public or community as well as the beliefs or attitudes they hold; cultural artefacts or activities that are intended for ordinary or common people, or which are made appropriate for their consumption; cultivating favour with

1

or supporting common people; or, more familiarly, liked or admired by many. The word may also be used to distinguish taste. Popular, in this sense, would refer to the culturally un-refined; as the OED defines it – 'vulgar, coarse, ill-bred'. In other contexts, you may find the word interchanged with the words *folk* or *mass*, as in folk or mass culture. Applying just a few of these definitions to performance would quickly generate a very extensive list.

It is understandable, therefore, why the field of popular theatre is a tricky one. The difficulty of defining it has meant that many of the available books on the topic are collections of essays that give isolated critical attention to specific practices, practitioners and forms as opposed to historical narratives of the field. This modern tradition of anthologizing the popular theatre began in the 1970s with David Mayer and Kenneth Richards's now out-of-print *Western Popular Theatre* (1977), a collection of essays covering a diverse range of performances and performance forms, including Aristophanes' *The Frogs*, Restoration pageants, and nineteenth-century American Wild West exhibitions. This was followed by a far more substantial collection edited by David Bradby, Louis James and Bernard Sharratt entitled *Performance and Politics in Popular Drama* (1980). Broken down into two thematic sections – nineteenth-century spectacle and twentieth-century political theatres – the book covers impressive territory, including melodrama, circus and equestrian performance, the work of Russian theatre director Vsevolod Meyerhold, the international communist-oriented Workers' Theatre Movement of the 1920s and 1930s, and German theatre director Erwin Piscator. The book's continuing relevance stems in part from the editors' deliberate choice to attempt to understand the popular on its own terms, giving consideration to the techniques and skills of the specialist popular performers as opposed to applying critical academic models of analysis borrowed from the study of theatrical texts. Bradby and his collaborators understood that such an approach contradicted the spirit of the popular, which, more often than not, had been deliberately excluded by the cultural authorities because it could not conform to the aesthetic criteria they set. The essays in Ros Merkin's edited collection *Popular Theatres?* published over a decade later (1994), grapple with the popular theatre in more contemporary performative contexts, acknowledging its role in the avant-garde as well as its incorporation into certain experimental theatre practices of the twentieth century. The most recent collection of essays on popular theatre is Joel Schechter's *Popular Theatre: A Sourcebook* (2003). Principally consisting of articles submitted to *The*

Drama Review since the 1960s, the book covers a range of periods, styles and practices, from *commedia dell'arte* to the work of contemporary American theatre director Julie Taymor. Like Bradby's text, it, too, groups practices and forms together in distinct thematic sections and offers rationalizations for these groupings in helpful introductions, giving a good sense of the linkages that can be found between popular theatre practices.

Combined, these collections usefully demonstrate the sheer variety of popular theatres and performance forms, as well as giving some sense of the character, skill, and politics that performing popular theatre involves in specific contexts. But, ultimately, they offer isolated snapshots of the popular from various historical and critical perspectives. Beyond very general thematic categories that serve to anchor particular essays together, little attempt is made within these collections to historicize or rationalize the field as a whole. While I acknowledge the complexity of such a task owing to the tremendous scope of the field – as those earlier studies demonstrate all too well – I have written this book in order to do that, albeit with a principal focus on twentieth-century popular theatre. What a survey of these earlier collections also reveals is a limited engagement with the immense body of popular culture theories developed throughout the twentieth century, such as the important work done by Pierre Bourdieu, John Fiske, Stuart Hall and Raymond Williams, among others. This book aims to remedy this as well.

Definitions and Central Concerns

Popular theatre is often generically defined as theatre by and for the people. One of the principal methodological problems with studying popular theatre is determining who those people are at any particular point. Cultural theorist Stuart Hall, among others, has critiqued the ambiguity of the collective subject 'the people', which enables it to be all too easily co-opted by those who seek to realize their own agendas (2009, p. 518). There is a clear danger in believing in a social and historical category known as 'the people' that neutralizes individual differences to make room for sweeping generalizations and assumptions about distinct cultures. It also makes the field of popular culture, including popular theatres, exceedingly large and subsequently difficult to study. A short discussion of the lineage of the word popular and how it has been applied to 'the people' will help narrow the field.

The Popular versus Power

The English word popular has its roots in the Latin word *populāris*, which, in ancient Rome, meant belonging to, supported or admired by ordinary people, and was opposed to *patrician*, or the upper classes. The term arrives in English from both Latin and French sources. Popular appears in English for the first time in the fifteenth century in a translation of French physician Guy de Chauliac's important medical treatise *Chirurgia Magna*, where he explains that to be '*populer*' is to be 'knowen to the common pepul (sic)' (OED). While 'common' in this context appears to imply a class division, Chauliac is referring to what might be understood now as *common knowledge*. In French, the word *populaire*, used to describe 'ordinary people', emerges sometime in the thirteenth century, while its extended use to describe the general public at large emerges in the early fourteenth. It is thus likely that a version of the word in English was already in circulation, borrowed from the French, by the time Chauliac's text was translated into English.

By the sixteenth century, the term appears to be more widely used in English and it possessed multiple meanings. The use of the word to designate the general public was cemented by the legal practice of *action popular*, which first began in England in the late fifteenth century. *Accions populers*, as they were known, enabled citizens to sue, for themselves or on behalf of the monarch, anyone found in breach of a penal statute. Writing about the practice in the late sixteenth century, Morag Shiach points out that they were 'not given to one man specifically but generally to any of the Queen's people' (1989, p. 22). A similar use of the term appears in the writings of William Thomas, a scholar and clerk of King Edward VI's Privy Council. In his essay 'Whether it be better for a Commonwealth that the power be in Nobility or in the Commonality', written for the young king in the early 1550s, Thomas categorizes everyone but the king and nobility as the 'commonality', or general public.

What thus emerges early in the history of the term is that popular implies a division between the people and those who control them. Understanding this, Hall came to see the popular as 'the people versus the power bloc' (2009, p. 517). It is thus the politics of the relationship between the general public and those in the 'power bloc' that is involved in establishing each category. That is, the popular is defined, in part, by its exclusion from power; and power is defined through its domination and oppression of popular classes. For this reason, many cultural theorists discuss popular culture (which would include the theatre) as a cultural struggle, a process of negotiations, dominations and subordination that operate to establish the popular in relation to power in any given period.

While there is a tendency to view the power relationships bound up in the popular in terms of the class-consciousness and cultural struggles brought on by economic capitalism, it can be seen by how the term was used in the sixteenth century – 200 years before the Industrial Revolution and the onset of modern capitalism – that there was an awareness of power relations and a dominated social category known as the popular even then. Furthermore, if understanding of the term is limited only to social class, this overlooks other forms of subordination that produce similar, i.e. popular, cultural struggles. As historian David Mayer observes in his seminal essay 'Towards a Definition of Popular Theatre', while the popular theatre may well serve 'the masses', it has historically tended to emerge from the 'lower' in society: 'lower per capita income, lower level of education and literacy, lower interest in or knowledge of aesthetic criteria, lower level of political influence' (1977, p. 263). The term may thus be applied sweepingly to theatres intended for all subordinated peoples within a society, as in 'the lower classes', or marginalized social groups, like ethnic minorities or lesbian, gay, bisexual and transgender (LGBT) people. Even with these qualifiers, the performative scope of the popular theatre is tremendous, from performances found entertaining by popular audiences, as the early nineteenth-century music hall was for the British working class, to those that openly address the issues and needs of specific communities. In this regard, the popular theatre might be viewed as a form of theatre that reflects the needs and tastes of subordinated peoples and the communities with which they identify.

Low and High Art

So the word popular can be used not only to distinguish who has or does not have power in a society, but also to discuss the activities, behaviours and general culture of subordinated social groups. Part of the cultural struggle played out between the people and the power bloc is found in the establishment of low and high cultural categories. The art of the elite, or those in a position of dominance, is usually considered to be 'high art'. High art is constructed according to specific aesthetic criteria and designed to appeal to those who have received the education required to understand or appreciate it. French sociologist Pierre Bourdieu refers to this as the 'pure gaze', which he explains is a 'historical invention [...] which imposes its own norms on both the production and consumption of [art]' (1984, p. xxvi). Low art, by comparison, is defined against high: instead of emerging from specifically constructed aesthetic criteria, low or popular art emerges from the ordinary experiences of the people. In contrast to the pure gaze, Bourdieu explains that low art, which he refers to as the popular aesthetic, embraces human experiences and tends to construct artistic representations that are familiar to its audiences (ibid., p. 24). The 'pure' aesthetic, on the other hand, rejects this familiarity, perceiving it to be common and 'easy' (ibid.). Bourdieu fundamentally believes that the dichotomy between high and low art has been constructed by the dominant classes 'to fulfill a social function of legitimating social differences' (ibid., p. xxx). The distinction between high and low art is thus one component of the cultural struggle between subordinate and dominant social groupings embedded in the term popular.

On one level, the low/high categories when applied would see the division of what are generally perceived as easy forms from more sophisticated ones; for instance, this might mean pitting the circus (low/popular) against the plays of Samuel Beckett (high/pure). However, if the popular is viewed as being applicable to a range of subordinated cultures, from the generic to the more specific, then such a straightforward application of Bourdieu's distinctions is limiting. There are occasions when work developed for or on behalf of specific subordinated social groups may have more in common with high art aesthetic strategies than low, but it is the content of the work, its venue or its audience that prevents it from being accepted as 'high art'. Work that openly champions LGBT communities, for instance, may have been historically discriminated against owing to its articulation of what dominant classes had established to be sexual taboos. Consequently, a performance that transgresses the ethical censors regardless of its aesthetic may be labelled as crude, vulgar or controversial and subsequently categorized as 'low' art.

Hegemony and Popular Prejudice

While high and low artistic categories may imply a cultural break between the people and those in power, this does not mean that power is not interested in what subordinate groups consume. Those in power are often acutely aware of the influence popular theatre has with the communities it controls and have subsequently sought to co-opt it for their own purposes. David Mayer has identified three principal ways in which this has occurred. Firstly, government officials might commission popular performances to appeal to the masses in order to impress 'symbols and personalities of authority […] upon [them]' (Mayer, 1977, p. 263). The opening ceremonies for the Olympic Games are a modern example of this. For these, host nations *stage* their cultural and political achievements in a spectacular way to impress not only their own citizens but also a global televised audience. Power thus exploits an impressive popular mode – the spectacle – in order to demonstrate its strength and bolster its position in world politics. The second way power co-opts the popular is by commissioning popular entertainments for their own pleasures, thus *appropriating* the form and making it part of the dominant culture. The *commedia dell'arte*, the Italian form popular across Europe between the sixteenth and eighteenth centuries, is often given as an example of this kind of co-option. As Eugene van Erven has observed, 'This type of improvisational farce originated as a theatre form for and by the people, but was later absorbed by the aristocracy', principally through the act of patronization (1988, p. 6). Where this occurs with popular theatre, two things happen: firstly, the subversive potential of the form (that is, its ability to speak on behalf of the people) is neutered; and, secondly, the form is placed out of reach of its traditional popular audiences. On a much darker level, the co-opted form may be reintroduced in an amended form to popular audiences as a mouthpiece for the powerful. Hence, a form's popularity becomes confused when co-opted by power. This is closely connected to Mayer's third and final observation regarding power's influence on the popular: if the form is seen as openly resistant to the will of those in power, it will be corrected, and if it cannot be, it will be outlawed (1977, pp. 263–264).

In contemporary popular culture studies the attempts by those in power to label (low/high) or co-opt popular forms are recognized to be strategies by which *hegemony* is established and maintained. Coined by Italian Marxist Antonio Gramsci in the early twentieth century, the term hegemony is used to signify the process by which the powerful seek to impose their own interests on those they dominate. By imposing and naturalizing their views as *the* views of society, the dominant classes marginalize those of subordinate groups, which results over time in the acceptance of the dominant views as if they were their own. Consent, Gramsci explains, is fundamentally achieved through a process of education and state coercion. At the social level, 'organic intellectuals', or class specialists, help social groups understand (and accept) their place in society (Gramsci, 1971, p. 5). This includes educational institutions and 'organisms to promote so-called "high-culture" in all fields of science and technology' (ibid., p. 10). The State's role is more disciplinary, offering corrective training through the laws created in the dominant group's interests (ibid., p. 12). Readers familiar with philosopher Louis Althusser's concept of the Ideological State Apparatus (ISA) will likely sense similarities between the two.[1] Althusser builds on Gramsci's notion of hegemony to explain how the State achieves consent through ideological manipulation of the masses. An ISA can include religious and educational institutions, the family, culture, laws and forms of communication (like television or the Internet), which train people to think and behave as the dominant groups need them to in order to retain power.

The popular is one of the major battlegrounds on which hegemonic wars have been fought. As well as the strategies already exposed by Bourdieu and Mayer, there were other ways in which those in power have historically discredited the popular. Central to this was the way the popular became defined by dominant prejudices. It is not difficult to find examples dating back to the sixteenth century of subordinated people being discussed as ignorant, ill-behaved and prone to violence. In Thomas's essay mentioned earlier, for instance, he explains that '[N]one is to be compared to the frenzy of the people' (Thomas, 1721 [1550], p. 374). While he acknowledges the oppression of common people at the hands of the nobility and concedes that such tyranny is unfortunate, he ultimately believes that the people are too ignorant and irritable to rule. The Italian variant *popolaccio*, meaning 'the grosse, vile, common people', was also in circulation at the time (Skeat, 1911, p. 402). This definition not only characterized the people, but also was extended beyond social categories to define their 'low' behaviours and culture. For instance, in John Florio's Tudor translation of *The Essays of Montaigne*, an extensive collection of essays written by Michel de Montaigne of France in the latter part of the sixteenth century, there is a reference to the behaviour of popular men:

> it is a custome of popular or base men to call for minstrels or singers at feasts [...] and pleasing entertainment, wherewith men of conceit and understanding know how to enterfeast and entertain themselves (sic). (Montaigne, 1967, p. 380)

Montaigne makes a crucial distinction here regarding class and behaviour. The conflation of popular and base suggests that Montaigne is intending to be disparaging about the behaviours of those from the lower classes. A related derogatory use of the term can be found in the writings of Gabriel Harvey. Writing about a series of uninspiring debates he attended in 1573, he lamented their 'popular and plausible themes' (quoted in Shiach, 1989, p. 27). In this sense, popular is used to describe anything perceived to be naïve, simple or uncomplicated. Combining all of these definitions, a fairly unsavoury profile emerges. To be popular is to be ignorant, irrationally violent, crude, uncouth and to be easily amused by vulgar and mindless things.

The Working Class

These particular prejudices intensified with the onset of economic capitalism in the West in the late eighteenth century. During this period of dramatic social change, the working class emerges for the first time as a coherent social body. This was the consequence of a number of factors, chief among them the processes of industrialization – the catalyst for the new economic system – and the workforce required to run and maintain new manufacturing technologies. E.P. Thompson observes that during the latter part of the eighteenth century and the first part of the nineteenth many 'English working people came to feel an identity of interests between themselves and against their rulers and employers' (2009, p. 43). While the working class was in effect forming, the dominant classes were being radically restructured. The new middle class, or bourgeoisie, was struggling to win recognition of its power from other historically dominant groups, like the aristocracy. John Storey observes that this resulted in the dominant classes losing, for a short period, 'the means to control the culture of the subordinate classes' (2006, p. 13). Once this was regained in the nineteenth century, the new working class came to be regarded as the popular 'masses' and a new term, 'popular culture', began to be used to describe or qualify their culture (OED).[2] The scorn once reserved for generic popular social categories was subsequently transferred to the working class and to discussions of their popular culture. An example of this can be found in Matthew Arnold's book *Culture and Anarchy*, published in 1869. He wrote:

> Every time that we snatch up a vehement opinion in ignorance and passion, every time that we long to crush an adversary by sheer violence, [...] every time that we are brutal, [...] every time that we trample savagely on the fallen, – he has found in his own bosom the eternal spirit of the masses. (2009 [1869], p. 9)

Arnold's principal concern in *Culture and Anarchy* was over the preservation of high culture. For him, culture was the study of perfection: 'the best knowledge and thoughts of the time', which he believed only a small minority of trained individuals fully understood (ibid., p. 7). The presence and power of the working class suggested to Arnold that this was in danger of being lost, either because of a levelling down of culture so that the working classes could grasp it or through the imposition of the workers' popular culture from below. Arnold's proposed solution to this problem was the development of a strong centralized State that would educate the working class into submission. In contrast, he believed that the State should provide middle-class children with an education that would prepare them to assume power.

Arnold was not alone in his fears of the working class's newly found power. Many of the discourses around culture that emerged in the nineteenth century pitted the 'barbaric' and immoral popular culture of the workers against the 'refined' and moral high culture of the bourgeoisie. Texts like Arnold's might thus be seen as a kind of cultural propaganda against popular culture, certainly intended to help curtail its spread and influence. The press, literature, theatre and other forums where ideas were rehearsed or exchanged offered the means by which these disciplinary discourses could be inserted and circulated through society. An example that John Fiske gives in *Understanding Popular Culture* (1989) is cockfighting. In the nineteenth century, cockfighting was a popular activity among working-class men. However, many in the upper classes regarded cockfighting as vulgar. Consequently, a public discourse soon emerged making it responsible for high crime rates and moral corruption in rural areas (Fiske, 1989, p. 71). Often, Fiske points out, the social threats identified by the middle classes focused on the unruly worker's body: 'the pleasures and excesses of the body – drunkenness, sexuality, idleness, rowdiness – were seen as threats to social order' (ibid., p. 75). It should come as no surprise then that Britain's popular music halls, which invited all of these excesses in various ways, also became a prime target for legislation.

In terms of defining the popular theatre, the cultural struggles that characterize working class and bourgeois relations in the nineteenth century are especially important. From the point at which the working class becomes politically and socially visible, the popular theatre is seen as accommodating their interests and pleasures. In addition, due to the intense political battles fought between the working classes and the bourgeois in the nineteenth century and well into the twentieth, the popular theatre acquires a distinctly political reputation. Even now the popular theatre is often regarded as a radical, politically progressive form of theatre that is hostile to mainstream and/or commercial forms of theatre.

Folk, Mass and Popular Culture

As well as popular culture, folk and mass culture also began to be used in the nineteenth century to signify non-elite cultural activities and forms. While these terms have been used interchangeably in certain critical and historical contexts, contemporary cultural theorists tend to frown on such laxity. This is because, technically, each term refers to quite specific *processes* by which culture is produced.

Of the three terms, *folk* and *popular* share the greatest similarities. Folk stems from the German *das volk*, meaning the people. Thus, folk culture refers to, as popular culture does, a people's culture. The distinction, however, is that folk cultures are typically considered to be pre-industrial and non-commercial, formed by communities or tribes outside of the direct influence of power. For this reason, Stuart Hall and Paddy Whannel have defined folk cultures as being 'created by the people from below' (1964, p. 59). This is congruent with Fiske's definition, although he clarifies that it is a 'social culture [that] [...] is typically produced and reproduced communally' (1989, p. 173). Examples of this would include the folk songs of the Appalachian region of the United States, or the powwows or other cultural practices of Native American tribal communities. Unlike a popular form, such as the British music hall, these forms developed as expressions of the values, faiths or other beliefs of their originating communities/cultures without a concern for wider systems of power or for the commercial potential of the materials produced. By contrast, the popular performances associated with nineteenth-century British music halls were not constructed as expressions of the everyday practices of working people, but by others (sometimes from the same class, sometimes not) in order to amuse and delight them. Still, it was in the financial interest of music hall owners to accommodate its spectators' tastes and, therefore, the acts they programmed would be constructed as a 'negotiation' of sorts, taking into consideration what the intended audiences may appreciate and the resources and talent at their disposal. So while *folk* and *popular* may be used to label the culture of 'the people', current thinking suggests they refer to different cultural formations and to the distinct processes they undergo to construct their cultural resources.

With folk, that culture is people-led; with popular, it is what the people make of the resources available in the social system in which they are dominated.

While I fundamentally agree with the definitions offered by Hall, Whannel and Fiske, it is also important to recognize folk culture as a nineteenth-century invention that forms part of the disciplinary discourses levelled at the working class discussed earlier (i.e. Arnold). As Georgina Boyes helpfully clarifies in her book *The Imagined Village*, folk culture emerged in Britain both as a discipline of study and a cultural movement at a point where people were beginning to sense the cultural impact of industrialization and urbanization – in particular, it was discovered that people's non-literary cultural traditions, especially songs and dances, were being forgotten. Once again, the working class was blamed for failing to maintain its own culture. Boyes writes:

> The Folk, it was authoritatively maintained, had imperilled the existence of their own culture. When they moved into towns during the Industrial Revolution, they abandoned their priceless heritage of folk traditions – songs, dances, customs, and stories all ceased to be performed. [...] Folk culture hadn't simply proved incapable of transference into a new urban context, an irreplaceable loss had almost occurred because the Folk had been wilfully derelict in their duty towards their culture. (2010, p. 63)

Folk culture was framed by leaders of the British Folk Revival as a heroic, organic culture of the people.[3] It was argued that this stood in sharp contrast to the vulgar popular culture the nineteenth-century worker showed a preference for. Instead of seeing the popular culture as evolving with the people who make it, the folk revivalists had an invested interest in highlighting the distinction between the pre- and post-industrial 'people'. The folk revivalist argument was that prior to the onset of the Industrial Revolution, the people happily accepted their place in society and went about singing songs and devising dances as expressions of their everyday experiences for their own amusement. After they left the country to find work in industrial cities, so the argument goes, they became politically restless mobs with an appetite for vulgar popular forms. This clearly rewrites history, as the discussion of the term popular earlier demonstrates.

So folk culture, as a concept, was a nineteenth-century invention used to distinguish between the popular cultures of the pre-industrial period from the popular culture of the newly formed working class. This is why theorists, including Hall and Fiske, mark the historical distinction between folk and popular culture as falling at the point of the Industrial Revolution. Another reason this periodization has been applied is due to the emergence of an industry producing cultural commodities targeted at the 'masses'. These commodities are usually referred to as *mass culture*. Unlike folk culture, which apparently comes from the people without coercion or influence from power, mass culture is produced by the dominant and imposed onto the subordinate classes. Popular culture, therefore, stands as the middle point between the two. A list of mass cultural products at the present time would include, among other things, pop music, Hollywood films, and magazines concerned with fashion or celebrities. Most commercial productions, like Broadway musicals, can also be classified as forms of mass culture because they are mass-produced, branded commercial 'products'. For this reason, this book treads carefully around blockbuster musicals and other commercial theatre productions because they resist straightforward classification under the term popular.

While scholars like Dwight Macdonald saw mass culture as revolutionary and democratic, 'breaking down the old barriers of class, tradition, taste and dissolving all cultural distinctions' (1953, p. 5), others saw it as diluting high culture and imposing dominant views on the undiscriminating masses. In the latter category there is the literary critic F.R. Leavis and his wife, Queenie, who were particularly influential in developing thinking about mass culture in the early twentieth century. In *Mass Civilization and Minority Culture* (1933) Leavis extends Arnold's argument regarding the erosion of culture to the tastes of the working classes. Like Arnold, Leavis believed that culture had historically been the concern of 'a very small minority' who were 'capable of unprompted, first-hand judgement' on aesthetic matters, and that it should continue to be so (2006 [1933], p. 12). He believed industrialization and a consumer culture were working to erode the role of these cultural gatekeepers, as people were led to choose cultural products through the popular press, the radio and advertising. The Leavises also believed that some of the new cultural modes were addictive, distracting and promoted a dangerous form of passivity. They saw the cinema, for instance, as involving 'complete surrender' and fostering a kind of 'hypnotic receptivity' (Storey, 2006, p. 18), while the radio was putting an end to critical thought (ibid., p. 19).

Members of the Frankfurt School, the affiliation of Marxist critical theorists that emerged in the 1920s, shared some of the Leavises' views. Chief among these were Theodor Adorno and Max Horkheimer, whose seminal text *Dialectic of Enlightenment* (1944) offers an incisive critique of the 'culture industry', which they believed was responsible for reducing cultural products to a series of formulaic, easily reproducible, hypnotic pleasures that functioned to pacify the masses into subordination. Just like the mass-produced cultural commodities consumed by the public, Adorno and Horkheimer believed 'The culture industry as a whole [had] molded men as a type unfailingly reproduced in every product' (Adorno & Horkheimer, 1997 [1944], p. 127). Their complaint was not so much about the taste of the working classes – although, it is clear that they found much of what was consumed by the working class 'popular' in the worst sense of the word – but, instead, that popular amusements had been co-opted by those in power, repackaged and returned to the people in a much more dangerous form.

There are two principal concerns informing Adorno and Horkheimer's argument – and both are connected to Gramsci's concept of hegemony discussed earlier. Firstly, in light of the Second World War, both writers (who were Jewish) were seeking to understand how the German people could have allowed something as colossally horrible as the holocaust to happen. Complacency brought about by the manipulation of the culture industry was just one explanation. Secondly, as fellow Frankfurt School theorist Herbert Marcuse would later argue in *One Dimensional Man* (1964), the democratization of culture that the culture industry had imposed was 'historically premature; it established cultural equality while preserving domination' (1968, p. 64). In other words, the equality one might perceive through a culture of choice is illusory in a society in which domination still exists. Most worryingly, it fixes those inequalities by depoliticizing the subordinated classes by means of manipulative cultural products.

The ideas of the Frankfurt School make several problematic assumptions about the working classes and consumer habits that have provoked criticism. Among the earliest critics to counter these views was Raymond Williams, who pointed out that equating mass culture and the working class is unfair because mass culture is produced by the 'commercial bourgeoisie, so that their use became, and has remained, characteristically capitalist in its methods of production and distribution' (Williams, 1957, p. 30). The attack here is mainly directed at those, like the Leavises, who fail to grasp that it is their class, the bourgeoisie, that manufactures the culture they are taking issue with. Equally critical of this viewpoint were Stuart Hall and Paddy Whannel. In their book *The Popular Arts* (1964) they make the point that artefacts that may become popular culture are not simply mass-produced products of the culture industries, but are instead artefacts which are able to reinstate the relationships familiar from folk culture: 'Such art has in common with folk art the genuine contact between audience and performer: but it differentiates from folk art in that is an individualized art, the art of the known performer' (Hall & Whannel, 1964, p. 66). This sees mass culture as not simply one-directional (imposed from above), but influenced significantly from the folk cultures from below. While Hall concedes that mass culture can be manipulative – as a capitalist creation it needed to be so in order to survive – it never operates without the consent of the people (2009, p. 508). Fiske concurs:

> A homogenous, externally produced culture cannot be sold ready-made to the masses: culture simply does not work like that. Nor do the people behave or live like the masses, an aggregation of alienated, one-dimensional persons whose only consciousness is false, whose only relationship to the system that enslaves them is one of unwitting (if not willing) dupes. (1989, p. 23)

While it is true that banal, mindless or even manipulative cultural commodities do become part of the popular culture, many are outright rejected. Others, still, are edited by the people before becoming part of their culture. Fundamentally, the people will recognize a popular text as being relevant to their personal circumstances. As Fiske observes, the popular text will 'contain both the forces of domination and the opportunities to speak against them' (ibid., p. 25). The whole of a society's popular culture will often bear the scars (hypocrisies, tensions, contradictions, etc.) of the struggles that made it, with power, complacency and dissent usually constituting parts of its very fabric. It is also important to recognize that this is a constantly changing process. It is wrong to assume that once something has become part of the popular culture, a performance or other cultural artefact will not later be rejected and replaced by something else. This is what the folk revivalists failed to understand. Popular culture changes with the needs and tastes of the people. Popular theatre is thus culturally subjective and evolving, and popular theatre forms are especially prone to changes and mutations.

Recognizing the differences between folk, mass and popular culture is important in understanding what popular theatre is. My suggestion here, and one that has proved a guiding principal in selecting the theatre practices discussed in this book, is that popular theatres are of interest to or operate on behalf of subordinate social groups. They are produced out of a collection of cultural resources available to the people in developed societies – which may very well include 'folk' traditions of the past and 'mass' culture of the present – and so are a complex expression of the will, knowledge and interests of peoples and those who dominate them. Hall describes this as 'the double movement of containment and resistance', which is found in all popular culture (2009, p. 509). The popular forms of performance discussed in this book all carry this double movement, although this may not always be equally distributed through a practice. Inevitably this means that some popular theatres may seem simple, naïve or spectacularly vulgar and thus appear to satisfy the historical popular stereotypes developed by the culturally elite. Others, however, will openly seek to dismantle those stereotypes and the dominant positions that developed them by placing greater emphasis on the forms' potential for resistance. Regardless of where this emphasis rests, it must be remembered that in each case the performance is designed to appeal to the interests or needs of a specific target audience. I shall make no value judgements about which strategy is better, more interesting or politically meaningful. In this book, the focus is on recording popular practices, not contributing to historical prejudices about what constitutes good or bad art. But any book which seeks to give an account of the popular theatre will need to grapple with those prejudices on some level as they form part of the critical dominant discourses which have given shape to many, particularly resistant, popular forms.

People's Theatres: Theories and Early Practice

While the subject of this book is explicitly that of the modern popular theatre, the question of what might constitute a meaningful modern people's theatre dates back to the eighteenth century. One of the first major calls appears in the writings of Genevan philosopher Jean-Jacques Rousseau (1712–1778), who was largely dissatisfied with the theatrical offerings of his time. In fact, in his *Letter to M. D'Alembert on the Theatre* (1758), his most important text on theatre, he advocates censoring it. His reasons were political. Dramas about former 'tyrants or heroes', he claimed, 'give us vain admiration for power and greatness' (Rousseau, 1960 [1758], p. 116), while comedies which seek to provoke laughter through satire or caricature 'serve as an instrument for factions, parties, and private vengeances' (ibid., p. 121). In a democratic republic, which Rousseau advocated for in place of autocratic governance, it would be disastrous if immoral behaviour or radical political ideas, like those often implicitly promoted through drama, were allowed to take hold in a portion of a society in which everyone has input into how it is managed. Doing so, he believed, would jeopardize its success. The most appropriate performances for republican audiences would be able to both educate the audience and promote positive social values. While some plays might do this, like 'those of the Greeks, from the past misfortunes of the country or the present failings of the people' (ibid., p. 120), Rousseau saw the most potential in public festivals. He regarded these to be unifying, educational and entertaining, thus promoting a more harmonious, unified society.

Alongside Rousseau, French philosopher and critic Denis Diderot (1713–1784) was also interested in people's theatre, although he saw potential in something more akin to that of the ancient Greeks. This can be seen in his '*Deuxieme entretien sur le Fils naturel*' ('Second Interview on Natural Son') (1757), where he writes of the 'power' to be found in the 'great assemblage' of ancient Greek audiences, and the impact such gatherings were to have on the population (Diderot, 2011 [1757]).[4] Rousseau's disciple Louis-Sébastian Mercier (1740–1814) also contributed to the debate, more or less unifying Diderot's and Rousseau's thoughts into a proposal for a theatre 'inspired by and intended for the people' (Rolland, 1918, p. 67). Mercier did not call for a theatre as restricted in content or form, as Rousseau's had been; rather, he conceived of it as being 'as broad as the universe', allowing for multiple perspectives and interests to be taken into account (ibid.). And yet the outcome of such a theatre would be to produce a 'moral spectacle' capable of 'mould[ing] the morals and manners of the citizens', and would thus still be Rousseauian in its functionality (ibid.).

The immediate impact of these ideas can be seen in the republican performances given around the time of the French Revolution (1789–1799), most especially Rousseau's with the revolutionary *fêtes*, which were public festivals and celebrations. These were used frequently during and after the French Revolution to celebrate victories, commemorate the dead and to bolster support for the war. Many of the Parisian *fêtes* took place on the Champs de Mars, the large esplanade to the north of the *École Militaire*, which was then used for military drills and public gatherings. The spectacle of a *fête* could consist of many features: military parades, mock battles, the singing of patriotic songs and anthems, the staging of military plays, firework displays, the burning of effigies, and other pageantry. For Maximilien Robespierre's 'Festival of the Supreme Being' in June 1794, designed by artist Jacques-Louis David, a mountain was built in the centre of the Champs de Mars on and around which grand parades, speeches and music were set. It was considered one's patriotic duty to attend, which meant that usually thousands of people were in attendance. As this suggests, the *fêtes* produced during this period were large-scale public performances designed to communicate, in essence, the ambitions and pride of the new republic, while simultaneously legitimizing its power and mobilizing support from citizens.

Another kind of people's theatre that emerged during the French Revolution is represented by Sylvain Maréchal's *The Last Judgement of Kings*, a revolutionary drama first performed in October 1793 at the Théâtre de la République in Paris.[5] The play mixed spectacle, audience participation and blatant anti-monarchist politics, and was made and performed for *sans-culottes* audiences.[6] *The Last Judgement of Kings* tells the story of a Robinson Crusoe-like figure, known simply as Old Man, who has been living on a semi-deserted volcanic island, having been banished there by the French monarchy after he protested the rape of his daughter at the hands of the aristocracy. One day, a ship of *sans-culottes* arrives on the island, seeking a place to deposit all the monarchs of Europe who had been overthrown in a collective uprising by the people of all European nations. The Old Man welcomes the news and invites the *sans-culottes* to deposit the former rulers on his island. The rulers, which include the Pope and Russia's Catherine II, are presented as comic caricatures that bicker and fight with one another for small scraps of food. The island quickly descends into chaos, made worse by the eruption of the island's volcano. In the play's final moments, the ground opens up and consumes the former rulers while the *sans-culottes* safely sail back to their new republican nations with the Old Man.

While this may not have been exactly what Mercier had in mind when he theorized a people's theatre, it was certainly 'inspired by and intended for' a targeted, subordinate audience (i.e. the *sans-culottes*). It also deliberately broke with the neo-classical style characteristic of other French theatre of the period, in favour of a bluntly political and spectacular approach more in keeping with the cultural and political views of its spectators. Scholar Erica Joy Mannucci has pointed out that in drawing on archetypal imagery, like the deserted island, primitivist ritualism and the old wizened man, Maréchal also 'set out to involve them on an emotional level' and in a more 'immediate way' than other performances did at the time (Mannucci, 2004, p. 242). Interestingly, *The Last Judgement of Kings* also had the support of the new government, which ensured there was sufficient gunpowder for the performance's spectacular volcanic finale – a rather remarkable fact considering the country was engaged in counter-revolutionary battles with Austria, Britain and the Dutch Republic. That a performance such as this was recognized as important enough to justify the use of valuable gunpowder during a time of warfare is no doubt indicative of how fragile the political conditions were in France at the time, and how vital it was to keep the revolutionary audience on the side of the new republican government.

In the latter part of the nineteenth century the theory and practice of Naturalism emerged as a theatrical form that sought to represent the lives of ordinary people. Influenced by Darwin's theory of evolution and developments in photography, naturalists sought to make theatre within four walls relevant to society once more by depicting everyday life through objective imitation. This meant that social concerns, such as the contrast between the rich and poor, gender inequality and even sexual taboos, among other issues not traditionally explored on stage, were chosen and represented in near photographic detail. Spectators who chose to go to these productions were being asked to consume more explicit material than they had previously encountered on the stage. The movement's leader, Émile Zola (1840–1902), was motivated by the belief that human behaviour was directly linked to heredity and social environment, and argued in 'Naturalism in the Theatre' (1881) that the theatre needed to be able to show this connection and its material consequences. Zola's ideas were ideologically and politically congruent with those of many socialists, who saw opportunities for representing the plight of the industrial working class. Naturalism's recognized appeal to socialists, paired with what some believed to be inappropriate subject matter, made it doubly problematic with the authorities. Consequently, many naturalist plays were banned from being given public performances throughout Europe.

Many wished to see the possibilities of this theatre and sought ways to bypass the censor and get new plays produced. While censors could ban a play from being given a public performance, they had little jurisdiction over what was performed inside private theatres. Consequently, many early naturalist dramas received their premieres in exclusive members-only theatres. These included André Antoine's Théâtre Libre in Paris, Otto Brahm's Freie Bühne in Berlin, and J.P. Green's Independent Theatre in London. Each of these venues produced similar repertoires of plays, including works by Henrik Ibsen, Gerhart Hauptmann and Leo Tolstoy. Although some may have acknowledged that the work they produced had socialist undertones, many were not deliberately presenting it for political reasons. Their motivations, instead, were largely aesthetic. And while some of the material performed might be loosely defined as 'popular' in the sense that it dealt with issues affecting the working classes at the time, the clubs' memberships, consisting primarily of the literary and cultural intelligentsia, could hardly be defined as such. Even had workers wished to join the Théâtre Libre, the Freie Bühne or the Independent Theatre to experience the new naturalist drama, the subscription fees would have prevented many from doing so. Due to their financial and intellectual exclusivity, then, one might see these organizations as distinctly *un-popular*.

It was in part the frustration arising from the conflict between the inaccessibility of these venues and the recognized social value of the new works they produced that led to one of the most significant people's theatres in history: the Freie Volksbühne (Free People's Theatre). The Freie Volksbühne was established in Berlin in 1890 by Bruno Wille, Wilhelm Bölsche and Julius Türk with the intention of staging contemporary, socially relevant plays, and informative talks about them, for working-class audiences. Like the other independent theatres mentioned, the Freie Volksbühne was a members-only organization, but the subscription fees were set at prices workers could afford to pay. While subscriptions fluctuated significantly throughout the first season, which included productions of Ibsen's *Pillars of Society* and Hauptmann's *Before Sunrise* – plays already staged by the other independent theatres – upward of around 4000 people are thought to have seen a production in the theatre's inaugural year.

By the start of the second season, divisions developed within the organization about its political commitment. Some members argued for a more openly socialist programme that could give the workers a political education. Others, notably Wille, insisted that to align their work with a specific political system or party would make the association less appealing to some members of the public. Art's role, in his view, was not to indoctrinate but to aesthetically enrich.[7] The issue would eventually split the organization. At the end of the second season, Wille left and formed the Neue Freie Volksbühne, which would remain a politically neutral organization. Despite their different attitudes towards the function of their theatres, John Willett points out that the programmes for both organizations were remarkably similar (1988, pp. 21–22). Perhaps the most significant of the early productions was Gerhart Hauptmann's *The Weavers*, which was produced by all three of the Freie theatres before 1895. The play depicts the events leading up to the Silesian weavers' rebellion of 1844, which was predicated on the use of new, machine technologies in the weaving industry that made weaving fabric by hand a nearly obsolete occupation. This resulted in widespread poverty, starvation and anger among weaving communities. In the play, the character of Dreissiger, a bourgeois manufacturer who purchases fabric from the weavers, is equally troubled by the rapid changes taking place to his industry, and the impact this was having on his business and the weaver community. Despite poor business, he tries to create opportunities for the weavers, even purchasing their cloth when he knows it is unlikely he will be able to sell it on. Nonetheless, anger among the weavers spreads, resulting in a rebellion in which Dreissiger's home is destroyed. In the final moments of the play, the rebellion is forcibly quashed by the Prussian military.

The Weavers proved to be a hit with working-class audiences. With a cast of over fifty performers and five distinct realistic settings needed for the play's five acts, it was not just its politics that pleased audiences, it was also the spectacle, especially that of the full-blown weavers rebellion that results in the destruction of Dreissiger's house. In Davies's account of the Freie Volksbühne production, the cheers and applause were so extensive following that scene that the police apparently did not believe it would ever end (2000, p. 52). Perhaps ironically, while some audiences regarded the play as championing the cause of the working class, and therefore politically progressive, through its depiction of mob-like behaviour it also reinforces the prejudices about workers articulated by critics such as Arnold in his *Culture and Anarchy*, discussed earlier. As a text, its politics are decidedly confused, which is perhaps why it could so easily serve both an aesthetic elite, as a model of Naturalism, as well as the developing socialist movements.

Two other theorists and theatre-makers who would theoretically and practically advance the notion of a people's theatre in the later nineteenth and early twentieth century were Romain Rolland (1866–1944) and Maurice Pottecher (1867–1960). Rolland's book *The People's Theatre* (1918) offered both a critical evaluation and an overview of people's theatres throughout history. The first part of his study interrogated existing theatrical models for their suitability in a modern people's theatre, including the comedies of Molière, the classic French tragedies of Racine and Corneille and the Romantic plays of Dumas. His assessment was that the outlook was not good. In relation to comedy, he concluded that while Molière's works were pleasurable, contemporary audiences '[got] nothing from [him] but the low comedy' (Rolland, 1918, pp. 13–14). Classical tragedies, meanwhile, lacked pleasure for popular audiences and tended to better serve the aristocracy, who could appreciate their form and poetic language (ibid., pp. 23–24). He was equally dismissive of melodrama and Romantic drama – the latter of which he considered to be 'a lion's skin thrown over a bit of trifling nonsense' (ibid., p. 28). By Rolland's assessment, none of the theatres of the past were appropriate for popular audiences. Drawing on the lessons of performances the working classes seemed to enjoy, such as melodrama and popular entertainments, Rolland offered in the second part of his study a series of proposals for the establishment of a modern people's theatre. He believed such a theatre would need to include:

(1) *Varied emotions* – because, he noted, 'people come to the theatre to feel, not to learn'.
(2) *True realism* – for one of the reasons why melodrama has remained so successful, he argued, was because of 'the exactitude with which such and such a well-known place is reproduced'.
(3) *Simple morality* – which meant ensuring that plots showed that 'good will eventually triumph over evil'.
(4) A *square deal*, or an efficient cultural experience, for audiences – a call to dramatists and playhouse managers not to rob the public of their time by making dramas too long or by scheduling lengthy programmes. (ibid., p. 121)

Rolland believed Maurice Pottecher's Théâtre du Peuple, established in 1895, met his criteria for a people's theatre. Like Rousseau, Pottecher's principal goal was to promote social unity through the arts. This was reflected in his theatre's motto, 'Through art for humanity', which was written across the stage's proscenium (Bradby & McCormick, 1978, p. 32). This belief was also realized through the way Pottecher ran his theatre, which appears to have had an inclusive policy of hiring local people as performers, builders and stagehands.

Located in the small village of Bussang in north-eastern France, Théâtre du Peuple was built in a field up against the side of a mountain. Each summer, between the months of August and September, Pottecher would stage two productions, usually of his own authorship, with a team of local people. According to Rolland, one of the productions would be a revival of a play produced the previous year, which was offered free to the public. The other would be a new play, which audiences had to pay a small entry fee to see (1918, pp. 83–84). Pottecher's plays varied greatly in content and style, from the historical epic *The Mystery of Judas Iscariot* (1911) to more didactic works about the evils of alcohol, e.g. *The Merchant Devil Drop* (1897). The aim, of course, was to write plays that would resonate with local people, to entertain and educate them in some way, and therefore Pottecher's understanding of the preferences and concerns of local people would have shaped their content and style. The Théâtre du Peuple in Bussang still exists today and continues to programme summer seasons, which now consist of concerts, new plays, shorter performances, and community events and activities.

Plan of the Book

As this whistle-stop tour demonstrates, since the eighteenth century there have been two predominant forms of people's theatre that have been fundamental in shaping our understanding of modern popular theatre. The first, following Rousseau's model, sought to unite all people together, regardless of class, through communal performances and festivals. The second, best exemplified by the Freie Volksbühne, had its origins in conventional theatre spaces and spoke to the concerns of 'the people', in particular the lower classes. As consciousness of working-class issues became more pronounced in the early twentieth century, this particular strand of popular theatre would become more politically radical – and, as the century progressed, it would evolve into a mouthpiece for subordinated peoples to speak against power in many cultural contexts. In the process, it would take on many forms, informed by the needs, tastes and influences of the people making or receiving it: from didactic political theatre to abstract performances made from deconstructed or reconfigured popular modes. It is this form of popular theatre – the political variety – that is the primary focus of this book. A third form of popular theatre, not discussed in the previous section, is popular entertainment, which would include pantomimes, circuses and music halls. While popular entertainments such as these did not play a major role in the theorizing or defining of people's theatres in the eighteenth and nineteenth centuries, they were undeniably popular with members of the public. Recognizing the appeal of these forms, makers of politically committed popular theatre repeatedly turned to them throughout the twentieth century in order to make their political messages more attractive to audiences. Consequently, entertainment forms do appear in this book, but they are primarily discussed as aesthetic resources drawn upon by twentieth and twenty-first century theatre-makers seeking to do much more than entertain spectators. Popular entertainments are subsequently not given extensive isolated attention here. What readers can expect, however, is a discussion of the ways in which some of these forms have been appropriated, reworked or revised by theatre-makers over the last century.

To be explicit, this book offers an investigation into the evolving concept of the popular in modern and postmodern theatre. It traces manifestations of the popular in the theatre chronologically across two major parts, covering the pre- and post-war periods up to the present time. In Part I, entitled 'The Revolutionary Impetus', I establish the political tone of the study by looking at theatres that emerged in conjunction with the rise of socialist political theory and practice. In Chapter 2, I trace a history of revolutionary popular theatre starting from the October Revolution and the rise of the Soviet Union, where theatre-makers including Vsevolod Meyerhold and Vladimir Mayakovsky put their creative talents, and popular entertainment forms like *commedia dell'arte* and the circus, into the service of the Bolsheviks. As well as professional theatre-makers, the chapter looks at the role of the worker-amateur and the various attempts that were made to fashion a Soviet proletarian cultural identity. The amateur element is also considered in relation to propaganda and education with the development of the enormously successful Blue Blouses, which were companies of workers that performed Living Newspapers and agitational one-act plays and sketches in order to spread news and Bolshevik propaganda to the masses. Chapter 3 looks at the revolutionary theatre in the Weimar Republic in the corresponding period. In that chapter, I introduce the ways in which the avant-garde movements Expressionism and Dada sought to engage with proletarian issues after the First World War and how this affected the work of key theatre-makers, including Erwin Piscator and Bertolt Brecht. As well as the avant-garde, the chapter considers the ways in which these theatre-makers were influenced by popular forms, including cabaret, clowning and variety theatre. Combined, the two chapters show how theatres with similar political positions work in fundamentally different ways. In the Soviet context, 'the people' may have engineered a particular brand of revolutionary popular theatre, but they did so under the watchful and controlling eye of an increasingly authoritarian government. In the Weimar Republic, where communism was not the dominant political force, the revolutionary popular theatres worked to liberate the working classes from an oppressive capitalist system. Consequently, it is argued that in the Soviet Union in the 1920s, certain forms of popular theatre may be seen as hegemonic and manipulative, whereas in the Weimar Republic roughly similar forms were considered to be marginal and radical. Thus, the chapters demonstrate a problem I referred to earlier in this chapter about the popular's relationship to power. While all popular theatres will be people-focused in some way, the people may not always be fully in control of those theatres.

The international Workers' Theatre Movement, which is the subject of Chapters 4 and 5, grew out of the revolutionary theatres of the Soviet Union and Germany. From 1926 until around 1935, communist parties across Europe and the United States began developing theatre troupes in order to conjure support for revolution, teach workers about the importance of unionizing, and to recruit members to the party. Remarkably, volunteer communist activists with limited experience of theatre mostly staffed these theatres. Workers' theatres, as they were known, typically worked as collectives and shared responsibilities for devising, directing and performing material. In Chapter 4, I look at the starting points for the international movement, focusing on early forms of socialist drama in Britain and the United States. I then consider workers' theatres in Germany in the latter part of the 1920s, which became one of the strongest arms of the movement. This discussion is carried over into Chapter 5, which concentrates on the development of the Workers' Theatre Movement in Britain and the United States. The practice of agitprop as it evolved and changed under different cultural conditions is explored throughout both chapters, as is the ongoing, and sometimes troubled, relationship between the amateur groups and the Soviet Union, who endeavoured to maintain, through various means, aesthetic and political consistency across the international movement. In the 1930s, the Soviet Union's attitude towards the theatre began to change and it denounced the agitprop method that it had made popular internationally. This, and the rising threat of fascism in Europe, would eventually put an end to the movement. During its peak in the early 1930s, there were thousands of amateur workers' troupes spread around the world, but by the start of the Second World War, hardly any remained. Chapter 5 ends with a discussion about the end of the Workers' Theatre Movement and considers its wider legacy.

Following Part I, readers will find an 'intermezzo' entitled 'The Popular and the Avant-Garde', which offers a brief, supplemental history to that discussed in the first part. In it, I rewind back to the late nineteenth century to consider the popular theatre's role in the shaping of avant-garde practices. Although there are some political similarities between the avant-garde artists and the revolutionary workers' theatres, the aims and aesthetic strategies of the avant-garde artists seemed to me sufficiently different to warrant isolated attention – hence the separation of this history from Part I. In Chapter 6, I draw on the ideas of Peter Bürger, who has suggested that the avant-garde's use of popular forms was in part intended as an attack on the 'status of art in bourgeois society' (as well as an attack on modernism more generally), in order to consider the ways in which early cabaret artists, Meyerhold, Futurists, and the Bauhaus incorporated popular performance forms into their art, as well as their objectives for doing so (1984, p. 49). While the aesthetic strategies are fundamentally very different to those discussed in Part I, as the chapter demonstrates, many avant-garde artists were just as politically motivated as the revolutionary theatres of Soviet Russia or the international Workers' Theatre Movement. But rather than indoctrinate the masses or recruit for a political party, many in the avant-garde sought to shock, provoke critical thinking or encourage new modes of looking at the world with their art. While the aesthetics of these artists are distinctly *un*popular, I argue that an investigation of the avant-garde's appropriation of the popular is fundamental to understanding modern popular theatre history, as well as to improving our understanding of the malleability of popular forms altogether.

Part II, entitled 'Contemporary Resistance', looks at popular theatre in the post-war period and its evolution up until the present time. After the Second World War, several key developments, including the onset of the Cold War between the Soviet Union and the West, a growing suspicion of Soviet-style communism, and rapid technological and economic developments, radically reconfigured the political left and, consequently, the popular theatres that developed from it. While the effects of economic capitalism were still a fundamental concern, in the 1960s politics expanded to include gender politics, sexual politics and racial politics. The New Left, a revisionist Marxist movement that sought to revive radicalism, established itself as the theoretical and ideological anchor to unite the new, more diverse political scene. In Chapter 7, I introduce readers to the New Left and some of the theatre groups, like the Bread and Puppet Theatre, Gay Sweatshop, and 7:84, that emerged out of it. The chapter concludes with a discussion of this work today and how it has been affected by further changes to left-wing politics.

Chapter 8 focuses on popular theatre in the postmodern era. Borrowing from Susan Sontag, the chapter looks at the 'new sensibility' of post-war culture – a consequence, she argues, of the abundance and speed of new technologies and commodities in the mid-twentieth century – which has destabilized traditional high and low art categories. This has meant greater slippages between popular and high art, leading to the development of performances that fuse forms from across the aesthetic spectrum. The chapter is subsequently divided into two sections. The first looks at theatre-makers and other artists which, owing to the ideas informing their work, the venues in which they perform, or the audiences they target, would have historically been classified as 'high art'. But having consciously appropriated and re-presented popular performance forms in their practices, their work operates between the two aesthetic binaries. Artists and theatre-makers discussed in this section include: Forced Entertainment, Richard DeDomenici, and Tristan Meecham. In the second part of the chapter, I reverse this strategy and look at the ways in which high art practices now routinely inform the popular – in particular, I highlight contemporary puppetry and the circus, and consider work developed by Blind Summit Theatre, Cirque du Soleil and Camille Boitel, among others. This is the only instance in the book where I give isolated attention to forms of what would have historically been seen as popular entertainments. This may seem to some readers like a lapse in the book's focus, but the chapter's primary argument relies on demonstrating the reciprocal and cross-pollinating effects of postmodernism and the way this transforms and changes popular culture. Thus, in my view, a brief discussion of popular entertainment under postmodernism is necessary. Throughout both sections, my interest is in demonstrating the interconnectedness between art forms in the contemporary period and the ways in which they can be critically resistive of hegemonic systems. In the conclusion, I summarize and offer some observations on what I believe can be gained from looking at the modern history of popular theatre. I also offer some provocations about its future.

I shall end this chapter with a polite disclaimer. While my principal aim is to record and document popular theatre practices, I construct my accounts with the recognition that the performances I discuss are only a few of the many intellectual and imaginative outputs of the cultures from which they emerge. In acknowledging this here, and where it is appropriate to do so throughout the text, I aim to avoid the problem of making the few performances I describe stand in for all the members of a social group and their views. While the popular theatre may very well aim to work for or on behalf of a community, it cannot speak to or for everyone. I am conscious of these issues and have no wish to misrepresent. Yet, the focus of the book is, of course, the theatre, and so the contexts I include are designed to aid readers better understand the practices. The book is not intended to be a peoples' history or a critical overview of popular cultures.

It is also plainly not possible to provide a detailed account of all the theatre practices that have been identified as being popular or that have incorporated popular elements, so I have had to be selective. Readers familiar with the field will feel the absence of extended discussions on many important practitioners, including Dario Fo and Franca Rame, El Teatro Campesino and Augusto Boal. There are hundreds of examples like these – artists who clearly fit the scope of the book but receive little or no attention in the coming pages. As exhaustive and detailed as I would have liked to be, space limitations necessarily dictated that I be selective in choosing which artists to write about. Additionally, my personal approach has been to privilege the argument and the construction of a coherent historical arch over exhaustive detail, which I very much hope has resulted in a more useful text. Another scholar would have inevitably made different choices. While the work cannot be exhaustive, it aims to be thorough and critical. It is designed to be introductory, but not elementary. I can only hope I have got the balance right.

Part I
The Revolutionary Impetus

2 Popular Revolutionary Theatres I: The Soviet Union

In a secret gathering in Minsk, Russia, in 1898, the Russian Social Democratic Labour Party, a party intended to unite a number of socialist parties in Russia, was formed. As socialist activities were considered treasonous in autocratic Russia – and, indeed, many other European countries, too – for much of the party's early history it existed underground. Given that the party was formed of different socialist strands, it was inevitable that tensions would develop over its ideological direction. One of its members, Vladimir Ulianov, better known as Lenin, believed that in order to achieve the proletarian dictatorship outlined in Marx's *Communist Manifesto* (2000 [1848]) the workers would need to be led by a professional revolutionary elite who possessed specialist knowledge of Marxism. Lenin and his followers believed that if workers were left to their own accord, they would only ever develop what he called 'trade unionist' consciousness – i.e. an individualized consciousness that placed too much emphasis on one's material conditions. With such an individualistic focus, workers would never see themselves as part of the bigger 'working-class' picture, which would subsequently prevent them from mobilizing to overthrow tsarist autocracy and the social and economic systems responsible for their oppression.

Others in the party, led by Julius Martov, believed that Lenin's approach created unnecessary hierarchies, and that it would be in their best interest to promote a united working class that would work collectively towards shared social goals instead (Priestland, 2009, pp. 76–77). These disagreements caused the party to split in 1902 into two factions, the Bolsheviks, led by Lenin, and the Mensheviks, led by

Martov. Eventually the Bolsheviks would drop their affiliation with the minority faction and become known as the Communist Party. The following two decades were tumultuous for Russia, as people demanded a more active role in how the country was governed. Some democratic powers were gained after a revolution in 1905, but Tsar Nicholas II still retained executive power up until 1916 when his long absence from the country during the First World War resulted in nation-wide riots and uprisings. Following revolution in February 1917, Nicholas abdicated and a provisional government was established. Between February and October of that year, there was considerable unrest in Russia, which was punctuated by a number of peasant and worker uprisings around the country. During this time, Lenin and the Bolsheviks' influence with worker councils (better known as soviets) grew, and, in October 1917, in what is now referred to as the October Revolution, Lenin and his party voted to attack government offices in Petrograd (Saint Petersburg), ultimately seizing power from the provisional government. This was followed by four years of civil war. Intense, bloody battles were fought between the pro-Bolshevik Red Army and the White Army, whose members tended to hold nationalist and pro-autocratic views. The Red Army was eventually victorious, resulting, in 1922, in the formation of the Union of Soviet Socialist Republics, or USSR.

The Bolshevik government had already begun its overhaul of Russian political and economic systems following the October Revolution, but after their victory in the civil war they were able to continue to do so with the benefit of complete authoritarian power. Members of Lenin's professional elite monitored everyone and everything in the new state to ensure all was functioning to advance socialism and achieve the 'dictatorship of the proletariat', or working class.

One of many concerns held by the Bolsheviks was how the proletariat would represent themselves and their ideas culturally. Even before the revolution, questions were being asked about what constituted 'proletarian culture'. There were those, like Anatoly Lunacharsky, the appointed head of the Commissariat of Public Education (also known as Narkompros), who saw potential in the existing popular culture and wished to see proletarian culture develop, if not completely organically from the workers themselves, with some encouragement from the Bolshevik cultural elite.[1] Other Bolsheviks, including Lenin, were less keen on this approach. As Geldern notes:

> Russian popular culture seemed too vulgar and too familiar to most Russian intellectuals, and they ignored its distinct features in their

sincere quest for a people's culture. [...] Most older Bolsheviks considered high culture good, popular culture pernicious. (1993, p. 104)

While the debate largely centred on high and low culture, there was
also the more fundamental issue of representation involved. Older
cultural forms that may have emerged from or accommodated popular
audiences had done so under the old autocratic regime. To draw upon
traditional popular practices signified allegiance to the past, not to
the revolutionary present or the Bolsheviks' plans for a proletarian-
controlled future. So it was not simply about protecting the people
from their 'vulgar' tastes. Many Bolsheviks wanted to see a heroic, new
culture emerge that could both serve and glorify the revolutionary present and pave the way for a communist future.

A Revolutionary Theatre: Meyerhold

From early in his career, Vsevolod Meyerhold (1874–1940) believed
that the theatre might be used as a tool for encouraging and/or promoting social discourse. Following his departure from the Moscow
Art Theatre in 1902, where he had worked as an actor, Meyerhold
began working as a director. Having become frustrated with the
artifice of Naturalism, Meyerhold experimented with different performance forms and styles in order to develop an aesthetic which
could capture the essence of (as opposed to the likeness of, as in the
naturalist theatre) contemporary social realities while simultaneously
involving the audience on a more interpretative and intellectual
level. In the period between 1904 and the Revolution, Meyerhold
frequently turned to popular performance forms to do this, especially circus and the *commedia dell'arte*. As Schechter has pointed
out, the decision to work with popular forms at a point in history
where Naturalism and other realistic modes were privileged was a
'rebellion against the illusions of realism', particularly the 'privacy
and other-worldliness accorded characters in a play' via the convention of the fourth wall (1985, p. 12). The popular, therefore, might
break these artificial barriers down and, as a consequence of the
participatory nature of these forms, facilitate more active responses
from spectators. I will return to Meyerhold's practice in more detail
in Chapter 6, which looks at the popular theatre in avant-garde
practices. For now, I will concentrate on his work to support the
Bolshevik Revolution.

During the First World War, Meyerhold's work became more directly politically engaged. His 1914 production of *Mademoiselle Fifi*, an adaptation of Guy de Maupassant's short story about national and class divisions set during the Franco-Prussian War, appears to mark this shift. As scholar Edward Braun points out in his study of Meyerhold's work, the production was his first encounter with 'agitatory theatre' – theatre designed to advocate a particular political position (1995, p. 151). Following the October Revolution, Meyerhold joined the Bolshevik party and became more strident in his efforts to use his theatrical style for revolutionary purposes. He grew increasingly frustrated by theatres with politically neutral policies, and when he briefly took over the Narkompros Theatre Department from 1920 to 1921, from which he oversaw all professional theatres in the Soviet Republic, he initiated sweeping reforms that he referred to as the 'October Revolution in the theatre' (Braun, 1995, p. 160). His frustration with non-political theatres is revealed in a speech he gave in 1920:

> it is utter nonsense to speak of an apolitical attitude. No man (no actor) has ever been apolitical, a-social; a man is always a product of the forces of his environment. And is it not this which determines the nature of an actor throughout all his individual, social and historical metamorphoses? (Meyerhold, 1988a, p. 168)

Meyerhold's views on what constituted a revolutionary theatre were surprisingly diverse. While emerging Soviet drama, such as Vladimir Mayakovsky's *Mystery-Bouffe* (1918) and Alexander Vermishev's *The Red Truth* (1919), were perhaps obvious examples, he stressed that many plays, from Shakespeare's *Hamlet* to Oscar Wilde's *Salome*, could be revolutionary if interpreted as such by their director (Meyerhold, 1988a, pp. 168–169). What appears to be consistent in Meyerhold's work, though, is his belief in the value of popular performance forms, which he continued to draw on as a committed revolutionary theatremaker. His productions of Vladimir Mayakovsky's (1893–1930) *Mystery-Bouffe* in 1918 and 1921 demonstrate this well.

Mystery-Bouffe is considered to be the first post-revolutionary play to fully adhere to Soviet ideology (Braun, 1995, p. 155). The play is a propagandistic, proletarian allegory drawing on the biblical story of Noah and the great flood. Rather than cleansing the earth of sin, however, the flood is used to represent the international socialist revolution and the cleansing of the world of capitalism. Surviving on board the ark are seven 'clean' and 'unclean' couples. The clean consist of members of the international bourgeoisie, while the unclean is formed of proletarians. In the course of the play, the class conflict comes to a head aboard the ship, as the clean wish to dominate the unclean as they had done before the flood. Guided by the visionary character Man (who was played by Mayakovsky), the unclean win control over the ship and are commandeered through hell, paradise and onto the 'promised land', a commune in which machines and other tools of labour serve the proletariat.

For the original production, commissioned by Narkompros in 1918 to celebrate the first anniversary of the October Revolution, Meyerhold drew on *commedia dell'arte* and circus techniques, which by that time had become characteristic of his work. Braun describes 'the clean' as being depicted in a 'broad, knockabout manner', thus caricaturing and further propagandizing the play (1995, p. 157). This was contrasted with the heroism of the proletariat, which at one point saw Man suspended from a harness five metres above the stage and flown over the heads of the unclean while delivering a rousing, heroic monologue. The *commedia* and circus elements became even more prominent in the 1921 production, which contained an updated text by Mayakovsky. For this production, the stage's proscenium was removed and the set, which consisted of a series of platforms, stairs, ramps and a revolving hemisphere, to represent the ark and the flooded earth, spilled out into the auditorium in which the first several rows of seats had been removed. Braun describes the theatre as 'bursting at the seams' with acrobatics, clowning and other spectacular effects (1995, p. 169).[2] While the production was dismissed by Soviet critics for being too abstract and excessive, it was popular with audiences, playing for nearly five months for an estimated 60,000 people (ibid.).

Proletkult

Another significant presence in the development of a revolutionary theatre in the Soviet Union was the Proletkult. The aim of the Proletkult movement was to promote the vision of a people's culture, or, as Lynn Mally notes, 'a new morality, a new politics, and a new art' for the new worker-centred social system (1990, p. 1). Founded by Bolshevik theorist and physician Alexander Bogdanov (1873–1928), his brother-in-law and Narkompros head, Anatoly Lunacharsky (1875–1933) and the prolific revolutionary and author Maxim Gorky (1868–1936), the Proletkult set out to provide workers with the tools and spaces in which to learn new skills and work together to develop their own culture based on heightened class awareness. Collectivism was central to Bogdanov's vision, which he contrasted with the liberalist attitude of the bourgeoisie. Between 1917 and 1921, the Proletkult would operate as a largely autonomous organization (despite being funded by Narkompros), running courses in theatre, music, literature and visual arts, as well as publishing and finance (Stourac & McCreery, 1986, p. 26). While some communists saw the organization as controversial because it did not strictly follow the party's views, it was popular with the working classes. At its peak in 1920, it is believed that the organization worked with half a million people spread across 300 Proletkult centres throughout the country (Mally, 1990, p. 221).

One of the most subscribed sections of the Proletkult was its theatre division, which was headed by playwright and arts theorist Platon Kerzhentsev (1881–1940). Kerzhentsev was an admirer of Rolland and Rousseau and had a particular interest in collective creation, especially mass theatre, which was the subject of his 1919 book *The Creative Theatre*. Robert Leach explains that Kerzhentsev's 'collectivism' would involve 'all the people of a neighbourhood' working together to put on plays in 'neighbourhood theatres' (1994, p. 24). In reality, of course, this kind of collectivism was difficult to achieve since many proletarians were untrained and saw their activities with the Proletkult as an after-work pastime. So, rather than the proletariat developing its own theatre, professional theatre artists were required to train participants and direct Proletkult productions. While training was tailored to the amateur, this was usually quite rigorous and, in many respects, quite experimental. Sayler offers a prospectus from a course led by Meyerhold and fellow actor-director Leonid Vivien for the Petrograd Proletkult demonstrating the scope of the training workers might receive. The course considered:

> The meaning of the 'refusal'; the value of the gesture in itself; the self-admiration of the actor in the process of acting; the technique of using two stages [...]; the role of the outcry in the moment of strained acting; the elegant costume of the actor [...]; little canes, lances, small rugs, lanterns, shawls, mantles, weapons, flowers, masks, noses, etc., as apparatus for the exercises of the hands [...]; various forms of parade in conformity with the character of the general composition of the play; geometrization of the design into the *mise en scène*, created even *ex improviso;* the mutual relation of the word and gesture in existing theatres and in the theatre to which the Studio aspires. (1922, pp. 216–217)

Despite what this might suggest about the rigour of the actor-training programme, the aim was not necessarily to transform amateurs into professionals. Kerzhentsev strongly believed that amateurism was important and that Proletkult performances should be constructed out of the experiences of its worker members. While professionalism might produce more polished work, it would not be 'rooted in the class position of its creator[s]', ultimately defeating the purpose of the exercise (Leach, 1994, p. 38). What this privileging of amateurism meant in practice was that traditional character-led drama requiring psychologically developed characters was often beyond the skill level of the performers. To overcome this, a technique referred to as mass declamation was introduced, in which an ensemble would speak text simultaneously, much like a choir. Choreographed actions and movement sequences would be added to the chant, so as to further emphasize the unity of the collective and, more broadly, the proletariat. The shift in dramatic focus from the solo protagonist to the collective did not lend itself well to the existing dramatic repertoire, however. In addition, many established dramas did not contain the kind of class-conscious discourse the Proletkult wished its participants to be exposed to. This became clear to Kerzhentsev, who lamented, '[the] number of authors and works that reflect the aspirations and spiritual needs of the proletariat is extraordinarily thin' (quoted in Geldern, 1993, p. 31). To overcome this, Proletkult directors began to adapt material from non-dramatic sources, usually prose and poetry.

This was the case with the Second Central Theatre Studio's production *The Mexican*, which opened on 10 March 1921. The script for *The Mexican* was written by Boris Arvator following improvisations undertaken by the company (Zolotnitsky, 1995, p. 1). The production was directed by Valentin Smyshlyaev, better known for his work as an actor with the Moscow Art Theatre, with set and costume designs by Sergei Eisenstein, who would later become well known for his pioneering work in film. Adapted from Jack London's 1911 short story, *The Mexican* concerns a successful Mexican boxer who uses his winnings to support the *Junta*, a group of exiled revolutionaries battling against an oppressive Mexican regime during the Mexican Revolution. The production, which featured clowning, masks, circus techniques paired with abstract and expressive gesture and movement, and a bright cubist set made up of colourful geometric shapes and lines, was heavily influenced by the work of Meyerhold, with whom Eisenstein had studied. The geometry of the set was reflected in the spatial and topographical configurations of performers on stage, a decision that held revolutionary significance. As Zolotnitsky points out, Smyshlyaev believed that these shapes and how they were realized on stage signified 'the revolutionary work was still in a phase of conspiracy and isolation' and that changing patterns symbolized a 'fermenting' of revolutionary ideas (ibid., pp. 1–2).

In sharp contrast with the production's overt symbolism, certain scenes, including a pivotal boxing match, were played realistically to emphasize the seriousness of the boxers' (and the performance's) revolutionary politics. There was also a more concerted effort to bridge the gap between the stage and the audience in the production. At certain points slogans were shouted at the audience, small clowning scenes designed to get a response from spectators were placed in intervals between acts and some of the action was staged directly in the auditorium (Leach, 1994, pp. 73–76). While the production clearly bore all the hallmarks of the 'futurist'[3] approach that the Bolsheviks frowned upon, the production was regarded a success, with critic Samuil Margolin observing that it 'turned the Central Workers' Studio into a genuine theatre overnight' (quoted in Leach, 1994, p. 76).

But the larger the Proletkult grew, the more suspicious the Communist Party became of it. Even with Lunacharsky doing his best to protect the organization, many high-ranking Bolsheviks were concerned by its independence and by what they saw as its flawed ideology. As Lenin's draft resolution for the First All-Russia Congress of Proletkult, held in October 1920, makes clear:

[The] Congress rejects in the most resolute manner, as theoretically unsound and practically harmful, all attempts to invent one's own particular brand of culture, to remain isolated in self-contained organizations, to draw a line dividing the field of work of the People's Commissariat of Education and the Proletkult, or to set up a Proletkult "autonomy" within establishments under the People's Commissariat of Education and so forth. (Lenin, 2008, p. 142)

Lenin had had enough. To him, the question of what constituted a proletarian culture already had an answer: it was to be repurposed bourgeois culture. Attempts to force or manufacture a new culture – even if it emerged from the people themselves – went against the official views of the Party. In December of 1920, two months after the All-Russia Congress and Lenin's resolution, the Proletkult was officially absorbed into Narkompros. Although it would continue its work until 1932, at which point the Communist Party would dissolve all literary and cultural groups, replacing them with professional unions, it never regained the momentum it had as an autonomous organization between 1917 and 1920. Even by 1924, due to severe financial constraints, it had shed all but eleven of its Proletkult centres (Mally, 1990, p. 221). Although the theatre continued to prosper, especially the First Workers' Theatre created in 1921 and directed by Sergei Eisenstein until 1923, it primarily did so by supporting smaller workers' theatres and other cultural groups (ibid., p. 241).

Monuments and Mass Spectacles

It had become clear through the state's dealings with Proletkult what its views regarding a proletarian culture were. While it criticized the Proletkult for trying to manufacture an artificial proletarian culture, it was simultaneously promoting one by choosing which projects to fund. In this context, what might constitute a new proletarian art was secondary to the more immediate task of submission. And with illiteracy high and dissent widespread in the first years of the new government, it was vital that strategies for disseminating information widely, through visual and aural means, were found. Lenin's 'Plan of Monumental Propaganda' was one scheme, which saw tsarist monuments replaced with new ones celebrating important revolutionaries. When architect Nikolai Vinogradov-Mamont, who was to realize the scheme, enquired about the significance of the plan, Lenin is said to have replied:

> The decree is extremely important. After all you cannot liquidate illiteracy immediately. Just imagine: a statue to a revolutionary has been put up. There is a solemn ceremony … an imaginative speech is made … and imperceptibly we are achieving our first goal: we have touched the soul of an illiterate person. (Tolstoy, 1998, p. 17)

The monument plan is a good example of the problems faced by the Bolsheviks. There was a clear need to quickly replace signs and symbols of the old regime with those of the new. Simultaneously, constant reminders about the newness of the regime might equally undermine its authority in the eyes of the people. The task was extraordinarily complex: they would need to introduce new national symbols to replace the old ones while retaining a sense of history and importance. This would not only require developing a (new) coherent Soviet iconography, but also the (re)development of national myths to help stabilize their public image and reinforce their claim to power. Ironically, their task was not dissimilar to that of Meyerhold and Mayakovsky. They would need to find a way to blend the best of the past with the present to forge a unique and powerful identity that people could understand; the difference, of course, was that the Bolsheviks' aim was to convince the public to value the new system and submit unconditionally to their power. And, much like these artists, one of the early solutions to this problem was discovered in popular theatre. In the Bolsheviks' case, this was in the form of mass spectacles.

The appeal of mass spectacles to the Bolsheviks is unquestionably connected to Rousseau and the popular *fêtes* of the French Revolution discussed in the previous chapter. In the Russian context, the spectacles drew on traditions which had been popular in Russia throughout the eighteenth and nineteenth centuries under the autocratic tsarist regimes, so in many ways the Bolsheviks were appropriating a popular cultural tradition that was, as Geldern observes in his study of Bolshevik festivals, 'alien to their goals' (1993, p. 8). Still, by all accounts, many of the mass spectacles were well received and, due to their success, the government gave a significant amount of money to them throughout the period of the civil war. The Mass Presentations and Festivals division of the Narkompros Theatre Section (TEO) oversaw the development and execution of most of these so as to ensure they were constructed according to 'correct' national histories and utilized icons significant to the Bolshevik regime.

It was Lenin's monument builder, Vinogradov-Mamont,[4] who would introduce mass spectacles into the Soviet Republic. His vision for what he called 'monumental theatre' would see large numbers of participants improvise performances through games and other forms of structured play. Vinogradov's ideas were particularly well received by the military, leading to the creation of the Theatrical-Dramaturgical Studio of the Red Army, better known as Red Army Studio, where he could implement his ideas. The first performance, *The Overthrow of the Autocracy*, was performed in March 1919. It saw real-life soldiers re-enact the February Revolution of 1917. The performance, which took place in the Steel Hall of the People's House in Petrograd, was a kind of game in which soldiers were instructed to improvise, or play out, the very battle many had actually fought in. Many scenes were performed on two large platforms located on opposite sides of the hall, while battles were played in a large aisle through the centre that the audience were also allowed to pass through (Geldern, 1993, p. 126). No costumes were used; instead, soldier-actors were dressed in their own clothes.

They were then distributed across the platforms and throughout the audience so as to confuse the boundaries of the performance. The idea was to unite the performers and audience in a collective remaking of the Revolution. Meyerhold, who was in attendance, recognized what the objective of the game was, and when one of the soldier-actors was 'killed' in battle, he picked up the actor's rifle and joined in (ibid.).

The most famous mass spectacle produced by the Bolsheviks was Nikolai Evreinov's *The Storming of the Winter Palace*, which was performed on 7 November 1920. The performance took place in Uritzky Square, Petrograd, and in and around the General Staff and Winter Palace buildings that surround it. Up against the General Staff building, two large platforms were constructed, one for the 'red' workers and the other for the 'white' Provisional Government, which had assumed power following the February Revolution. The main workers' platform was a staggering 55 metres long by 16 metres wide; it was subdivided into three levels and surrounded by a constructivist set of worker interiors, e.g. brick walls, factory chimneys and machinery (Deák, 1975, p. 15). The equally large white platform, located to the left of the red one, was subdivided into four levels, allowing space to depict the Provisional Government, the bourgeoisie and bankers. Many of the staged battles between the two sides were performed on a bridge that connected their platforms. On these platforms, a loose account of the months between the February and October revolutions was played out, although, as Deák points out, '[t]he two individual images did not have a strictly narrative relationship, but rather created two independent lines of events that met at certain points' (ibid., p. 20). The worker platform, which was bathed in red light, showed a beleaguered but honourable working class performing 'large gestures and exaggerated postures' that would not be out of place in heroic drama (ibid.). In contrast, the figures on the white platform were performed much more ridiculously, incorporating, according to Deák, elements of 'variety theatre and circus' (ibid.). The levels were also used to demonstrate Prime Minister Kerensky's, and the Provisional Government's, loyalty to the bourgeoisie, a point that was punctuated by scenes of bribery with comically large bags of money. For the first part of the performance, then, the estimated 100,000 spectators, occupying the centre of the square, would have seen two clearly juxtaposed images: the noble workers versus the ridiculous and corrupt Provisional Government.

In the second part of the performance, the battle between the workers and the Provisional Government became more pronounced, and the square came alive with military vehicles, parades of soldiers and flag-waving revolutionaries. The action eventually made its way into the Winter Palace, located on the opposite side of the square. The original warship that had fired the first shot in the revolution three years earlier was fired again, at which point the Palace literally came alight with combat. Shadow fights and battles could be seen through shaded Palace windows, and the sounds of machine gun and artillery fire filled the city. Several minutes of intense, noisy fighting were followed by darkened silence. Red stars then started to appear in the windows of the Palace, signalling the victory of the Bolsheviks. The spectacle then came to a close with a military parade and fireworks (Gorchakov, 1957, pp. 149–150).

The sheer scale of this performance is difficult to grasp. It has been estimated that over 8000 performers in total took part, which included professional actors, circus performers, dancers, actual military personnel and volunteer amateurs. According to Deák, the white platform alone required nearly 3000, which included 125 ballet dancers, 100 circus performers and over 700 extras (Deák, 1975, p. 16). The Opening Ceremony for the London 2012 Olympic Games offers a close comparison: it featured 7500 mixed-ability performers performing to a stadium audience of 80,000 (McVeigh & Gibson, 2012). It was, to be sure, a grand spectacle designed to make the Bolsheviks' rise to power look difficult and heroic.[5]

Agitprop

But securing the public's faith in their ability to lead was only part of the Bolsheviks' problem, they also had to get people to understand and comply with the political and economic changes they were introducing. One of the ways the government disseminated information such as this was through mobile agitprop theatres. Like agit-trains and agit-ships, agit-plays were a simple and effective means of quickly disseminating *agit*ational *prop*aganda to the masses. Agitprop can take many forms, from short, one-act plays constructed around a single topic, to variety-style programmes offering songs, sketches, recitations and movement pieces covering a range of issues. Throughout the early years of the Soviet Republic and up until the early 1930s, agitprop was widely performed across Russia, coordinated by both amateur and professional theatre troupes. Many of these groups were funded by the TEO and ROSTA, the Russian Telegraph Agency (Leach, 1994, p. 37).

Formed in 1918, ROSTA was the state-controlled news agency. At the direction of Narkompros in 1919, they began developing posters to help spread important news and information to the masses.[6] The posters were based on the *lubok*, a popular Russian print featuring a well-known story, usually a folk tale or Bible story, narrated in simple text and organized in strip form, much like a cartoon. Mayakovsky designed some of the better-known examples of the ROSTA poster, in the new constructivist style, which had only started to be theorized at the Institute of Artistic Culture by artists Alexander Rodchenko and Liubov Popova, among others.[7] While the posters were designed to be accessible, some level of literacy was required in order to comprehend their message, which meant there was still a large percentage of the population for whom the posters were of little value. It was the director of the Vitebsk ROSTA, Mikhail Pustynin, who first saw the potential of performance to help disseminate the news (Curtis, 1990, p. 220). His idea was for a Living Newspaper, in which different parts of a newspaper, including political stories, feature articles or even letters to the editor might be acted out for the masses. The result was the establishment of the Theatre for Revolutionary Satire, better known by the acronym TEREVSAT, in 1919 (Casson, 2000, p. 108).

Much like a newspaper, TEREVSAT programmes would consist of a range of items ordered in a revue-like format. In addition to news stories, a typical programme consisted of political songs and sketches, plays, folk dances, gymnastics, parodies and, as A.L. Tait reports, Petrushka puppet acts (Tait, 1974, p. 242).[8] As well as current events, performances might address personal hygiene, give farming advice or even recruit for the Red Army. Programmes were not usually thematically linked or contextualized by a master of ceremonies, as would become the norm with later agitprop; instead, an agitational prologue delivered by a professional 'agitator' was used to focus the audience's attention on crucial pieces of information, and to punctuate messages they were expected to take away from the performance (Leach, 1994, p. 83). Because of the revue format, programmes could vary in length from half an hour to several hours, depending on the time the venue hosting the performance had available. As performances might be given in a number of locations, including workers' halls, union offices or even on the front lines of the civil war, such flexibility was important. But portability did not mean that the work sacrificed aesthetic elements. In contrast with later mobile troupes that would, out of financial and practical necessity, adhere to a more minimalist aesthetic, TEREVSAT performances were usually aesthetically rich. Their productions typically employed elaborate costumes and hand-painted backdrops (Leach, 1994, p. 83).[9]

The TEREVSAT actor was expected to be proficient in speech, movement and improvisation, while simultaneously keeping up to date with official state news. He or she would also need to be able to bear the strain of touring. Leach describes the work as being similar to the *commedia dell'arte*, because, like that form, performances contained a simple structure and identifiable archetypal characters, and were typically constructed out of improvisations undertaken by the company – in this case, around a selected news story or political topic. Curtis sees stronger connections between the popular cabarets and variety theatres which had been allowed to continue to operate by the Bolsheviks after the Revolution, as the material – often short sketches – tended to resemble, at least structurally, the kinds of acts one might find in those venues (Curtis, 1990, p. 223). The versatile TEREVSAT actor was usually rewarded with payment in the form of food items, like potatoes and grain, which were highly prized during the years of the civil war.

In its first year in operation, TEREVSAT toured the Red Army front lines, towns and villages, giving over 300 performances for an estimated audience of 200,000 (Curtis, 1990, p. 220). The success of the TEREVSAT clearly rested in its ability to address topical issues of concern quickly and in a manner that was easily understood and enjoyed by a wide range of audiences. Owing to its success, the TEO gave TEREVSET the Nikitsky Theatre in Moscow to continue to develop its practice. This appears to be in keeping with the theatre's changing objectives, which, as Curtis notes, was a consequence of the changing conditions of the Soviet Union itself (ibid.). Rather than inform, the theatre saw its role as 'consolidating the achievements of Soviet power', during the delicate years of the civil war (ibid.). Unfortunately, while the group's work certainly possessed traditional theatrical features – costumes and settings, for instance – it was not fully prepared for the challenges a permanent theatre offered. Their reputation had been built on a flexible programme of material they improvised and one-act agit-plays written either by brigade members or by individuals closely associated to the group.[10] A permanent theatre demanded a different kind of repertoire. Full-length plays soon found their way into the programme, including some by George Bernard Shaw and Lunacharsky. As Leach observes, 'the agit pieces were too bald for traditional theatre, and the conventional plays lacked the element of agitation which was TEREVSAT's *raison d'être*' (1994, p. 88). The group suffered its identity crisis for over a year when, in June 1922, the theatre was renamed Theatre for Revolution and handed over to Meyerhold to run (ibid., p. 94).

Following in the footsteps of TEREVSET was Blue Blouse, which was formed in 1923 by Boris Yuzhanin at the Moscow Institute of Journalism. Like TEREVSET, the idea behind Blue Blouse was a desire to perform important news stories for popular audiences. In common with the Proletkult movement, Yuzhanin strongly believed in the value of amateurism – and that workers should educate members of their own class; consequently, Blue Blouse troupes were made up of amateur worker performers. To signify the working-class status of the performer and to express solidarity with their worker audiences, the troupes performed in a familiar working-class uniform: a blue shirt and black trousers or skirts. It was from this simple costume that Blue Blouse got its name.

The programme of the Blue Blouse started off closely resembling those of TEREVSET, consisting of sketches about topical news items, patriotic songs and political recitations. This familiar approach proved popular with audiences and the government, and by the end of the first year, there were fourteen mobile Blue Blouse troupes. In 1924, Blue Blouse became the official cultural representative of the Moscow Council of Trade Unions, resulting in further expansion (Stourac & McCreery, 1986, p. 40). To ensure standardization across the growing network, Yuzhanin began publishing *Blue Blouse*, a biweekly magazine, which featured models of good practice, notes on programme structures and texts that groups were encouraged to perform (Deák, 1973, p. 44).

Yuzhanin's desire that troupes be kept amateur meant that assistance from professional writers was not initially accepted. Instead, he encouraged groups to write their own sketches and submit the best of those to *Blue Blouse* magazine for dissemination. He further advised troupes to devise their own materials using a technique known as *literary montage*, which consisted of assembling text from non-dramatic sources, such as 'poems by the proletarian and LEF poets' and 'texts from humorous soviet journals and magazines' (Blue Blouse, 1995 [1925], p. 182).[11] Yuzhanin believed that such a technique was inherently agitational because it resisted the traditional one-author model that characterized the bourgeois theatre. The strategy appears to have been influenced by Eisenstein's 'Montage of Attractions', a revolutionary technique strongly influenced by his work with Meyerhold, the Proletkult and the First Workers Theatre. In his essay 'The Montage of Attractions', published in 1923, Eisenstein defines an attraction as 'any aggressive moment in theatre, i.e. any element of it that subjects the audience to emotional or psychological influence' (1995 [1923], p. 88). While individual attractions, he argued, are capable of producing 'shocks' in the spectator, when ordered alongside other attractions they can be made to suggest a 'specific final thematic effect' (ibid., p. 89), revealing to spectators the 'ideological aspect of what is being shown, the final ideological conclusion' (ibid., p. 88). In practice, the montage technique requires juxtaposing seemingly unrelated images/scenes in a manner that invites a particular reading. It is a technique now more commonly associated with film, as it was in his films, most notably *Strike* (1924) and *October* (1927), that Eisenstein mastered it. By 1925, the *literary montage* had become a permanent element of all Blue Blouse programmes, although how well it was understood and practised across the Blue Blouse network is unclear. Despite Yuzhanin's efforts, scripts were not forthcoming. Although he had tried to author many himself, as membership grew, he was unable to keep up with demand. Eventually, he relented and allowed troupes to use professional writers. Adopting Eisenstein's montage technique and the use of well-known constructive writers gave the Blue Blouse network a distinctly constructivist aesthetic, particularly in its later years.

It is possible to get a sense of what a Blue Blouse performance was like, largely thanks to the magazine *Blue Blouse* and the investigative work of Richard Stourac, Kathleen McCreery and František Deák. Each performance began with a parade *entrée*: set to upbeat music, the parade involved all twelve to twenty members of the company. Performers would march through the hall and, one by one, introduce themselves and the major headlines that were to be performed. This was followed by an *oratorio*, which is a piece of music, usually written for a symphony, choir and soloists, featuring some kind of story and characters. It was amended by the Blue Blouse troupes to report on current events. Following the song, the troupe would give an account of international events, focusing particularly on the perceived failure of capitalism in the West, in an act entitled, 'international survey'. A vaudeville-style sketch known as a *feuilleton* followed, which explored urban or rural themes; it was most often used to promote positive social values, like avoiding alcohol and treating women fairly.[12] After the *feuilleton*, the troupe would perform a *lubok*. As with the ROSTA posters, the *lubok* was amended by the Blue Blouses to deal with social and political themes. In this context, the *lubok* would be realized by cutting holes into a large poster through which actors would place their heads and 'perform' its content to the spectators. The poster would be followed by one or more dialogue duets or dances, which presented an opportunity for a more intimate examination of an issue.[13] These could be either serious or comic.

After the duet, a solo performer would perform a topical *rayok*, a quickly spoken, rhymed comic speech, which was then followed by the *chastushki*, an upbeat song about topical issues, performed by several members of the troupe. The penultimate section of the programme featured sketches on issues of concern to the local audience. While these may have consisted of materials amended from *Blue Blouse* to appear localized, it may have also involved improvising a sketch prior to a performance from research undertaken by the company, which could have involved speaking to people from the community or scouring local newspapers for topical issues. Not dissimilar to the opening, the finale-march would include all members of the company. In it, key points and messages would be emphasized and the troupe's working-class unity with the audience would be stressed once more (Stourac & McCreery, 1986, pp. 30–39).[14]

Unlike the TEREVSAT brigades, the aesthetic of a Blue Blouse troupe was considerably less decorated. Apart from their basic uniform, the troupes were advised against settings and 'clumsy props' (Blue Blouse, 1995 [1925], p. 181). Instead, the stage was to remain clear, barring a piano, which would provide regular accompaniment, the 'bough of a tree' and 'things necessary for demonstration', such as crucial furniture and placards (ibid.). Anything that would not be used directly was to be eliminated, as it might slow down the tempo of the action.

Like many of the practices discussed so far, the Blue Blouse troupes looked to the *commedia dell'arte* for inspiration. They were drawn especially to the form's reduction of personalities to easily identifiable social types articulated through exaggerated gestures and physicality. Blue Blouse would amend the conventional types of servant, master and lover, however, to fit the Soviet narrative, which included the 'fat-cat capitalist', and the 'heroic social revolutionary' and 'noble proletarian' (ibid., p. 182). As the above structure indicates, such typing was probably necessary because the sketches and songs were too brief for considerable exposition and character development. What was important was that information could be relayed quickly and in a manner that could be understood by spectators with mixed levels of education and literacy. As *Blue Blouse* made clear, the troupes were to 'influence the brain of the spectator with all scenic means' in order to 'prepare [him or her] for the perception of the new social condition' (ibid.). Drawing on familiar cultural forms, like the *lubok*, and recognizable archetypal characters, allowed the Blue Blouse troupes to do that more efficiently.

At its peak in 1927, Blue Blouse membership stood at a staggering 100,000 participants, who were spread across 5000 troupes (Drain, 1995, p. 183). It is the largest agitprop movement in the history of theatre, and one that should be recognized not just for its effective dissemination of propaganda but also for introducing avant-garde aesthetic and literary approaches to new audiences across Soviet Russia. The movement was also hugely influential in the development of workers' theatres internationally. In October 1927, the Moscow Blue Blouse troupe toured Germany at the invitation of International Workers' Aid, sharing its methods and techniques with its workers' theatres.[15] The Living Newspaper and revue style model of agitprop refined by the Blue Blouses proved to be attractive to those involved with the proletarian theatres in Germany and was subsequently widely emulated around the country. By the end of the century, workers' theatres around the world were adapting Blue Blouse techniques for their own contexts. The organization would last, despite being forcibly merged with other organizations in the late 1920s, until 1933, by which time it had gone out of favour with the government and had become the Soviet's exemplar of how *not* to perform revolutionary theatre (Mally, 1990, p. 329). The Soviets' shifting attitude towards revolutionary theatre will be discussed in greater detail in Chapters 4 and 5.

3 Popular Revolutionary Theatres II: Germany

In Germany, while socialist theatre groups appeared before 1914 – notably the amateur groups affiliated with the German Workers' Theatre Federation, formed in 1908 – the appearance of a revolutionary theatre can be traced to the latter years of the First World War and the German Revolution (1918–1919) that followed it.[1] As with Russia, the first artistic responses to these crises would emerge from the avant-garde, notably through Expressionism and Dada. Although works with characteristics now typically associated with Expressionism – e.g. a concern with modernity and its impact on humanity, the symbolic treatment of characters, heightened and extreme representations of emotions, and a mix of poetic and broken language – did appear in Berlin prior to the War, it would not be until 1917 that a distinctive theatre movement began to take shape.[2] It would become associated with, in particular, opposition to the First World War. Unlike naturalist plays, which prioritized the appearance of external or surface realities, the expressionists sought to represent subjective emotional experiences. Emerging as it did towards the end of the war and as a response to the catastrophic effects it had on the German people, Expressionism, as Willett observes, came to be associated with the 'the empire's decline and demolition' (1988, p. 56).

These characteristics are identifiable in the works of Ernst Toller (1893–1939), a left-wing activist and playwright who served a five-year prison sentence for his role in establishing (and briefly presiding over) the short-lived Munich Soviet Republic in April 1919. Toller believed Expressionism capable of articulating proletarian concerns in a way that had universal appeal. He would write that 'Proletarian art can only exist where the creative artist reveals that which is eternally human in the spiritual characters of working people' (quoted in Bradby & McCormick, 1978, p. 69). This spirituality and concern for humanity can be seen in Toller's first play, the semi-autobiographical *Transfiguration* (*Die Wandlung*) (1919). The play concerns a Jewish intellectual, Friedrich, who struggles to understand his cultural identity, believing the faith he was born into makes him 'homeless' in his own country (Toller, 1935, p. 63). In order to prove his Germanness, he joins the German army during the war and is later injured in battle. After his recovery, he continues his journey to personal discovery by becoming an artist, a medical student and eventually a prisoner. Throughout, he is haunted by skeletons and soldiers disabled by the war. In the play's final scene, enlightened by his experiences, Friedrich calls on people to remember their 'real selves' and to have faith in humanity once more (ibid., p. 105).

The play's premiere, which was directed by Karlheinz Martin and starred Fritz Kortner in the leading role, was held at the Tribüne Theatre in Berlin in 1919. According to Willett, it was a critical and commercial success, running for 115 performances (1988, p. 62).

Later that year the Tribüne would lend its support to writer Rudolf Leonhard's efforts to establish a German version of Proletkult, which was called the League for Proletarian Culture. The League soon established the Proletarian Theatre, which sought to 'break the cultural stranglehold of the bourgeoisie' by organizing performances of new and classic works for the masses (Rorrison, 1980, p. 37). In many respects, the Proletarian Theatre was not vastly different to the early Volksbühne, although it was conceived as a more openly political venture that would do more than just provide the working classes with a cultural education – it also sought to advance proletarian concerns. The Proletarian Theatre's only production, Herbert Kranz's *Freedom* (*Freiheit*), also directed by Martin, was performed at the Philharmonic Hall in Berlin on 14 December 1919. Both the League and its Proletarian Theatre disbanded soon after, principally because it lacked the support of the German Communist Party (KPD), which had been established the year before. As Bradby and McCormick have observed, there was a recognized conflict between the new League and the Russian Proletkult model it sought to emulate: while the Russian Proletkult had emerged from a socialist revolutionary context, the other had not. Hence, many in the KPD felt that the League's ambitions were premature (1978, p. 63).

Dada, Erwin Piscator and an Epic Theatre

The avant-garde, anti-art movement Dada, which gained momentum at the Cabaret Voltaire in Switzerland in 1916, shared with German Expressionism a critical stance against the war. However, the Dadaist's approach was more antagonistic. They were considerably more direct in their attack of bourgeois culture and values, which they held responsible for the war. Dadaist's 'anti-art' rejected bourgeois artistic principles outright, often appearing nonsensical, slovenly and irrational. After the completion of his military service, the young Erwin Piscator became involved with members of Berlin's Dada circle, alongside artists George Grosz and John Heartfield, publisher Wieland Herzfelde and poet Walter Mehring, among others. At the start of the war, Piscator had considered himself an actor, but as he later recalled in his book *The Political Theatre:*

> The moment I uttered the word *actor* among the exploding shells, the whole profession for which I had struggled so hard and which I held so dear in common with all art, seemed so comical, so stupid, so ridiculous, so grotesquely false [...] that I was less afraid of the flying shells than I was ashamed of my profession. (1980 [1963], p. 14)

The war and immediate post-war period was one of significant personal change for Piscator. His attitude towards the theatre, particularly the bourgeois/commercial theatre, had hardened. He also became an active member of the Communist Party, lending his support to the Spartacist Uprising in January 1919 (Piscator, 1980 [1963], p. 21). He and the other artists he associated with would spend hours discussing the value of art and its social responsibility, eventually deciding that if art was to be made meaningful it would need to be put into the service of the class struggle. But the reality was that Piscator was not entirely sure how to achieve that. Working under the slogan 'Art is shit', he and fellow Dadaists would develop aggressive political artistic interventions, such as: 'recitations of simultaneous poems of the most incomprehensible sort, using toy revolvers, toilet paper, false beards and poems by Goethe and Rudolf Presber' (ibid., p. 22).[3] While Piscator's direct involvement with Dada appears to have been brief, he seems to have been deeply affected by the ideas motivating their work – especially in their repositioning of proletarian arts outside of traditional high art models and the aesthetic standards valued by the bourgeoisie. He later noted that

'[the Dadaists] changed the notation, abandoned the bourgeois position they had grown up in, and returned it to the point of departure
from which the proletariat must approach art' (ibid.). After gaining
more practical experience with expressionist plays after founding a
short-lived expressionist theatre in 1919,[4] Piscator came to the conclusion that the genre was in conflict with his personal politics and he
subsequently started to experiment with other theatrical forms (ibid.).[5]

In 1920 Piscator returned to Berlin permanently, where he set up
a new theatre, the Proletarian Theatre. The aim of the theatre was to
produce agitprop plays that would promote class-consciousness and
unity among the working classes. As Innes observes, 'The framework
for his [a]gitprop style was formed [...] by the notion that only "proletarian" art could have social relevance in the predicted Marxist mil-
lennium and that this should embody working class experience' (1972,
p. 25). In prioritizing the propagandist function over artistic quality of
the work, Piscator openly aligned his theatre with the Dadaists. Like
them, he saw the work of the company not just as a form of cultural
intervention but as a form of protest. He hoped that the performances
he and the company created 'would have an effect on current events, to
be a form of political activity' (Piscator, 1980 [1963], p. 45). In order
to achieve these goals, he knew that new forms of writing and acting
would be required. In an article for the Dadaist journal *The Opponent*
(*Der Gegner*) in October 1920, Piscator theorized how the Proletarian
Theatre would attend to these issues. Modern writers, he observed,
would need to get over their autocratic tendencies, which the bourgeois
theatre had fostered, and focus instead on educating the masses (ibid.,
pp. 46–47). In order to do this, he advised writers to look to popular
forms that 'have the merit of being clear and easily understood by all'
(ibid., p. 47). As for the Proletarian Theatre performers, they would
need to learn to prioritize the political cause over their role, ensuring
that 'every word, every gesture [was] an expression of the proletarian,
Communist idea' (ibid., p. 46). Realizing, too, that there was a conflict
between the traditional artistic hierarchies of theatre organization and
the politics of his new theatre, Piscator called for collective management in which directors, designers, actors and spectators were on equal
footing. In this new theatre, everything from the smallest physical
gesture to the way the company was managed was designed to be revolutionary and to propagate the class struggle.

The Proletarian Theatre's first season included six plays, including
Franz Jung's *The Kanakans*, Karl August Wiltfogel's *The Cripple*, Gorky's
Enemies and Lajos Barta's *Russia's Day*. Of these, only Barta's play, which

crudely depicts workers battling against personified political forces, like 'World Capital', the military and the church, has survived. It bears many of the hallmarks of the Soviet agitprop performances discussed in the previous chapter, including stereotypical characters, slogan shouting and a rousing, musical finale in which the performers and audience sang the 'Internationale' together (Rorrison, 1980, p. 39). What seems clear from this programme is that the right kind of writing did not yet exist for the revolutionary theatre that Piscator imagined. The problem of suitable revolutionary texts would be one that would continue to haunt him throughout the decade. Apart from a few professionals who shared his political views, the theatre consisted mainly of proletarian amateurs whom Innes describes as 'unrehearsed and often unskilled' (1972, p. 25). The texts performed, therefore, had to accommodate their limited abilities, as well as the limited financial resources available to the company (ibid., p. 26). Unsurprisingly, the aesthetic standards of these performances were often low. The experience appears to have altered Piscator's views on proletarian performers. He came to believe that performers first and foremost needed a fundamental understanding of their role and its political function in the text and, secondly, the ability to develop convincing characters in order to perform effectively in the revolutionary theatre (Piscator, 1980 [1963], pp. 49–50). To insist that only proletarian amateurs could be used in this kind of theatre, Piscator would eventually realize, was a mistake.

While Piscator forbade mainstream critics from observing the productions because he saw them as propaganda and not art, this did not prevent the odd critic from coming along to have a look. One of the reviews that particularly disappointed Piscator came from Gertrud Alexander, critic for the Communist Party publication *Die Rota Fahne* (*The Red Flag*). In an article appearing on 17 October 1920, Alexander called foul on the whole project:

> We read in the programme ...that this is not supposed to be art but propaganda [...] To this we would say: In that case, why choose the name theatre? Let us call a spade a spade and label it: propaganda. The name theatre commits you to art and to an artistic level of performance! Art is too sacred a thing to lend itself to *propagandistic concoctions*. (quoted in Piscator, 1980 [1963], p. 51)

As Willett notes, though the party's official arts policy was unclear at the time, Alexander's remarks on the debate about art and propaganda were not uncommon, suggesting that many in the party may have held views on the matter similar to that of Lenin, which, as discussed in the last chapter, were not always favourable (1986, p. 48). At any rate, Piscator claims that there was a great deal of interest in the work developed by the Proletarian Theatre, which recruited between 5000 and 6000 members during its short existence (Piscator, 1980 [1963], p. 50). Even with the support of the workers, however, the project would be short-lived. In the spring of 1921, the Berlin chief of police refused the theatre a licence to perform, on the grounds that the company's work was not art but propaganda. Without a licence, the theatre was unable to complete its first season. Even had it been given a licence, however, its business plan was also proving unworkable. While the venues – mostly union, school and concert halls – were full for most performances, the low cost of tickets and the decision to allow members of the theatre and the unemployed to attend for free meant that the project was financially unsustainable (ibid., p. 52). Although Piscator's Proletarian Theatre did not last long, it is significant for being one of the earliest models for a mobile workers' theatre outside the Soviet Union – one which not only refocused the theatre's attention onto the politics of the working class, but which sought to realize those politics through its organization and management. By the end of the decade, as Chapters 4 and 5 will demonstrate, this kind of workers' theatre was far more common in Germany and throughout Europe.

Piscator's influence on the German Workers' Theatre Movement can also be found in his cultivation of forms of popular entertainment for use in agitprop. Three years after the Proletarian Theatre was dissolved, and the KPD's attitude towards art and propaganda had started to change, Piscator was commissioned by the party to create a political revue in the run-up to the 1924 elections. The *Revue Roter Rummel* (*Red Riot Revue*), as it was eventually called, was co-authored by Felix Gasberra, Piscator's mentor in the Communist Party.[6] It contained over a dozen political sketches, mixed with songs, speeches, acrobatic acts, live action cartoons, and films (Innes, 1972, p. 44). Piscator saw great potential in the revue format, believing it capable of achieving greater propagandistic effects than plays, which, he explains, 'tempt you to psychologize and constantly erect barriers between the stage and the auditorium' (Piscator, 1980 [1963], pp. 81–82). The revue format, on the other hand, allowed for small bursts of propaganda in a format known to hold favour with working-class audiences. Willett notes that with *R.R.R.*, 'Piscator had discovered the value of the revue form as a kind of elastic montage which embraced a wide range of theatrical devices and could continually be changed and brought up to date' (1986, p. 51). The episodic nature of the revue format, and subsequently montage, later became central to Piscator's conception of epic theatre, which will be discussed shortly. It also became a crucial form for the growing network of amateur workers' theatres in Germany. Due to touring and skill-sharing visits with other countries, such as Britain's Workers' Theatre Movement (WTM), a London-based proletarian agitprop theatre, in the early 1930s, the revue format would become the staple form for workers' theatres internationally. As Piscator had discovered, it was popular, adaptable and pedagogically and politically effective.

Piscator's role in the development of what is more generally known as epic theatre is also important to note, as it would have a significant impact not just on the way in which political theatre was thought about and made, but would also play an important role in twentieth-century theatre-making more generally. Today, epic theatre is understood as a combination of dramaturgical and staging techniques designed to minimize the audience's emotional investment in the theatrical illusion and promote, instead, critical spectatorship. To achieve this effect, epic theatre performances tend to be constructed so as to disrupt conventional psychological or emotional responses to narrative and character. This can be done in several ways, including having a performance acknowledge its construction by exposing and sometimes emphasizing the theatrical frame, and/or by making familiar events appear unfamiliar so as to make audiences question what they are seeing. So, for instance, projected text or placards might give away the plot before a scene is played; stage equipment, such as lighting, may not be disguised so that patrons do not forget that they are in a theatre space; or an actor may step in and out of character, etc. These elements stand in direct opposition to the kind of illusory experience provided by the naturalists, and were intended to ensure that audiences retain their ability to keep an objective, and therefore critical, view of the play's action. It is theorized that by maintaining their senses and a safe critical distance from the action on stage, spectators will process those events in a more meaningful and critical way that might feed into their understanding of the issues addressed in the production.

Piscator believed one of the fundamental problems faced by the revolutionary theatre was the lack of appropriate plays. To him, many of these were indebted to the bourgeois theatre, and a meaningful revolutionary theatre would require new material and a new stage style. When these were not forthcoming, Piscator started to work closely with playwrights to help fashion something better suited to his political goals and aesthetic vision, and it is in these experiments where Piscator's major contributions to epic theatre can be found. The first epic drama Piscator encountered was Alfons Paquet's *Flags*, which he would direct for the Volksbühne in 1924. Paquet's play, a dramatization of the 1886 Haymarket bombing in Chicago, consisted of twenty loosely connected scenes documenting the incident and its aftermath.[7] In order to expand and contextualize the performance, Piscator mounted two screens on either side of the production's large revolving set on which he projected text and images in between and during certain scenes. Piscator claims that he considered the screens to be 'blackboards' designed for 'reporting and documentation' (Piscator, 1980 [1963], p. 75). Furthermore, the projections could serve as an 'extension of the action and the clarification of the background to the action [...] a continuation of the play beyond the dramatic framework', and in this regard could be used to (re)contextualize the action allowing for emphasis to be placed on particular events that might contribute to a clearer political interpretation of the work (ibid., p. 75). Piscator later described the effect of mixing text and media as a kind of revue made up of 'chopped up' moments (ibid., p. 81), which may go some way to explaining why the play and its unconventional structure appealed to him. Willett also usefully points out that this was, in effect, a form of montage, which Piscator would have been familiar with from his Dada days (1986, p. 108).

While Piscator had only made minor amendments to *Flags* to accommodate his interest in a more fragmented, epic dramaturgy that could be expanded and (re)contextualized through scenic effects, this was not the case with other plays he chose to direct. Piscator significantly reworked Paquet's play *Tidal Wave* (*Sturmflut*), which he directed for the Volksbühne in 1926, during the rehearsal process because he was not satisfied with its revolutionary message or its characters, which he believed had been left without discernible characterization (Innes, 1972, p. 127). The problem of locating appropriate plays was so critical that upon setting up the first Piscator Theatre (Piscatorbühne) in 1927, Piscator established a dramaturgical collective to oversee the development of a suitable programme for his theatre. The original collective was overseen by Felix Gasbarra (who had worked with Piscator on the *Red Riot Revue*) and included among its members Walter Mehring and Bertolt Brecht. Two of the four productions developed with the assistance of the collective, with their careful balance of context, didactic political message, and propaganda, perhaps come closest to Piscator's vision for revolutionary theatre. These were *Rasputin* (1927), adapted from the play by Alexei Tolstoy and some thirty other sources, including Churchill's *The World Crisis* and Stalin's *The October Revolution*, and an adaptation of Jaroslav Hašek's novel *The Adventures of the Good Soldier Schweik*, entitled *Schweik*. Unfortunately, due to major debts, the first Piscatorbühne was closed down in 1928, thus prohibiting further experimentation with the dramaturgy collective. The second and third Piscator theatres, which operated in 1929 and 1930–1932, respectively, and on much-reduced scales than the first, also did not provide much opportunity for Piscator to continue to experiment with the epic form. With massive debts and an opportunity to direct films in the Soviet Union, Piscator left Berlin in 1931 – two years before Adolf Hitler was appointed German Chancellor. He did not return to Germany again for twenty years.

Bertolt Brecht and His Pedagogies

Bertolt Brecht's contribution to the development of epic theatre theory and practice is more widely known, but a discussion of his work here in the broader context of revolutionary popular theatres will be useful. Like Piscator, Brecht was drafted into military service during the First World War, although this came about a month before the war's end. Although he did not see any frontline fighting, his politics would be profoundly shaped by the war and its aftermath.[8] At the end of the war, the living conditions of the newly formed Weimar Republic were impoverished, as unemployment and inflation were high and hunger and poverty widespread. Unlike Piscator, however, his frustration with the conditions around him did not translate into immediate political activism or commitment to any of the socialist political parties. In the mid-1920s he would take up the serious study of Marxism – study that he would maintain throughout the rest of his life – although he never became a member of the KPD. As Mumford notes in her study of Brecht, he preferred instead to be critical from the sidelines (2009, p. 10). This somewhat loose connection with the KPD can be seen as early as 1922 with his semi-expressionist play *Drums in the Night*, which is set at the time of the Spartacist uprising. The play presents a sympathetic portrait of a war-weary soldier, Andreas Kragler, who returns from the war-front to find his fiancée, Anna, engaged to the war-profiteering/bourgeois Frederick Murke, at her parents' behest. As events intensify, Kragler and Anna are reunited and decide to forgo participation in the uprising in favour of the stability of home. While it is not exactly a scathing attack on the revolution, the refusal of the protagonist to commit to the uprising can be seen as reflecting Brecht's critical view of it. He is said to have thought the revolution 'ridiculously incompetent' (Mumford, 2009, p. 11).

Brecht began to use the term 'epic theatre' to discuss his experiments in developing a critical social theatre in the mid-1920s. As discussed, Piscator was by this time already working in this area – and no doubt Brecht's familiarity with his work and his participation in the Piscator Collective in 1927–1928 for the first Piscatorbühne shaped his views of it. Willett and Mumford acknowledge Piscator's didacticism, his use of music to disrupt the action and comment on it (Willett, 1986, p. 109), the use of film, and the 'decentralization' of the individual to the collective as being particularly influential to Brecht's practice (Mumford, 2009, pp. 22–23). And yet, it is also important to recognize that some of these features were already apparent in Brecht's work before his time with the Piscator Collective, especially the use of music (cf. *Baal*, written around 1918). His use of music and the episodic 'epic' structure was as much influenced by his fondness for popular forms of performance, especially the cabaret, as it was Piscator. Brecht was an avid cabaret spectator and sometimes performer who is known to have been a fan and personal friend of Bavarian clown and cabaret star Karl Valentin.[9] The two are even known to have performed together in a cabaret act the early 1920s (Calandra, 2003, pp. 190–191). A cabaret performance, like variety or music hall, usually consists of a programme of self-contained acts loosely connected by a master of ceremonies, or other host figure, who introduces each performance and makes banter with the performers and the audience. In addition to its frequent use of music, this episodic structure is quite clearly reflected in epic theatre dramaturgy, as are the linking and contextualizing devices, such as placards, projections or narrators to introduce scenes. The cabaret performer's performed persona, a mix of self with artificial 'show' personality, is also reflected in Brecht's attitude towards the epic actor. Unlike the realist theatre, where the actor is expected to fully embody a character, the Brechtian actor is asked to demonstrate it, thus allowing the actor to comment on their character's actions within the narrative. Finally, the cabaret's tendency to ridicule through parody and satire are also very firmly embedded into Brecht's theatre practice.

It is easy enough to misinterpret Brecht's theatre as one that privileges the intellectual over the pleasurable, but with popular forms scattered across his work there can be little doubt that he also sought to appeal to audience's want for amusement. He makes this point clearly in his essay 'Theatre for Pleasure or Theatre for Instruction':

> Generally there is felt to be a very sharp distinction between learning and amusing oneself. The first may be useful, but only the second is pleasant. So we have to defend the epic theatre against the suspicion that it is a highly disagreeably, humourless, indeed strenuous affair. (Brecht, 1964d, p. 72)

But the popular forms also served the political and critical objectives of the work. Placing familiar popular forms into different historical and cultural settings was a useful way of bridging the past and the present, and in many of Brecht's plays he dramatizes historical events in order to comment on the present, so bridging the periods was essential. This anachronistic laying of popular forms into the past was also a useful way of defamiliarizing familiar forms. It was this reciprocal relationship of (de)familiarization that might help achieve the *Verfremdungseffekt*, an effect which Brecht explains in 'A Short Organum for Theatre', is 'designed to free socially-conditioned phenomena from that stamp of familiarity which protects them from our grasp today' (Brecht, 1964a, p. 192). There is evidence of this in many of Brecht's plays: the jazz-infused songs of *The Threepenny Opera* (1928); the band of clown-soldiers in *Man Equals Man* (1926); and the echoes of the *commedia dell'arte* in his *Mr Puntilla and his Man Matti* (1940), among others. While this could be seen as simply a continuation of the experimental merging of elite and popular forms dating back to Meyerhold and the symbolists, it is more likely that Brecht's interest in cross-form pollination was more directly influenced by his understanding of Marxist dialectics, which conceives of social change as the consequence of the conflict of contradictory social forces. In fact, later on in his career, Brecht started using the term 'dialectical theatre' in preference to 'epic theatre', as it more clearly reflected what he wanted the work to do. So it is the contradiction between popular and elite forms that may help to explain why conjoining them appealed to Brecht.

Pedagogy was also central to Brecht's work. He conceived of education through theatre in two distinct, but connected, ways that he referred to as Major and Minor Pedagogies. The former was theorized as a way in which the public might be transformed into socialist 'statesmen' in an imagined post-revolutionary period (Brecht, 2003, p. 88). This particular pedagogical approach is most clearly found in his *Lehrstück* (learning plays), which were developed between 1926 and 1933. In a *Lehrstück*, the performer is expected to be both participant in the action and a spectator. The effect is similar to Augusto Boal's Forum Theatre, which would come about much later, in which 'spect-actors' are invited to propose and, at times, act out solutions to problems depicted in scripted performances about social issues. The performer in a *Lehrstück* is expected to learn positive social lessons by taking part in the performance, usually imitating scripted character's actions or creating alternatives. As Mueller confirms, the intended outcome was 'a total abolition of the division between performance and audience' (Mueller, 1994, p. 83). Choice was often central to these plays, which can be seen in texts like *The Boy Who Said Yes* and *The Boy Who Said No*. These related texts tell of an ill schoolboy who, in the former text, sacrifices himself for the greater good, and, in the latter, elects not to. In the *Baden Baden Cantata*, concerns are raised over the complicity of the individual in his personal destruction by placing one's trust in the wrong places, which was vividly demonstrated by the clown protagonist being sawn apart on stage by allegedly 'helpful' sources. Aesthetically, the performances were more indebted to the workers' choirs and theatres that were widely popular during this period than to the great epic experiments of semi-realist designs, revolving stages, and projections for which Brecht is perhaps better known. Photos taken of some of the plays show that many were performed on raised platforms with minimal settings and properties. But there were more than just aesthetic similarities between the workers' groups and Brecht's conception of the *Lehrstück*. As Mueller points out, he conceived of this kind of performance predominantly for the working class (1994, p. 82).

In contrast to Major Pedagogy was the Minor Pedagogy, which Brecht describes as 'a democratization of theatre in the transitional era of the first revolution' (Brecht, 2003, p. 88). The purpose of these plays was thus regarded as preparation for the post-revolutionary communist society. It is this category of work that constitutes the majority of his epic plays, which he spent the greatest amount time theorizing and practising, and subsequently where the bulk of our contemporary understanding of epic theatre stems from. The central component of Brechtian epic theatre is *Verfremdung*, which I briefly introduced earlier. It is a much-debated term that has been variously translated as alienation, defamiliarization and estrangement. The most recent, and perhaps clearest, translation comes from David Barnett in his book *Brecht in Practice*, which is 'making the familiar strange' (Barnett, 2014, p. 76). The aim of this strategy was to make elements and issues that had, through their familiarity, become naturalized appear sufficiently strange so that spectators could see and think about them differently. In his writing, Brecht offers several ways of realizing this effect. I have collated some of these below.

1. Prevent audiences from getting 'swept away' into the illusion by keeping them firmly grounded in the theatre space. This might include keeping lighting and sound equipment exposed; the use of placards and projections which indicate what will happen in a scene before it is played; and avoiding exhaustively detailed naturalistic settings, favouring instead only crucial realistic components so as to set the play and reveal/punctuate its social messages (Brecht, 1964c, p. 136).

2. In contrast with the Stanislavskian actor, the epic actor should not seek to psychologize his or her character. They should not seek to embody the role either. Instead, the actor is advised to remain conscious and critical of the character's actions at all times (ibid.).

3. Much like a comedian or variety show performer, the actor is instructed to 'show' their role and their critical attitude towards it in performance. This is known as *Gestus*, and it is intended to reveal the underlying social relations depicted in a scene. Despite the way it may sound, a *gest* may be revealed through the delivery of text, an expression, a gesture or a whole stage picture. In his essay 'On Gestic Music', Brecht explains that a social *gest* 'allows conclusions to be drawn about the social circumstances' (Brecht, 1964b, pp. 104–105).

4. Historicization is another defamiliarizing device. It is the process of repositioning an important social event in the past in order to place historical distance between it and the audience (Brecht, 1964c, p. 140). As Barnett points out, historicization also works to 'point out the differences [between two periods], [and] to stimulate the audience's curiosity and invite them to consider why such differences exist' (Barnett, 2014, p. 76).

The anticipated result was not intended to be dry or emotionless, as some have interpreted it to be, nor, as Brecht notes, is it to be 'as unnatural as its description' (Brecht, 1964c, p. 140). It is also important to recognize that while Brecht spent considerable time writing down the results of his own experiments, the techniques he used are by no means the only ones in which to achieve the *Verfremdungseffekt*. As Mumford helpfully reminds us, '*Verfremdung* is not about grafting artistic devices mentioned in his essays [...] onto a production. Rather, it is a matter of employing devices in accordance with an interventionist interpreta-tion' (2009, p. 65). Given the rigour with which he pursued methods to effectively mobilize 'the children of the scientific age' (Brecht, 1964a, p. 204) and realize his Marxist beliefs, Brecht would probably be disap-pointed to see his approaches treated as historically unalterable.

Like Piscator and many other leading left-wing artists, Brecht went into exile when Hitler came to power. As early as 1923, his work had already attracted the attention of the Nazis who protested a production of his play *In the Jungle* with gas bombs, claiming that it sought to glo-rify communism (Mumford, 2009, p. 11). During his sixteen years in exile, spent largely in the United States, Brecht wrote some of his most important epic plays, including *The Life of Galileo*, *Mother Courage and Her Children*, *The Good Person of Szechwan* and *The Caucasian Chalk Circle*. In 1949, Brecht and his wife, actress Helene Weigel, formed the Berliner Ensemble in East Berlin, where he focused entirely on the development of his practice until his death in 1956. The Ensemble remains a significant presence in European theatre today.

Conclusion

The revolutionary theatres that emerged in the Soviet Union and Weimar Republic in the early part of the twentieth century are good examples of Hall's 'double movement of containment and resistance', discussed in the introduction to this book (Hall, 2009, p. 509). As I explained, the popular theatre, while of interest to or directed at subor-dinate social groups, may not always be prepared in the interest of their welfare. As Mayer pointed out, it may just as well operate to impress 'the symbols and personalities of authority [...] upon the public' (Mayer, 1977, p. 263). One is faced with a particularly striking example of this paradox in the case of revolutionary popular theatre in Russia. On one hand, the performances created were intended to advance the revolution and its aims – the end of oppressive ruling and economic systems, which would see the liberation of the working classes. On the other hand, during the civil war and through the early years of the Soviet Republic, the same theatre was being used to indoctrinate the masses into submitting to an authoritarian communist regime. Given the political climate, such performances may have certainly appealed to, and found sympathetic reception with, many Russian people; but it cannot be convincingly argued that they were in control of the aesthetic or content of these works. Indeed, as discussed, Narkompros closely monitored this work to ensure 'official' Soviet narratives were being communicated to audiences. Aesthetically and politically, the work changed very little after the Bolsheviks assumed power. What changed was who was in power and how those in power used the theatre. What had started as bottom-up theatres, emerging from a place of subordination and directed at oppressive economic and ruling systems, became, after the revolution, the theatre of power, and it was directed from the top back down. This change in direction does not necessarily jeopardize the form's popular status, but it usefully demonstrates how slippery the slope between the people and power can be in popular culture. Such shifts are inherently part of how popular culture works.

Outside Soviet Russia, the October Revolution and its aftermath were an inspiration to many on the far left. In Germany, theatre-makers, including Toller, Piscator and Brecht, developed unique aesthetic systems for articulating their political views to audiences. These were aimed at provoking critical thinking about social and economic inequalities, and mobilizing audiences into action. In this sense, Germany at that time supplies another case of bottom-up popular theatre, emerging from outside power and directed at it. While Brecht's work has unquestionably had the most long-lasting impact on political and popular theatre practice, in the 1920s it was Piscator's work that would have the greatest impact on proletarian theatre. His 'discovery' of the revue format for creating revolutionary performance was especially important, for it was a model that could be – and was – easily reproduced by other artists and activists to feed into the growing worker-focused movement. As discussed, the revue format would also be influential in the development of Piscator's brand of epic theatre, especially its fragmented dramaturgy, which was better suited to historicization, juxtaposition and didacticism than other available dramatic models. By the time the Moscow Blue Blouses toured Germany in 1927, bringing with them their own revue/variety format, Piscator had already demonstrated how such a form could be used to promote the revolutionary cause.

The popular theatres developed in Russia and Germany between 1917 and 1930 would prove hugely influential on politically committed workers seeking better working and living conditions. Owing to the abolition of many autocratic regimes in Europe and the success of the Bolsheviks in Russia, the promises of socialism started to be viewed as less utopian and much more like realizable prospects. The economic crisis of 1929, leading to the worldwide Great Depression in the 1930s, was also a signal to many that capitalism was a far from stable system, further enhancing socialism's appeal. Out of this grew an international movement of left-wing political parties and socialist organizations, and from these a network of theatres, which had as their goal the mass education of the workers by workers, to see an end to capitalism and the establishment of more equitable social and economic systems. The next two chapters will consider the workers' theatres that developed in Germany, Britain and the United States, and how these became unified under the banner of the Workers' Theatre Movement.

4 The Workers' Theatre Movement I: Starting Points, and Germany

As Chapters 2 and 3 showed, there was a growing international awareness of the struggles of working-class people in the nineteenth and early twentieth centuries. A significant development in this history was the revolution that occurred in Russia in 1917, which became a beacon of hope for socialists internationally. In the quickly changing political contexts following the First World War, the working classes (and those working for their emancipation) took the opportunity to participate and gain recognition in a way they had not been previously allowed. A notable sign of this change was the rise in the number of workers' organizations, including theatre and film groups, throughout the 1920s and early 1930s. Not only were these groups seeking to disseminate their ideas more widely in an effort to recruit more members and strengthen support for their cause, but they were taking advantage of new political environments that recognized their right to creatively and politically express themselves and their ideas.

Although some limitations on these activities still existed, it was no longer completely necessary for theatre groups to operate covertly through suggestive but often politically ambiguous naturalistic plays. Instead, they were freer to articulate their ideas more explicitly and through a wider array of dramatic means. Meyerhold's, Piscator's and Brecht's work are all manifestations of this new-found political freedom, but outside of their professional contexts, there were hundreds, if not thousands, of proletarian groups drawing on the theatre to spread socialist ideas. As with the Blue Blouse and TEREVSET in the Soviet

Union, amateur theatre groups thrived in conjunction with the professional theatre, and, due in large part to their mobility and the frequency with which they performed, they were seen by more audiences than the professional theatres.

While there were, of course, amateur workers' theatre groups performing before the First World War, such as the Clarion Players groups in Britain or the groups associated with the German Workers' Theatre League, they would become especially prevalent in many countries after the war, as many believed significant social change was imminent. By the mid-1920s, an international movement of communist-oriented popular theatres was starting to take shape, reaching its peak in the early 1930s. The Workers' Theatre Movement, as it was known, involved amateur and professional theatre groups from around the world, with the most significant activity coming from the Soviet Union, Europe, the United States and Japan. In this and the following chapter, the major developments of radical popular theatre practice between the two World Wars will be introduced. I will focus the discussion on linkages that can be found between groups internationally, and singling out, where appropriate, crucial variations between approaches.

Starting Points

The origins of the Workers' Theatre Movement can be found in a number of sources. In Germany, the impact of the pre-war workers' groups, allied together through the German Workers' Theatre League (Deutscher Arbeiter Theatre Bund), more popularly known by the acronym DATB, is one clear source, although not all of the theatres involved in the organization were exclusively socialist. In fact, there were nationalist, Christian and socialist factions – all producing performances of plays, readings, recitations and musical events, usually in association with either their workers' organization or the local branches of their respective political parties. While this might sound divisive, the groups usually shared a common goal, which, as Bradby and McCormick observe, 'was to find a way back to the medieval community of shared beliefs' (1978, p. 66). Similar developments took place in Britain and the United States, although they were more heavily influenced by the growing labour movements in those countries. In Britain, as well as the Clarion theatre groups and Cooperative drama societies that characterized socialist drama in the early years of the twentieth century, theatre groups affiliated with the Independent Labour Party and the Labour Party soon surfaced after the war.[1]

As well as being a recreational activity for people of shared political beliefs, the Labour Party saw propagandist potential in the theatre. A notice appearing in the *Labour Leader* in 1922, for instance, advised branches to start putting on plays to liven up weekly meetings, 'for as much propaganda is given in the sketches as is often supplied by the ablest socialist speaker' (quoted in Samuel, 1985, p. 21). Despite what this suggests about the politics of the performances developed, Raphael Samuel confirms most were usually politically 'centre-left', focusing on 'the sharpening of the class struggle and increasing polarization of British politics' as opposed to socialist revolution (1980, p. 216). In 1925, twelve labour drama groups were brought together under the London Labour Drama Federation, an initiative organized by Herbert Morrison, the Labour Party Secretary, and a group of Labour MPs and theatre professionals (Saville, 1990, p. 22). A year later, the Federation mounted a production of Czech playwright Karel Čapek's *The Insect Play*, a parable on human failing represented by insect species, at the Strand Theatre in London's West End. While the production appears to have been largely well received, it resulted in a deficit for the Federation and no further productions were given (Saville, 1990, p. 23).

The Independent Labour Party's Masses Stage and Screen Guild, formed three years before the London Labour Drama Federation, provided more sustained support for socialist theatre groups and would have a much more robust presence through its productions and other programmed events. Like the Federation, it was also supported by the professional theatre industry, with notable involvement from actors Sybil Thorndike, Lewis Casson, Melton Rosmer and Elsa Lanchester (Samuel, 1985, p. 22). The manager of the Strand Theatre in London's West End, Arthur Bourchier, was a member of the Guild and allowed the organization to use the theatre to programme events on Sunday evenings, leading to productions of *Hamlet*, Georg Kaiser's expressionist drama *Gas* and Elmer Rice's *The Adding Machine*. Perhaps its most significant production in terms of the Workers' Theatre Movement was its premiere of Upton Sinclair's *Singing Jailbirds* at the Apollo Theatre in the West End in 1925. The play, set in a jail after the 1923 California maritime strike involving the International Workers of the World (IWW), seeks to counter the extremist stereotype that prevailed in the media at the time of IWW members, known as Wobblies.

The text would be widely performed by workers' groups in Britain throughout the decade.

Despite the increase in political theatre activity, locating appropriate texts remained a challenge for groups internationally. The two options usually available to amateur theatres would be either to draw on well-known left-wing plays, of which there were few, or to author plays themselves. In Britain, London-based groups had the benefit of drawing on the drama library of the British Drama League, founded in 1919. The League's remit was not exclusively Labour theatre societies, but amateur and community theatres more generally, and thus the plays in its collections were wide-ranging. Of the 360 societies affiliated with the League in 1923, only a fraction of those were politically motivated (Browne, 1953, pp. 203–204). Apart from the League's library, groups could also consult two series of plays that were published specifically for use by amateur Independent Labour and Labour Party theatres. The first, *Plays for a People's Theatre*, published in 1920, included Ralph Fox's *Captain Youth*, a play about a young boy who fantasizes about defeating imaginary evil pirates and who then grows up to fight capitalism, and D.H. Lawrence's *Touch and Go*, about the problems faced by a rural mining village. The second series, *Plays for the People*, was overseen by the *Daily Herald*'s drama critic, Monica Ewer, and published by the Labour Publishing Company in 1925. Among the more spirited highlights from the eighteen plays in the series are Stephen Schofield's political farce *The Bruiser's Election*, A.J. Boothroyd's comedy *Foiling the Reds* and Margaret MacNamera's *Mrs Jupp Obliges*, a one-act play about a housekeeper who outwits her employer for a weekend cottage. While both series were widely applauded by labour critics for their originality and for the spirit in which they were published, many of the plays were considered to be gloomy and poorly written, which seemed contradictory to the goals of the movement.

Apart from these series of plays and promoting use of the League's library, the Independent Labour Party did little else to support its theatre groups in finding appropriate material. This left many groups electing to perform a few well-worn favourites. Among the most frequently produced were plays by Toller, especially *Masses and Man*, a tragedy about a female worker who seeks a pacifist solution to revolutionary violence, and his *Transfigurations*, as well as Čapek's *R.U.R.*, a dystopian sci-fi thriller in which the world is overtaken by mass-produced robots, and his *The Insect Play*, already mentioned. If in doubt, plays by George Bernard Shaw were usually considered a safe choice.

Labour in the United States

That Sinclair's *Singing Jailbirds*, an American play, would not receive its American premiere until 1928, by which point it was already well established in Britain as an important workers' theatre text, can be read as broadly indicative of the different cultural attitudes towards the labour movement and socialism in the United States at the time. While similar developments in the socialist and labour movements occurred in the United States at roughly the same time as they did in Europe, the people's relationship with socialism and the labour movement was fundamentally very different. One of the reasons for this may have been the country's comparative youth compared to European nations. In the eighteenth century, the United States was founded upon the rejection of autocratic rule, reflected in the humanist axiom that 'all men are created equal', first inscribed on the US Declaration of Independence in 1776. In doing so, the country chose to break, ideologically, with centuries of oppressive hierarchical social systems in Europe – such as feudalism and aristocracy – that would bring many oppressed Europeans to North American shores in the eighteenth and nineteenth centuries. While its axiom has not borne out particularly truthfully in practice, the country was considered to be a progressive alternative for working and lower-class immigrants from Europe, which I believe probably delayed the spread of working-class dissidence.

The second – and very much related – reason concerns the ethnic and racial makeup of the American working classes. The predominant oppressed body in the United States has historically been that of ethnic minorities, especially African Americans, who were constitutionally denied the same rights and protections as white Americans up until the 1960s. Add to this a heavy influx of immigrants from Europe throughout the late nineteenth and early twentieth centuries, and the picture that emerges of the working class in the United States is one that is much more ethnically and racially diverse than that in most European countries during the corresponding period. Racist attitudes and a distrust of foreigners at the time meant that a coherent class identity that could have driven a mass movement was difficult to establish. This is what Susan Roth Breitzer has referred to as 'unequal labour citizenship', in which narrow definitions of American-ness determined the levels of access one might have to the labour movement. Indeed, some trade unions, including the American Federation of Labor, the largest federation for labour unions in the United States for most of the first half of twentieth century, implicitly promoted discrimination by their unwillingness to acknowledge or punish union members for racist behaviour in order to remain attractive to white members (Breitzer, 2011, pp. 270–201).

In addition to the problem of race, government repression of trade unions and advocates of radical political alternatives in the United States was, as scholars including Robert Justin Goldstein have argued, significantly greater than that in Europe (2010, p. 275). Repression at the federal and state levels usually occurred in the form of court-ordered anti-strike injunctions, the use of the armed forces, as well as private and city police forces, arrests and imprisonment on a large scale. If these very public 'lessons' in the State's views about organized labour were not clear enough, they were compounded by negative representations of trade unionists in the media and popular culture, which depicted them as violent aggressors. In his study of American workers' theatre, Lee Papa has noted these representations had a profound impact on the drama that was developed. He writes:

> As the government attempted to crush the effort to form a labor community and further alienated and separated the radical union male from society, the artistic response attempted both to explain the original source of the workers' alienation and to offer rejoinders to the popular perceptions of the [union] male. (2009, p. 4)

This can clearly be seen in Sinclair's *Singing Jailbirds*, which takes audiences into the jail cell with the Wobblies, presenting them in a rational, romantic light, intentionally counteracting the media's portrayal of them as irrational, politically misguided social terrorists. Plays like Peter Yrondy's *Seven Years of Agony* and Maxwell Anderson and Harold Hickerson's *Gods of the Lighting*, about the highly publicized trial and execution of Italian anarchists Nicola Sacco and Bartolomeo Vanzetti, are other examples of this. These plays not only offered a sympathetic portrayal of the two men but also openly challenged the inherently racist legal system many believed had failed them. In the early 1930s, the Scottsboro trials would provide the inspiration for performances more closely concerned with race, with works ranging from the agitprop *Scottsboro*, developed by New York–based German-language group Prolet-Buehne, to Langston Hughes's *Scottsboro Limited*.[2] Throughout the 1920s and early 1930s, the workers' theatres in the United States were especially interested in counteracting misrepresentations of minority groups that jeopardized a unified image of the American working class from forming. Because of this, and the repressive contexts in which much of the work was written, the tone of the plays and their radical political position is often much sharper than those developed in Britain during the same time.

Comintern

Another major factor in the development of the Worker's Theatre Movement was the international expansion of the Communist Party following the establishment of Comintern in 1919. Comintern was the name given to the Third Communist International, which was established to promote the international proletarian revolution (Sandle, 2012, p. 41). The Comintern's agenda was agreed on at large meetings of international delegates, known as congresses, and by Moscow. Justification for educational arts activity was covered by one of the resolutions agreed by the First Congress in 1919, which was 'to explain to the broad mass of the workers the historic significance and the political and historical necessity of the new, proletarian, democracy which must replace bourgeois democracy and the parliamentary system' (Lenin, 1919). International branches of the Communist Party would look to Moscow to determine how best to do this, which is why the Living Newspaper and agitprop models developed and refined by TEREVSAT and Blue Blouse, and overseen (more or less collectively) by Narkompros and the Central Committee's Department of Agitation and Propaganda, would become the most emulated by workers' groups internationally. The establishment of the International Workers' Dramatic Union in Moscow in 1929, which became the command centre for workers' theatres internationally, would anchor the movement and give its growing ranks guidance on how to maximize their efforts. This was reinforced by bulletins put out by the Agit-Prop Department of the Red International of Labour Unions, a communist international trade union organization that had offices around the world, which reported on the union and its developments, ensuring the revolutionary theatre models developed in the Soviet Union were disseminated internationally. Simultaneously, it told workers' theatres everywhere that an international movement was underway (Saville, 1990, p. 53).

The shift in dramaturgical approach from the more conventional domestic labour dramas to agitprop should be read in the context of the Communist Party's shifting ideological position, as well as its rise internationally as a legitimate political alternative to the reformist socialist parties. As some well-established socialist parties splintered to form new communist parties, they took their amateur theatre groups with them, or built new ones, in order to carry out their revised political goals. From 1919 until around 1925, it is difficult to locate communist performances outside the Soviet Union and Germany. This was the result of a number of factors, including post-war recovery, the time it took for new parties to grow their membership, and a lack of clarity around the Central Committee's official views on using art for political purposes. The United Front policy, which allowed for alliances with moderate socialist groups, was almost certainly a factor as well. The propagandistic plays produced by workers' amateur theatres, while not strictly adhering to the 'correct' (that is, Soviet-Communist) ideology, were raising class-consciousness with working class audiences. For these reasons, the workers' theatres of the early 1920s remained predominantly socialist in their outlook.

Workers' Theatre in Germany

But this steadily changed. In 1922, just two years after dismissing Piscator's efforts at building a proletarian theatre, the German Communist Party (KPD) passed a resolution at a conference on education recommending that workers' groups start using mass chant, similar to those discussed in relation to the Proletkult in Chapter 2 (Bradby & McCormick, 1978, p. 66). As a result, the Central Sprechchor (speaking choir) of the KPD was established, assimilating the members of the Proletarian Travelling Theatre a year later to make a choir of approximately sixty members (Davies, 2013, p. 240). Around the same time, the Communist Youth League of Germany (Kommunistischer Jugendverband Deutschlands), known by the acronym KJVD, began producing 'Red Revels', revues made up of short satirical scenes anchored by a theme. The first of these was performed in 1924 for the Eleventh International Day of Youth and contained sketches including 'This is the way in which young workers shall be drilled in the Involuntary Labour School' and 'March of Our Enemies' (Stourac & McCreery, 1986, pp. 104–105). The idea for revels was as much about novelty as it was propaganda. In a 1927 edition of the KJVD's official journal *Der Junge Bolshewik*, it is noted:

> We must try to find lively vivid forms for our political agitation like those found in the fairground: the barker who attracts the masses with his quick-witted remarks, the fun house, etc. ... The Red Revels ... enabled

us to approach the most indifferent young people and arouse their interest and enthusiasm. (quoted in Stourac & McCreery, 1986, p. 104)

Later that year, bolstered by the success of its Red Revels, the KJVD
congress would recommend that revels be used to agitate nationally at
large political events and gatherings (ibid., p. 107).

The clearest sign of the KPD's changed attitude towards the use of
theatre for propaganda would come in 1926 when it sought greater
control over the German Workers' Theatre League (DATB) (ibid.).
In the same year, the professional actor Maxim Vallentin set up the
'First Agit-Prop Troupe of the Communist Federation', or more simply
Agitprop Truppe, becoming the first of many troupes associated with
the KJVD. Early experiments in mass chant gave way to a more Soviet-
influenced agitprop theatre as the troupe matured. Vallentin's faith
in the agitprop form was strengthened a year later upon witnessing
the Blue Blouse tour. The Blue Blouse programme, featuring songs,
political orations, sketches and musical numbers, was precisely what
Vallentin and other political activists in Germany had been looking
for – a hard-hitting revolutionary theatre in a more convenient, concentrated form that could be convincingly performed by workers. By
1928 the KPD takeover of the DATB was complete. The new organization was renamed Workers' Theatre Federation of Germany (Arbeiter
Theatre Bund Deutschland), or ATBD for short. Arthur Pieck, the
son of KPD politician Wilhelm Pieck and founder of the Red Blouses
agitprop troupe, led the federation. From this point, both the ATBD
and the KJVD oversaw amateur workers' theatres across the country.
While they remained separate organizations, both were directly associated with the KPD.

By the time the KPD's revamped theatre federation was fully opera-
tional in 1928, the Agitprop Truppe had changed its name to Red
Megaphone and had become the leader of a quickly growing field
of German revolutionary workers' theatres, which included Column
Left, the Hamburg Riveters and many troupes incorporating the word
'red' into their names, such as Red Hammer, Red Rocket, Red Tempo
and Red Smithies (Bodek, 1997, p. 81). While exact figures are difficult to establish, it has been estimated that the between 300 and 500
troupes were affiliated with the ATBD in 1929, reaching an audience
of approximately two million people (Stourac & McCreery, 1986, p.
300).[3] In terms of participants, Bradby and McCormick indicate that
by 1929 the whole of the ATBD would have nearly 10,000 active
members (1978, p. 79).

Programmes developed by troupes would usually consist of sketches, songs and political monologues, many of which were satirical. Borrowing from Blue Blouse, a programme would often begin with a parade introducing the company, which could consist of anywhere between eight and thirty members. Following the parade, troupes might take advantage of the full company's presence by offering a *sprechchor* or, following the Blue Blouse model they might decide to perform a Living Newspaper on a topical issue. This usually helped establish the theme for the programme, which could range from showing solidarity with the Soviet Union to an issue affecting local people. According to texts published by *The Red Megaphone*, one of the movement's official periodicals, the most popular subjects were the Communist Party, Comintern, Marxist education and youth (Bodek, 1997, p. 108). Willett notes that, above all, troupes were instructed by party leaders to propagate the proletarian class struggle (1988, p. 135). It was party politics, rather than aesthetics, therefore, that guided the troupes' performances.

The environment in which the work was to be performed, which might be a street corner, factory floor, cafeteria or a small stage in a workers' club, often determined the length of a troupe's programme. A programme organized for outdoor settings was necessarily different from that organized for indoor spaces. When developing programmes for the outdoors, troupes had to give careful consideration to a number of important practical issues around staging and audibility. Many groups performed on raised platforms or on truck beds when working outdoors so as to improve sightlines, although depending on financial resources or the urgency of the performance (if it was supporting a strike, for instance), then groups may have had to contend with performing at ground level. Sound and vocal projection were fundamental concerns for troupes. Although performers may have used vocal amplification devices like megaphones in order to be heard, many would have to learn to comfortably project their own voices without amplification. For this reason, the best sketches for outdoor settings tended to prioritize movement and gesture over verbal communication, and therefore economized on dialogue.

Police interference was also an issue that had to be contended with. Troupes performing in outdoor public spaces might be able to get through only the parade and a few sketches before the arrival of the police, who would end the performance and disperse the crowds. Therefore, programmes designed for public spaces needed to consist of a troupe's clearest and most politically poignant materials in order to ensure they could communicate their message as quickly and efficiently as possible. It may be for this reason that some troupes were criticized for 'sloganizing' instead of agitating. A carefully crafted slogan that audiences could repeat with the troupe not only helped strengthen the connection between the performers and their audiences, it also ensured spectators walked away from the show with a political message firmly embedded in their minds. Context was also important. If a troupe was agitating on their own accord, then they could organize a programme according to their own agenda. If they were invited to perform as an auxiliary for a larger political gathering, however, then their hosts may have set the troupe's agenda. All of these factors would have impacted the programmes they developed and how they performed when working outdoors.

Working indoors usually enabled troupes to expand their programmes. Although the performance style was carried over from the outdoors, the megaphones and other tools needed in the outdoors were usually not. Certainly, indoor spaces provided groups with an opportunity to perform wordier sketches and to develop programmes more tightly bound by a theme. Evidence of this can be found in a programme developed by Red Megaphone and performed on 29 March 1931 (Bodek, 1997, pp. 94–99). Entitled *Für die Sowjetmacht* (*For Soviet Power*), the programme was broken up into three distinct acts made up of approximately twenty individual scenes. Starting with the parade, the programme moved into a mass chant about the Soviet *Komsomol*,[4] which was followed by a brief historical play about the Russian Revolution and the formation of the Soviet Union; a short moral sketch about a distracted, leisurely worker; a monologue about grain; a song about agriculture; and a 'where are they now'–type comic sketch about the former higher classes of Russia. The first half of the programme concluded with a song further glorifying the Soviet system. In the second act, a series of monologues, collective speeches and a short scene made comparisons between the Weimar Republic and the Soviet Union, highlighting the superiority of the latter nation. The final act focused on the defence of the Soviet Union. It consisted of a political speech about the failure of Western capitalism and two short scenes about the military and the GPU (the Soviet intelligence service), respectively. The performance concluded with 'For Soviet Power', a song in ten verses that surveys major Soviet events, from the Bolshevik victory to Stalin's economic plans, better known as the Five-Year Plans.

Skill was obviously a key factor in developing a programme as well. While members were expected to be able to move, sing and act, some had strengths in particular areas and the flexibility of the revue format combined with the fact that troupes authored their own materials enabled individual specialisms, such as acrobatic skills, an especially beautiful voice or good comic abilities, to be showcased in the performance. Collectivism and unity were prioritized over individual virtuosity, for their politics demanded this, but troupes still needed to attract and entertain audiences, and so some showmanship was essential. Performers were, for the most part, untrained and had a limited understanding and experience of theatre. As with other amateur theatres discussed so far, this made performing conventional plays and developing convincing characters difficult, as it would expose the shortcomings of the performers. This was equally as concerning for the KPD, because productions that suffered from apparent amateurism and a lack of skill would not be useful in furthering the movement. Like Blue Blouse, the German troupes rejected Naturalism and other perceived bourgeois dramatic forms, instead favouring satirical sketches containing two kinds of characters: proletarian or capitalist. For the proletarian roles, actors were instructed to merely act themselves and to avoid excessive emotion. Capitalist roles, however, were usually performed in an exaggerated, caricatured manner. Sketches, then, often had a cartoonish quality to them, depicting the heroic, sensible proletarian in battle against the ridiculous and evil capitalist enemy. The anti-bourgeois position usually extended to the use of sets and costumes. While suggestive scenographic elements might be used – e.g. a top hat to symbolize a capitalist or a few stools to represent a factory office – it was predominantly up to the performer to signify both their character and setting through their performance, which likely contributed to the physical exaggeration which characterized the work.

While standards varied between troupes, the impression given by most accounts of German agitprop is that it was developed to a high standard. Tom Thomas, national organizer of the British Workers' Theatre Movement who saw the German troupes perform in 1931, recalled that their performances were 'absolutely smashing' (1985a, p. 89). He seemed particularly impressed by the calibre of the performers. 'They were all very fine actors,' he observed. 'They didn't change their clothes though they appeared physically different in each scene' (ibid.).

Troupe members authored most of the sketches, songs and other materials that were performed. While some groups worked with professional writers to help generate material, most did not. Without extensive knowledge of plays or playwriting, many groups undertook the responsibility of developing material together, basing their work on models they had either seen performed or that they borrowed directly from other groups. Some troupes would have taken ideas for material from the scripts published in the two journals that served the movement, the aforementioned *Red Megaphone*, co-produced by the KPD and NJVD, and *Workers' Theatre*, issued in Berlin by the ATBD. Available scripts, however, were not seen as being very good and, consequently, many groups sought either to heavily adapt available materials, hoping to improve upon them, or to develop their own. For those who chose to do the latter, the process for devising new material was not dissimilar to that of many contemporary theatre groups who devise their own work. Central to the process was research, observation, improvisation and reflection. The research element primarily consisted of collecting stories and other pieces of information that might be used to develop a sketch. Newspapers, pamphlets and interviews were common sources of information for troupes. Bodek reports that members of Red Megaphone constructed many of their performances from interviews conducted by Vallentin's wife, Edith, with patrons at working-class pubs (Bodek, 1997, p. 89). Her interviews were not recorded or written down, but were roughly transcribed from memory later on. Precision and detail were unnecessary – and in some ways a hindrance – as only essential details could be translated into a sketch, which was usually between three and ten minutes long. Troupe members would also conduct interviews with audience members from time to time, which ensured that they were developing material that responded to the needs of the people they performed for.

In addition to research, education was also key to the development of material, not just in the political issues they sought to address through their work, but also Marxism and KPD policy. Bodek has pointed out, however, that most worker-players' understanding of Marxist theory was much like that of the broader population: 'sketchy' (1997, p. 82). This was a concern since troupes trafficked on the illusion of their fluency with communist ideas. As Bodek notes, 'they did everything possible to act as organic intellectuals' (ibid.). While some groups tried to read and teach themselves, many others took advantage of the Marxist Workers' School, also known as MASCH, which offered courses in a range of subjects, including politics, history and literature – all from a Marxist perspective. Helmut Damerius and members of his troupe Column Left attended MASCH courses regularly in order to gain a better understanding of Marxism. Despite his and his troupes' efforts at self-improvement, he continued to believe that Marxist theory was the group's fundamental weakness (ibid., p. 84). The ATBD ran similar courses, although they also offered classes in making workers' theatre.

Once collected, materials would be presented and discussed by the group. If something was believed to have dramatic potential, it would be taken into rehearsals. While some groups chose to work with forms of collective writing, which may have involved a combination of improvisation and roundtable discussion, others relied more heavily on improvisation and critical reflection. At some point, regardless of method, a written text was usually produced. For troupes working with professional writers, the process was similar. It was rare for a professional writer to create without the input of the troupe. Because of this, professionals, when they were used, had to adhere to the ideology of collective development. Their professional status, while valued, would not give them authority over anyone else in the group.

Music was also an important feature of a troupe's programme. As well as political songs, instrumental music was used to underscore the action of a sketch or to punctuate a particular point. Bodek explains that some troupes even performed dance music for the audiences, so in some cases music not only served a dramaturgical function but a social one – helping the performers forge a stronger bond with spectators (ibid., p. 82). But developing original music for a performance was an even greater challenge to troupes than producing scripts. While some troupes had the benefit of having a musician or composer among its membership – such as Red Megaphone, of which composer Hanns Eisler was a member – others had to find a way to realize their musical ideas without specialist support.[5] To overcome difficulties such as these, many troupes chose to adapt music they were familiar with. Borrowing patriotic songs from the Soviet Union was also common. Another strategy was to alter the lyrics of popular songs from the period. Troupes discovered that one of the benefits of adapting popular melodies was that they were already known to audiences, which in turn helped draw them into the performance, perhaps even making them a little more receptive to its propaganda. It also gave many agit-prop troupes a contemporary, popular appeal. This would have been compounded by their youthfulness, with the average worker-player estimated to be twenty-three years old (ibid., p. 80). A number of conclusions might be drawn about the allure of young bands of radicals armed with cool music and short, punchy political sketches, especially for young working-class people. The troupes were tremendously popular in working-class areas across Germany, which they understood and worked to exploit. As Bodek confirms, 'They were lively; they sang, danced and acted [...] They brought a splash of colour into the otherwise dull routine of tenement life, party gatherings, and union meetings', which many people valued (ibid.).

While agitprop and revue were the most widely used forms of workers' theatre in Germany, they were by no means the only forms during the late 1920s. In a report for the first NJVT congress, the leader of the Red Rockets acknowledged at least three kinds of workers' theatre being practised at the time: (1) 'old club performance', a legacy of the DABT and the working clubs that characterized German workers theatre in the early twentieth century; (2) text-heavy pieces, like *sprechchor* and conventional plays; and (3) agitprop (Stourac & McCreery, 1986, p. 132). While no specific form was ever exclusively endorsed by one of the workers' theatre associations, it was clear to many troupes that the agitprop form best suited the goals of the communist Third Period and the abilities of amateur performers. And yet, the agitprop form was not so rigid as to prevent groups from experimenting with it. Groups including Red Rocket found it best suited to the humorous and satirical treatment of important issues, ridiculing capitalism through the use of stereotype and reduction. Vallentin's Red Megaphones, on the other hand, while certainly no stranger to political satire, wished for a more serious means of analysing issues for their audiences. The company's *Hello, Young Worker* can be seen as an example of this. The short, episodic sketch depicts the backstory of a young, suicidal worker, showing how his delicate mental state is a result of the oppressions he experienced throughout his lifetime: the stigma of his working-class upbringing; the hostile, authoritarian education system; and being fired from his job for refusing to work during a strike. The piece does not offer a tidy, happy ending for the worker, but leaves it open for the audience to conclude. So while agitprop was clearly widely used, it is important to recognize that it was an adaptable form that was aesthetically and stylistically altered by each troupe that performed it.

While the workers' theatre troupes were unquestionably popular with working class audiences, they were a consistent headache for other political parties, especially the ruling Social Democratic Party (SPD). In 1931, just as movements in Britain and the United States were starting to prosper, the German movement would suffer a fatal blow when the SPD passed the Law to Fight Political Excesses, which gave the police permission to ban agitprop troupes (Stourac & McCreery, 1986, p. 148). At this point, troupes had to decide whether to stop performing or continue and face possible arrest and imprisonment. This resulted in a shift in policy by the national organizations, which encouraged troupes to continue working but to make their performances more politically discreet. In an edition of the journal *Arbeiterbühne und Film* published in 1931, it was reported that 'we are not allowed to state explicitly anymore, but we may hint [...] one can achieve greater effects by hinting ... The audience understands and has the pleasure of thinking through what was only inferred' (quoted in Stourac & McCreery, 1986, p. 149).

The success of the Nazi Party in the 1932 election, followed by the appointment of Hitler as Chancellor in 1933, would effectively finish off the movement. Although some groups continued to perform more covertly as late as 1936, the Nazis aggressively pursued communists and communist organizations. Bodek notes that in the period after 1933, some troupe members were sent to concentration camps, some were drafted into the armed forces, while others escaped and emigrated to other countries (1997, p. 161). Many others were imprisoned, tortured and murdered to signal to others it was time to halt their activities (Stourac & McCreery, 1986, p. 304).

5 The Workers' Theatre Movement II: Britain and the United States

In Britain, the division between Labour and Communist-oriented workers' theatres would become more apparent following the 1926 National Strike, in which members of the Trades Union Congress stopped working for nine days to support 800,000 miners who had been locked out of mines during a wage dispute. The leader of the Labour Party at the time, Ramsay McDonald, fearing the strike's revolutionary undertones, refused to support it. For some Labour members, this was seen as a betrayal and many opted to leave the party. Tom Thomas, leader of the Hackney Labour Dramatic Group (soon renamed the Hackney People's Players), formed just months prior to the National Strike, was one of the defectors. He notes in his memoir essay 'A propertyless theatre for the propertyless class':

> in 1926 I left [the Labour Party] because of the way the General Strike had been betrayed. I could not continue under the MacDonald leadership which I was convinced would commit fresh betrayals, so I joined the only other socialist organization, the Community Party, and remained in it for many years. (1985a, p. 79)

The first leg of the British Workers' Theatre Movement (WTM) would emerge in the months following the strike. It is now largely regarded as the efforts of two organizations, the *Sunday Worker* newspaper and the Central Labour College, although it was artist and poet Christina Walshe who was the principal organizer (Samuel, 1985, p. 50). Equally important was the input of theatre critic and Soviet theatre expert Huntly Carter who advocated for a worker-driven theatre built not of old bourgeoisie techniques but of new modernist theatre forms. The goal, Carter claimed, was to find dramaturgical strategies that could represent 'the new machine age from a proletarian point of view' (ibid., p. 42).

The WTM's first production was Sinclair's *Singing Jailbirds*, discussed in the previous chapter, which was performed at Memorial Hall in London in July 1926, before embarking on a small tour. As the choice of text indicates, the division between the old labour drama groups and the emerging communist ones was not clear-cut. Indeed, as Samuel has pointed out, many theatre groups operating in Britain during this period were a conflation of Labour, Independent Labour and Communist Party members, including Thomas's Hackney People's Players (ibid., p. 38).

The WTM's second project was much more in line with Carter's view of the new theatre. The programme consisted of three shorter works: a satirical sketch about Conservative Prime Minister Stanley Baldwin, a naturalistic drama by miner and poet Joe Corrie about the miner's lockout called *In Time of Strife* and an expressionist play by students from Brookwood Labor College in Katonah, New York, about the 1926 textile workers' strike in Passaic, New Jersey. While Corrie's text was not aesthetically ambitious, it did satisfy one of Carter's criteria by being written by a proletarian writer and therefore could be said to represent a 'proletarian point of view'. The Brookwood drama, on the other hand, while also dealing with a topical industrial issue and written by labour students, was praised for its aesthetic ambition, with Walshe calling the play a 'very striking experiment in the new technique of revolutionary drama' (quoted in Samuel, 1985, p. 42). Of course, the techniques used by the Brookwood students were not new, nor was Carter's and Walshe's view that the new revolutionary theatre would, out of ideological necessity, need to reject bourgeois theatre forms. Still, in the British context, these pronouncements and the work of the WTM were significant for effectively making the ideological, dramaturgical and aesthetic divisions between the communist-oriented movement and the labour one more apparent. It had established new parameters in which the second and much more successful WTM would develop.

In 1928 the first WTM disbanded, but Tom Thomas and the Hackney People's Players (HPP) quickly resurrected it. In the two years since the Hackney group had formed, it had grown in membership to around twenty members and established a reputation as a useful auxiliary to political gatherings, which it had earned through its tours of workers' clubs and Labour and Communist Party events. Thomas's adaptation of Robert Tressell's 1914 novel *The Ragged Trousered Philanthropist* proved to be one of the more successful original works produced by the company. The novel shows how the working classes are complicit with the capitalist system that oppresses them, depicting them as tragically ignorant 'philanthropists' who work long hours for low wages only to make their employers wealthy. The protagonist of the novel and Thomas's play, Frank Owen, is a devout socialist who tries in vain to get his fellow workers to understand the consequences of their apathy. The novel ends tragically with the fatally ill Owen deciding to end his and his family's lives to save them from the hunger, desolation and humiliation they were certain to experience when he was no longer alive to provide for them. In Thomas's adaptation, however, he decided that such an ending sent the wrong message to audiences, so he chose to end the play with Owen delivering a stirring socialist speech designed to rally and energize the audience instead. In addition to its political directness, audiences seemed to appreciate the play's use of language, which was modelled on British working-class idiom. As Thomas would later observe, 'It was clear that there was a real rapport between the audience and the play. It was about a world they recognized and understood' (1985a, p. 84).

Even by the time Thomas and the HPP had taken over the WTM, they were starting to realize the limitations of conventional full-length plays. Not only did plays test the abilities and resources of the amateur performers and directors, but also they did not achieve politically what the group wanted, which was an optimistic, socialist theatre. While a play like Thomas's *The Ragged Trousered Philanthropist* had proven effective in articulating the group's politics, it was conventional in form. It required, among other things, actors who could act convincing characters, as well as appropriate settings and costumes. This meant time and money needed to be set aside to prepare each production. This was difficult for a theatre of volunteers who also held down full-time jobs. It was also difficult to finance, as the principal revenue stream was donations and small stipends paid by the organization or hall who invited the company to perform.

Alternative dramaturgical models were subsequently sought. The principal catalyst for the change seems to have been making contact with Arthur Pieck's Workers' Theatre Federation of Germany. Initial contact with the German workers' theatre movement appears to coincide with Thomas's involvement with the International Workers' Dramatic Union (IWDU), founded in Moscow in 1929. In June 1930 a German delegate is known to have spoken about the exciting work being developed in his country at a weekend school hosted by the British WTM. Later that month, Thomas visited Moscow to represent Britain for the First Congress of the IWDU. Following the congress, Thomas sent some of the WTM's materials and a report on their activities to Pieck for review. Pieck, in turn, invited Thomas and members of the WTM to tour Germany in the spring of 1931. Thomas was impressed by the scale of the German movement and the quality of the performances he saw. It became clear to the British delegation that the agitprop/revue form performed by the Germans presented a flexible, achievable model on which to build their own movement. As Thomas later recounted:

> We could not hope to emulate the brilliance of the German performances. But by adopting the revue style – which we had already been working towards – we could, almost at once, achieve the freedom of the streets, however crude our initial material and performance might be. (1985a, p. 89)

In many respects, seeing the German performances only confirmed to Thomas and the WTM delegation what they already knew about the shortcomings of their own. It was not simply about form, it was also about content and quality, which was difficult to oversee across a developing national movement. Already by 1930 the WTM had taken steps to help overcome these issues through a number of methods. Monthly all-London shows, for instance, brought troupes together to try out and get feedback on new material (ibid., p. 90). Troupes could also consult a bank of approved playtexts and music in order to develop their work. Many of these were written by Thomas or were developed collectively by the few troupes that existed before 1932. Groups were actively encouraged to amend or adapt texts from the bank to their own needs. Further ideas and models of good practice were also disseminated in the WTM's official periodical, *Red Stage*, which was first published in 1931. Edited by Charlie Mann, a member of the London-based Red Players, the aim of the journal was to publish reports on activities within the movement, as well as playtexts and critical articles about bourgeois theatre.

By 1932, Thomas and the WTM Central Committee saw agitprop, a 'propertyless theatre for a propertyless class', as they called it, as best suited to their needs (Thomas, 1985a).[1] This view was not exclusively adopted by all the troupes, however, and the pages of the aforementioned *Red Stage* and the *Monthly Bulletin* attest to the fact that the issue of form was frequently debated. Still, the Central Committee was unmoved. The movement's anti-bourgeois position, which had started out as a *suggestion* that troupes should avoid bourgeois theatre forms because of the challenges they posed to troupes – e.g. talent, preparation time, expensive visual elements like sets, props and costumes, and poor mobility – hardened to become an outright ban on most props and costumes from productions, which were regarded as trappings of the bourgeois stage. In addition, groups were discouraged from consulting theatre professionals because they represented the 'industry' and were therefore extensions of the bourgeois stage.

The WTM's periodicals became outlets for reinforcing the aesthetic policy of the movement, with strict guidance published on how to perform certain sketches and to reprimand troupes for performing incorrectly.[2] Charlie Mann's article 'How to produce *Meerut*', a play about the Indian railway workers strike, offered nearly three pages of instructions for a four-page play, with advice being given on everything from cueing speech to how to crescendo in order to capture the audience's attention (Mann, 1985 [1933], pp. 106–107). While such a rigid, detailed approach might sound at odds with the broader ambitions of the movement, it must also be remembered that having rejected the possibility of involvement from professional theatre artists, the WTM had to find ways of communicating standards across a growing network of troupes, consisting mostly of young workers with limited experience or knowledge of the theatre. Even Ewan MacColl, whose Salford Red Megaphones (later Theatre of Action) would be one of the more successful of the WTM troupes in Northern England, admits that when he set up the company he knew 'bugger all about theatre' (MacColl, 1985, p. 226). Still, what his group lacked in practical knowledge, they made up for in enthusiasm and quickly developed a clear vision of what it is they wanted to achieve; they subsequently undertook extensive study and experimentation to help realize their goals. Other troupes were not as clear about what they hoped to achieve. Combined with a lack of experience, this resulted in some very weak performances. For instance, on two separate occasions both Mann and Thomas had witnessed troupes recite stage directions during rehearsals as though they were part of the scripted dialogue (Stourac & McCreery, 1986, p. 240). Similarly, in recalling a visit to see Red Radio perform in London in 1934, MacColl would observe it struck him as the 'worst kind of amateur theatre' (1985, pp. 241–242). The professional theatre producer André van Gyseghem, whom the WTM had reluctantly allowed to lead the struggling London-based troupe Rebel Players, put it down to 'bad technique' across the movement (Stourac & McCreery, 1986, pp. 240–241). His suspicions about poor technique were confirmed at the International Workers' Theatre Olympiad in Moscow in 1933 when the British delegation came in last place in the competition with other nations.[3] Lynn Mally notes that condemnation of the British group was unanimous by the panel of judges, who complained that the work was 'primitive and uncoordinated' (Mally, 2003, p. 334). In this regard, the WTM's rigid approach and extensive guidance, designed to make setting up and sustaining a workers' theatre achievable by groups with hardly any background in the theatre at all, appears to have had limited impact on the quality of much of the work produced.

Although it continued for another two years, the WTM's heyday had passed by 1934. Thomas resigned as the national organizer in 1935 following a controversy surrounding a production of Clifford Odets's *Waiting for Lefty* by van Gyseghem's Rebel Players. The group had not been able to secure the rights to the play in time for their production and Thomas had requested that they hold off until their production was legal. The group ignored Thomas's advice and went ahead with the production, which was a huge success. The performance would mark the end of the group's time as the WTM Rebel Players and the start of what would be known a year later as the Unity Theatre. Following Thomas' departure, the WTM would be incorporated into the newly developed New Theatre League, which was intended to 'link all amateur dramatic groups with 'progressive' ideas and [to] obtain the cooperation of professional artists' (Samuel, 1985, p. 60). The Unity Theatre and its New Theatre League saw plays as the way forward, and street agitprop gradually went out of practice. Politically, the two organizations aligned themselves with the anti-fascist Popular Front adopted by the Comintern in 1934, but would also have strong affiliations to the British Labour Party. The period of sectarian revolutionary theatre in Britain had officially come to an end.

American Workers' Theatres

Like its British counterpart, the first significant activity of the American Workers' Theatre Movement emerged in conjunction with a strike – in this case, the communist-led textile workers strike in Passaic, New Jersey. To support the strike, two of the founders of the New Playwrights Theatre, Mike Gold and John Howard Lawson, established the Workers' Drama League (WDL) and produced Gold's play *Strike!*, which was the first in the United States to apply the mass chant and agitprop forms. One of the play's more notable elements was its attempt at promoting audience participation by placing actors in the auditorium, which was intended to blur the lines between actor and audience. As the actors increasingly interfere with the action and demand strike action, the audience, it was anticipated, would join them. As Gold notes in the preface to his play:

> The audience is swept more and more into the excitement all around them; they become one with the actors, a real mass; before the recitation is over, everyone in the hall should be shouting: 'Strike! Strike!' (quoted in Cosgrove, 1985, p. 266)

The New Playwrights Theatre, which Gold and Lawson had established with Emjo Basshe and John Dos Passos, also served as a committed radical theatre during this period and was influenced by the stage practices members were hearing about from the Soviet Union. But both organizations struggled to find audiences. The WDL existed until 1928, although few records remain of its activity. In addition to *Strike!*, the group is also known to have produced *The Biggest Boob in the World*, adapted from a German text by Upton Sinclair. Historian Douglas McDermott notes that the play did not do well with audiences (1965, p. 67). The New Playwrights Theatre was also short-lived, lasting a mere two seasons. Bradby and McCormick note that the failure of these organizations was predominantly down to their inability to reach working-class audiences. Instead, they endeavoured to perform class-conscious drama for the 'traditional theatre-going public' who were 'hostile' to the work (Bradby & McCormick, 1978, p. 101).

By the end of the 1920s, amateur workers' theatres were springing up around New York City and in other industrial centres across the United States, including Detroit and Chicago. Many of these groups were formed by immigrant workers with the intention of performing for members of their own communities. For instance, there was the Bronx Hungarian Circle; the Uj Elöre Dramatic Club, which was affiliated with the Hungarian-language communist newspaper of the same name; the Ukrainian Dramatic Circle; and the German troupe Die Natur Freunde. These groups specialized in performing in an agitprop style they had brought with them from Europe (Bradby & McCormick, 1978, p. 101). More indigenous minority workers' theatres also existed, such as the dramatic section of the League of Struggle for Negro Rights and the Jewish group Artef, which specialized in Yiddish agitprop performance.

Among the most influential of the New York troupes was the German-language troupe Prolet-Buehne and the Workers' Laboratory Theatre, both of which were founded in 1928. Originally established as a dramatic society for a New York workers' union in 1925, the Prolet-Buehne would become an independent company three years later under the direction of German émigré John Bonn and his wife Anne Howe (Cosgrove, 1980, p. 201). Bonn, who had been an active theatre director and dramaturg in Berlin between 1923 and 1928, was familiar with the workers' theatres in Germany, as well as Piscator's and Brecht's practices. Cosgrove also notes that a committed KPD member like Bonn would have most certainly seen the Blue Blouse tour of Germany in 1927, 'absorbing their phenomenal fusion of satire, music, jazz-gymnastics, acrobatics and propaganda' (ibid., p. 202). The group also borrowed the Blue Blouse's mobility and was the first of the workers' theatres in the United States to tour its work – performing for predominantly German-speaking New York neighbourhoods on street corners, in factories, and at trade union meetings and political gatherings. The influence of European radical theatre can be seen especially in its programme, which consisted of *sprechchor*, agitprop and political revues akin to those developed by Piscator. *Tempo, Tempo*, written and performed around 1930, for instance, is a classic European agitprop about workers who unite against their capitalist employer. Written in rhymed verse, the industrial rhythm and tempo established in the play is used to show competing notions of 'tempo' – that of the Capitalist, which is to increase productivity, and that of the workers, which is to accelerate the revolution. Upon realizing the workers' intentions, the Capitalist's tune changes:

WORKER:
  Production reaches higher stages,
  Shorter hours, higher wages.
CAPITALIST:
  Take your time and do not worry,
  Slowly, slowly, what's the hurry.
WORKER:
  Faster, faster, drive ahead.
  Tempo makes for triumph red. (Prolet-Buehne, 1980 [1930], p. 317)

While dealing with issues that American/German-American audiences would have understood, *Tempo, Tempo* was, in a sense, culturally neutral: it did not speak specifically to or about the American worker experience, but instead spoke in more universal terms about the exploitation faced by workers. This may account for the play's success, which Cosgrove acknowledges was one of the most popular by any troupe performed during the period (1980, p. 203). Other performances developed by the company, including *Vote Communist* and *Scottsboro*, were written with a more distinctly American flavour. *Vote Communist* demonstrates how the two principal American political parties, Democratic and Republican, share an interest in protecting capitalism, while *Scottsboro* is a mass recitation on the injustices of the Scottsboro trial. The performance marked a slight shift in the group's traditional emphasis on class struggle to include racial concerns. Race, as mentioned, was seen as a crucial barrier to the unification of the American working class. Hence, the highly influential Prolet-Buehne's treatment of the issue was significant, for it presented it as a component of working-class struggle and helped reposition race into the discourses of the movement.

The Workers' Laboratory Theatre (WLT) was, in part, a product of Workers International Relief, an organization set up in Berlin in 1921 to coordinate international aid for the famine-stricken Soviet Union and to disseminate communist propaganda (Cosgrove, 1985, p. 275). The company's early membership comprised several members of the failed Workers' Drama League, as well as newcomers Alfred Saxe, Harry Elion, Will Lee, Jack and Haim Shapiro and Ben Blake (Himelstein, 1963, pp. 13–14). Saxe, a recent theatre graduate from the University of Michigan, served as the company's creative director and directed most WLT productions. Elion was a writer and performer who later became the editor of the workers' theatre magazine *New Theatre*. Ben Blake was also a writer, but since the company often created collectively he would have an active, but usually not singular, role in writing sketches. Will Lee, an actor and self-proclaimed proletarian, was a recent graduate from the City College of New York, while the Shapiros were both metal workers who had first encountered social drama through their work with a New York settlement house (ibid., p. 13). The Russian Blue Blouse, who company members were in regular correspondence with in the early 1930s, was hugely influential to the company, and the WLT subsequently borrowed aspects of their practice (Mally, 2003, p. 327). Popular topics addressed by the troupe included the Great Depression, Roosevelt's New Deal and the capitalist media. Republican politician Fiorello La Guardia, who was a member of the US House of Representatives throughout most of the 1920s and, later, mayor of New York, was also a popular target. There was also a healthy exchange of texts between the WLT and other troupes, including the

Prolet-Buehne. Between 1930 and 1934, two of the WLT's most performed texts were English translations of Prolet-Buehne's *Tempo, Tempo* and *Vote Communist* (Cosgrove, 1985, p. 276).

The WLT's work did not consist entirely of making and touring political sketches, but shared similar goals to the early Soviet Proletkult. As Bradby and McCormick have indicated, the troupe's broader ambitions 'consisted of an attempt to find an alternative culture to that offered by the system' (1978, p. 102). In fact, this element was to some degree prioritized – to such an extent that by 1929 the troupe would establish a Proletkult centre in New York to help cultivate their cultural vision (ibid.). This vision included a broad network of workers' troupes performing around the country so as to rally workers to the larger communist cause.

While workers' theatres had consistently been used to support political activities throughout their brief history, the WLT placed greater emphasis on theatre serving as an auxiliary for direct political action. In order to do this, the troupe created offshoots in order to more effectively serve workers. Between 1931 and 1934, these would include the Shock Troupe, an 'on-call' emergency theatre collective designed to respond to strikes and other worker events at short notice; Red Vaudeville, which specialized in political revue; Theatre Collective, which was designed to stage more conventional realist plays off-Broadway; and a mobile puppet theatre group (Cosgrove, 1985, pp. 276–277). Of these, the Shock Troupe, formed in 1932, proved to be the most active.

The Shock Troupe was known to be a disciplined group. Work began at eight o'clock in the morning with collective members sharing domestic responsibilities, like cleaning and cooking, followed by practical training sessions, political lessons and rehearsals. The subjects studied by the group included biomechanics, dialectical materialism and current political events (ibid., pp. 272–273). In the early afternoons, new material would be devised and/or rehearsed, after which several hours would be spent rehearsing music. The evenings were usually set aside for performances. The collective lifestyle was intense, with members working, on average, fourteen hours a day. But the work put in by the group appears to have paid off. As Cosgrove has noted, the Troupe developed a reputation for perfection: 'The extensive practical work, self-criticism and theoretical study [...] help to explain their consistent ideological stance and the expertise they achieved in performance' (ibid., p. 273).

The Shock Troupe's practice was a composite of Marxist theory and revolutionary theatre practice. The troupe was especially interested in realizing a dialectical materialist critique of social phenomena through performance. Like Blue Blouse before them, one of the ways Saxe and the other collective members sought to achieve this was by applying Eisenstein's montage techniques, which allowed them to juxtapose images of wealth, class and social attitude in quick succession in a single performance. One of the clearest examples of this is found in the play *Newsboy*, first performed by the Shock Troupe in 1933. Based on Marxist writer and Communist cultural spokesman V.J. Jerome's poem of the same name, the play focuses on the ideological transformation of a 1930s newsboy from capitalist slogan-shouter to class-conscious communist. The text, which weaves original dialogue together with scenic fragments from Claire and Paul Sifton's play *1931*, Albert Maltz and George Sklar's *Merry Go Round* and Kurt Jooss ballet sequences (Saxe, 1985 [1934], p. 292),[4] juxtaposes the banality of sensationalist media headlines, such as 'Marlene Dietrich insures legs for fifty thousand dollars.' (Workers' Laboratory Theatre, 1985 [1934], p. 316), with the reality of Great Depression America: widespread hunger and poverty, unemployment, breadlines and racist attitudes. As the newsboy is exposed to these realities in the play, he comes to understand that the banal news he sells is no more than a distraction from the social injustices wrought by capitalism and is, in fact, a means of preserving it. In the final scene, his ideological transformation is signalled by his decision to swap newspapers, selling the communist *Daily Worker* instead. In this way, the text allies class-consciousness with agency, signalling to audiences that understanding alone will not bring about social change: that requires changing one's behaviours and encouraging those around them to change theirs too.

In an article for *New Theatre* in 1934, Saxe explains that *Newsboy* was not only a demonstration in Marxist dialectics, but that it reflected the impact of industrialization and modernization on perceptions of class, which had 'quickened the consciousness of the [historic] interplay of social forces' (1985 [1934], p. 290). In practice, this meant that the montages of ideological conflicts between the newsboy and the world around him, which lead to his political awakening, must occur frequently and be performed with machine-like efficiency. The result is an economic, politically efficient performance so full of ideas that the audience should feel as though they have 'lived through an entire evening' (ibid., p. 293). While audiences may feel as though they have encountered a full-length play's worth of material, *Newsboy* was to be performed in 'exactly 12 minutes' (ibid.). How was this achieved? By using easily identifiable social types, eliminating unnecessary dialogue, *showing* conflict rather than discussing it at great length, and having scenes seamlessly dovetail into one another. Crucially, 'There is no waste', Saxe reports: 'Say what you have to say – and be done saying it' (ibid.).

In line with other workers' theatres internationally, umbrella organizations and publications were developed to help oversee and support troupes, as well as help the movement grow. The first of these was the Workers' Dramatic Council, which was formed in New York in 1929. While focused predominantly on troupes in and around New York City, it also looked to support theatre groups in other large industrial cities across the United States. By 1930, the Council's membership stood at twenty-one companies from cities including New York; Cleveland, Ohio; Madison, Wisconsin; and Portland, Oregon (McDermott, 1965, p. 68). In 1931 further progress was made with the publication of *Workers Theatre* magazine. Much like Germany's *The Red Megaphone* or Britain's *Red Stage*, *Workers Theatre* specialized in publishing articles by and about workers' theatres, initiating debates about form, content and style, and circulating texts recognized by the co-editors, the Prolet-Buehne and the Workers' Laboratory Theatre, as models of good practice. When the League of Workers' Theatres was formed in 1932 – which replaced the Workers Dramatic Council as a national organizing body – they took charge of *Workers Theatre*, making it the movement's official publication. The development of the League occurred in conjunction with the first National Workers' Theatre Spartakiade, which was a competition designed to award the best practices and help promote the work of the movement. Prolet-Buehne's *Red Revue* was chosen as the winner out of the fifteen performances entered (Cosgrove, 1980, p. 209). The first official National Workers' Theatre Conference was hosted in June of that year, which set out an agenda for growth as well as a more stable artistic policy for troupes to follow. In a document prepared for the conference and published in *Workers Theatre* in May 1932, it was noted that there were several challenges facing the movement, including a lack of interaction between theatre groups and the need to develop stronger international contacts, and, as with the British movement, it was felt that the repertory needed to be quickly and significantly improved (National Workers' Theatre Conference, 1985 [1932], pp. 282–284). But whatever the shortcomings of the movement, Cosgrove reports that within a year of the conference there were approximately 250 groups identifying as workers' theatres in operation in the United States, a figure that would increase to 400 in 1934 (1985, p. 268).

Most American workers' theatre groups rejected bourgeois theatre techniques, just as their European counterparts had done. For the most part this rejection had extended to all commercial work and the professional theatre industry more generally, although attitudes were not as hard-line as they were in Britain. Still, the performances and the way in which they were developed were similar to that in other countries: the work was usually collectively produced; few costumes and props were used;[5] and performers of mixed abilities performed social types instead of realistic characters. Workers in the United States did, however, usually undergo some kind of actor training. Some groups, including the Workers' Laboratory Theatre and Artef, offered actor-training workshops for workers, with the latter sponsoring as many as six acting studios in New York City in the late 1920s and early 1930s (Bradby & McCormick, 1978, p. 103). Training would have principally concerned voice and movement. Writing at the time, Bonn noted that the key skills required of the worker-player were a 'clearness of diction, simplicity of movement and sincerity of utterance' (quoted in McDermott, 1966, p. 118). To attend to these areas, several exercises might be used to help prepare the performer. One common exercise was to ask two players to play out a conversation without speaking, which forced performers to find ways to articulate meaning through movement and gesture. To improve vocal projection, actors might be instructed to hold a conversation in separate rooms, the objective being to make oneself heard by the actor in the other room without shouting (McDermott, 1966, p. 118). How to develop convincing, realistic characters would not have formed part of the training – at least initially. Instead of a character, actors were instructed to perform, as Bonn dictated, 'a class angle or *conception* of [a] character' (emphasis added, ibid.). This would explain the proliferation of caricatures of social types upon the worker stage. Nonetheless, some level of proficiency was usually expected of the workers before they were allowed to go on stage.

To accommodate a movement that became increasingly more aesthetically and politically diverse as it grew, the decision was made to rename *Workers Theatre* the *New Theatre* in 1934. A year later, the League of Workers' Theatres would become the New Theatre League. At this point it was no longer fashionable or ideologically sound to think of the popular theatre in militant proletarian terms. Comintern policy shifted to the more relaxed Popular Front in 1934, which made collaborating with others broadly sympathetic with communism possible. In New York, the collaboration between the workers' theatres and the communist members of Harold Clurman's Group Theatre proved to be one of the most productive and, in terms of the movement's development, one of the most significant. Group Theatre members Art Smith, Elia Kazan and Clifford Odets, in particular, lent their support to the movement early on, arranging workshops for performers and directors to help improve the standards of the workers' theatre. The first theatrical collaboration came with Smith's and Kazan's anti-fascist play *Dimitroff* in 1934, which was produced with Theatre Union, the first professional workers' theatre in the United States, which had been established in New York in 1933. The Theatre Union specialized in one-act and full-length realistic plays. McDermott notes that it was due in large part to their discounted ticket prices that it became popular with working-class audiences (1965, p. 70).

More than any other play in the American workers' theatre, Odets's *Waiting for Lefty* shows the transition from rudimentary agitprop to more developed political dramaturgy most clearly. Based on the New York taxi drivers' strike of 1934, Odets's one-act play depicts a union meeting in which corruption is exposed among the union leadership and a strike is called. Throughout the meeting, the taxi drivers flash back to moments in their lives in which they made the transition from politically ambivalent to committed. The characters are, for the most part, social types. For instance, Harry Fatt, the union leader with a 'porcine appearance', is based on the 'fat cat' capitalist type common to agitprop (Odets, 1985 [1935], p. 326). The taxi drivers are depicted as a united force, but the play's focus on their individual circumstances through the flashback sequences gives them greater definition. Odets's decision to contextualize their political convictions through extended scenes of dialogue gives the taxi drivers more dimensions as characters. While this does not disguise the propagandist intention of the play, this more complex depiction of the protagonists gives the impression that the workers have considered their situations and the political choices they make more carefully. Aesthetically, the work retains the minimalism of agitprop, requiring little in way of setting and costumes, although distinctions between characters and their environments were more clearly marked through specific costuming, props and light-ing, gesturing towards a more developed scenography. Combined, these effects result in a play that argues its case more thoroughly than traditional agitprop, making *Lefty* a particularly convincing piece of propaganda.

In addition to its formal developments, *Waiting for Lefty* also marked a clear shift to the developing union between amateur and professional proletarian theatre that would become more pronounced throughout the 1930s. The original production of *Lefty* premiered on 5 February 1935 at the Civic Repertory Theatre in New York. The cast included Elia Kazan, Art Smith, Ruth Nelson, Phoebe Brand and J. Edward Bromberg – all of whom, including Odets, were playing on Broadway in the Group Theatre's production of Melvin Levy's play *Gold Eagle Guy*. The production was a huge success. Cosgrove has noted the enthusiastic response that greeted *Lefty*'s premiere: 'As the final lines were being delivered from the stage the audience ran to the front and joined in with the ritual chants of "Strike, Strike, Strike"' (quoted in Odets, 1985 [1935], p. 323). In March, the Group Theatre added *Lefty* to its repertory and it would run on Broadway for seventy-eight performances (ibid.). The play subsequently became one of the most popular of the workers' movement, with professional and amateur groups around the country seeking to perform it. In an ironic turn of events, the workers' theatres, which had firmly rejected Broadway for its bourgeois commercialism, were now desperate to obtain the rights to a successful Broadway play.

Increasingly, the mobile workers' theatres moved indoors. This occurred not just in the United States but also across the international movement. The two leaders of the early American movement, Prolet-Buehne and the WLT, who had continued to develop mobile performances, also succumbed to the changing conditions and moved their work indoors, although their heyday had already passed. In 1935 Prolet-Buehne officially disbanded when Bonn took up a post as head of the German-language section of the newly formed Federal Theatre Project. The WLT, meanwhile, changed its name to Theatre of Action and began producing full-length plays, starting with George Scudder, Peter Martin and Charles Friedman's *The Young Go First*, which was co-directed by Saxe and Kazan in May 1935 (McDermott, 1965, p. 73). What had started as a suggestion for broadening the aesthetic scope and improving the quality of the workers' theatre soon became a completely new way of working. As this new approach became more widespread, workers' theatres became more ambitious. As McDermott notes, there seems to 'have been an irresistible desire to compete on an equal basis with the theatre of the capitalist society' (ibid., p. 72). In addition to the more fundamental issues of form, acting style and scenography, which were now essentially borrowed directly from the professional theatre, the troupes' relationship with the workers also radically changed. No longer did the theatres seek out the workers to disseminate their message as they had done previously through their mobile performances; instead, many theatres now relied on the workers to come to them. Theatres like the Theatre Union were, for a time, the leaders of this new direction. Operating in a similar way to Piscator's theatres, Theatre Union attempted to woo working-class audiences to its productions with cheap tickets. Workers' organizations could purchase blocks of tickets for their members, and individual subscriptions were also available, which ensured significant advanced sales for many of the company's productions. While records indicate that these methods were successful in attracting audiences, the costs of producing plays to a professional standard in New York City proved too costly for the organization and it went bankrupt in 1937 (ibid., p. 74). Ironically, as many of the workers' theatres around the United States looked to Theatre Union as a model – especially for its new plays, as good revolutionary texts were still hard to come by – the Union's failure also signalled their own. What the gradual decline in workers' theatres indicated was that producing revolutionary theatre according to the aesthetic and literary standards established by the commercial theatre system was possible in places like the Soviet Union, where the resources to achieve those standards were provided by the government, but it was not possible in capitalist countries without significant arts subsidies.

Conclusions

By the start of the Second World War, agitprop and the Workers' Theatre Movement had run their course internationally. In Germany, the Nazis' seizure of power in 1933 effectively ended its workers' movement. While workers' theatres in Europe and the United States did not suffer the same kind of oppression as those in Germany, the official Popular Front policy, adopted in 1934 by the Communist Party, was not congenial to the militant agitprop form. Before the adoption of the Popular Front, the Party's goal had been to provoke international revolution, but the rise of fascism in Italy, Germany and Spain was regarded a significant enough concern to warrant a temporary change of course. The Popular Front essentially opened the doors to other progressive political parties from around the world willing to stand united against fascism. Agitprop was hardly unifying, and eventually, as the 1930s progressed, it went out of favour. The Soviet Union's denouncing of agitprop and shift to socialist realism, confirmed by 1934, also radically affected the movement. While socialist realism was equally as propagandistic, it was devoid of radical experimentation, fragmentation or any hint of avant-gardism. The Second World War would effectively put a temporary halt to the development of working-class drama everywhere.

As a popular theatre, workers' theatre is significant for a number of reasons. Firstly, at no other point in history has a mass theatre movement on this scale existed. That committed political activists and amateur performers, instead of trained theatre professionals, oversaw the movement's development makes its scale and reach all the more impressive. The workers' theatres really were a theatre by and for the people in an absolutely fundamental way. Secondly, the workers' theatres were important because of their complex relations with systems of power, both in terms of their own management and organization, and also how they responded to the powerful political forces in their countries of operation. Adopting the fundamental spirit of communism, the groups, where possible, resisted and often rejected creative hierarchies that privilege the views of a single director or playwright. This was forty years before the fashionable discourses of the late 1960s that paved the way for the collectives and devising ensembles such as the San Francisco Mime Troupe, People Show and Mabou Mines, which did away with, or endeavoured to reconfigure, the power such roles have traditionally held in the theatre-making process. Just like these more modern companies, the workers' theatres experienced at first-hand the difficulties of trying to evenly share the responsibilities of power across a company. This is, in part, what led to the uneven quality across the movement, which in turn made those in positions of leadership, like Thomas of the British WTM, impose rules with authoritarian vigour. But this is how the Soviet authorities wanted it. Through the International Workers' Dramatic Union (later renamed Union of Revolutionary Theatre), the Olympiad, and their internationally circulated journal, Moscow was also offering corrective aesthetic and ideological training so that the international movement moved in the direction it wanted. So, as with the revolutionary theatres discussed in Chapters 2 and 3, the workers' theatres relationship to power is not so straightforward. In capitalist countries, workers' theatres could be found promoting emancipatory ideas and working in an aesthetically progressive way that was in conflict with their 'bourgeois' hegemonic social and economic systems. But their actions were largely determined by the authoritarian Soviet regime. And where echoes of this authoritarianism crept into the tactics of national organizations or national leaders, as with Thomas, troupes did not respond well. This was one of the reasons the WTM ended. The other reason the movement fell apart was because of a reversal of the idea that it should be led by collectives of committed amateurs.

The Soviets' insistence that companies work with professional writers and strive for a more proficient aesthetic was not sustainable outside its own borders. The committed workers, the people, were the fuel that drove the movement, and when aesthetic demands were made that they could not realize, it was inevitable that the movement would have to end.

While it is impossible to measure the efficacy of the workers' theatres, their rapid international expansion in some leading capitalist countries between 1928 and 1935 suggest that there was an appetite for an alternative political and economic system. Some political institutions were also concerned by (or perhaps irritated by) the influence of the workers' theatres and, in some cases, took measures to prevent them from performing, such as legislation, heavy-handed policing or banning the performances from public spaces. That workers' theatre continued to be performed in spite of these measures, and to directly call out the corruption, injustices and economic failures of their political systems as a matter of routine, is testament to the political will and conviction of the people involved. In this respect they formed an effective movement, for those involved often jeopardized their own freedom and personal safety for a politics they believed would make the lives of so many others better. It was not until the 1960s that there was a return to this level of commitment within the popular theatre.

Intermezzo
The Popular and the Avant-Garde

6 Rejuvenation and Resistance: Popular Forms and the Avant-Garde

The theatre practices discussed in Part I were predominantly concerned with taking radical or left-wing political messages to popular audiences. This chapter is concerned with avant-garde and experimental performances that have a distinctly different rationale and aesthetic. While many of the tools used by the artists and theatre-makers mentioned in this chapter were borrowed from a similar repertoire of popular forms (*commedia* and puppetry, for instance), the work produced was, for the most part, not developed with a popular audience in mind. Still, in considering the vehicles that continue to drive the popular theatre in contemporary theatre practices, one cannot overlook the history of the avant-garde and its scavenging of popular and mass-culture forms. This chapter considers some of the histories of the avant-garde from the late nineteenth century up until the start of the Second World War, concentrating on instances where popular performance forms were used to, among other things, foster new aesthetic strategies for the twentieth century and to critique dominant aesthetic modes and the cultural prejudices of the bourgeoisie.

Rejuvenation and Resistance

As Peter Brook points out in *The Empty Space*, 'every attempt to revitalize the theatre has gone back to the popular source' (1968, p. 68). The reason for this seems clear. As discussions throughout this book have demonstrated, most popular forms are inherently adaptable and all too eager to bend to accommodate artist and audience needs and tastes. The motivations behind the kinds of artistic experimentation associated with modernism and the avant-garde in the late nineteenth century and the early decades of the twentieth emerge from the same radical and revolutionary impulse that informed the development of the performances discussed in other chapters: an awareness of significant social changes brought about by industrialization and the rise of economic capitalism. Modernists tended to be 'anti-bourgeoisie', as American writer John Barth observed, in both their politics and their aesthetics (1984, p. 199). Underscoring these concerns was the recognition that traditional forms of art, literature and theatre were outdated and irrelevant for an increasingly urbanized, industrialized society. This resulted in the rejection of what were perceived to be outdated modes of aesthetic representation, and chief among these was nineteenth-century realism. Consequently, the linear narrative, the coherence of character and plot, and aesthetic unity that one had come to expect of certain literary and dramatic forms were upended. As well as working against these conventions, modernists turned to irony, juxtaposition and self-mockery to question, as Barth puts it, 'the moral and philosophical "meaning" of literary action' (ibid.).

While some modernist forms were hostile to mass and popular culture, others, especially in the avant-garde, tended to be more embracing of it. For Peter Bürger, this is what distinguishes modernism from the avant-garde. In *Theory of the Avant-Garde* he argues that modernists' insistence on the autonomy of their works from other cultural forms, like mass or popular culture, essentially perpetuated a bourgeois ideology of superiority. Consequently, he regards modernist art as 'the objectification of the self understanding of the bourgeois class' (Bürger, 1984, p. 47). Historical avant-garde practices, on the other hand, were more forthcoming about their connections to other cultural forms; they not only acknowledged mass and popular culture, but also openly co-opted and integrated it into their artworks. Bürger sees this as part of the avant-garde's resistance to modernism, as well as its 'attack on the status of art in bourgeois society' (ibid., p. 49). Whereas modernists sought to position their artwork outside society to protect it, the avant-garde sought to eliminate the barrier between art and life and discredit the idea that art can somehow be set apart (or protected) from the conditions of the real world.

Bürger's views are not universally accepted, and while it is not the function of this book to solve the modernism/avant-garde dilemma, the tensions he highlights make for an interesting trajectory that will be pursued throughout this chapter.[1] The first concerns modernism's focus on developing artistic works capable of representing the complexities of post-industrial life. This goal, which one might regard as artistic rejuvenation, was theorized in many ways in the late nineteenth and early twentieth centuries. While certain theatrical forms were rejected on the grounds that they were no longer relevant, many practitioners turned to traditional popular forms to develop new theatrical styles and aesthetics which they believed to be more representative of, or appropriate for, contemporary society. Realistic literary and theatrical strategies were consistently rejected. This was not simply owing to the realistic theatre's need for the audience to be positioned on the other side of the 'fourth wall' in order to sustain an illusion of being 'a slice of life', but also because of a fundamental change in spectatorship throughout much of the West in the middle of the nineteenth century, when the houselights were turned off and theatre-going, which had been a communal, social activity, became a more personal one. By turning to popular forms, with their emphasis on participation, theatre-makers hoped to re-establish the connection between the auditorium and the stage and encourage a return to a more active form of spectatorship.

Another issue important to the discussion here is the notion of arts practices offering what Eric Bulson has referred to as 'resistance from within' (Bulson, 2013, p. 56). In terms of the practices of the avant-garde, this resistance is found on multiple levels. As well as critically engaging with artistic institutions of the past, artists challenged socially and culturally entrenched views of low/high artistic status and sought to question the broader effects of industrialization, notably the commodification of art and culture. The deliberate appropriation and reworking of popular and mass-culture artefacts in an avant-garde performance, then, had many critical objectives: to critique mass culture; to challenge notions of high art and the validity of established cultural institutions; and to chip away at the capitalist system responsible for the production of both mass-culture and high art. Working across the low/high artistic spectrum and in and outside of cultural institutions thus enabled the avant-garde to critique social and artistic systems from multiple angles.

Whether for rejuvenation or resistance (or both), the appropriation of popular or mass forms was usually not made in order to harness their potential to please or entertain, as was the case with practices explored elsewhere in this book. Rather, as Bourdieu has pointed out, it is often the case that such works borrow formalistic qualities only, deliberately detaching content from form (1984, p. 26). By doing so, artists were able to fill the gap left by the removal of content with ideas or concepts relating to their political and/or aesthetic goals. In this chapter, those goals are numerous: satirizing political events, parodying other artistic modes (usually 'high' art), shocking bourgeois audiences and their cultural critics, and challenging perceptions about what qualifies or disqualifies as being art. I make no claims that such work is popular in the same sense explored in earlier chapters. It is more often the case that such work is distinctly *unpopular* with popular audiences, owing to its unconventionality and aesthetic difficulty. However, in considering the constantly evolving practices of popular theatre, a critical examination of their appropriation and practice outside of popular contexts is important. Doing so can reveal a great deal about the flexibility of many popular forms as well as their broad appeal, even for those who did not wish to make popular art.

The Cabaret

Many of the ideas and aesthetic impulses now typically associated with modernity were cultivated in cabarets, which emerged for the first time in the late nineteenth and early twentieth centuries. While cabarets would eventually come to be recognized as centres of populist variety entertainment after the First World War, in their earliest manifestations cabarets were interdisciplinary arts spaces that brought together artists and writers from a range of backgrounds and perspectives to share and discuss their work. Even though views and practices may have differed, cabaret affiliates tended to share in their disdain for established arts practices and the bourgeoisie. As cabaret historian Harold Segal notes, fundamentally the artists in attendance at early cabarets sought to end 'the hegemony of art that was either elitist by virtue of patronage or audience, or bourgeois by virtue of its standards and conventions' (1987, p. xvii). As well as hosting discussions and debates about art's social function, early cabaret evenings featured poetry recitations, political speeches, the delivery of artistic manifestos, and performances of songs that reflected group members' views of society and the contemporary art scene more broadly.

Rodolphe Salis opened the first recognized cabaret, the Chat Noir, in an abandoned post-office in the Montmartre district of Paris in November of 1881. The Chat Noir was conceived of and designed as a *cabaret artistique*, a venue to accommodate artistic and intellectual activity. Even before it had opened, Salis had secured the support of Émile Goudeau (1849–1906), a well-known local poet and former president of a group known as the Hydropathes. Formed by Goudeau in 1878, the Hydropathes had prefigured the cabaret as an affiliation of artists, mostly poets, who met regularly in cafes to share and discuss their work and to amuse one another with silly songs and poems. Excessive drinking also formed a central component of the group's meetings. While the scope and content of the Hydropathes' work varied, much of it was in some way preoccupied with the tensions of modern Parisian urban life, such as the contrast between the aesthetic and intellectual energy associated with the Bohemian artistic community and the poverty and suffering of the Parisian poor and working class. While there were members of the group known for producing more serious work, such as the sombre (and occasionally morbid) poetry and songs of Maurice Rollinat (1846–1903), much of Hydropathes' output was deliberately, and playfully, unconventional. Segal points out that this playfulness was often nothing more than a 'barely concealed and intended mockery of convention, social as well as artistic' (ibid.). Charles Cros's poem 'The Salt Herring' is a prime example of this. In it, Cros describes a fairly unremarkable scene in which a man climbs a ladder, hammers a nail in a wall and then suspends a salt herring from it to dry. In the final verse, the poem's intention to irritate is highlighted: 'Now I have composed this story simple, simple, simple,/ To make all serious men mad, mad, mad/ And to amuse little children tiny, tiny, tiny' (Cros, 1987, p. 9).

Sharing the Hydropathes' anti-Establishment views, as well as some of their members, was Jules Lévy's *Les Arts Incoherents*, formed in 1882. Many of the group's satirical, ironic and at times controversial works were presented at public exhibitions. Of these, Sapeck's *Le rire* (1887), a photo-relief of Leonardo da Vinci's *Mona Lisa* with a smoking pipe in her mouth, is one of the more well known.[2] In Sapeck's work, the anti-establishment objectives of the Incoherents is made particularly clear through the playful defacing of a reproduction of a well-known classical painting.

The mischievous but critical attitude of the Hydropathes and the Incoherents has often been aligned with the trickster figure of Pierrot, star of the French pantomime with a history dating back to the Italian *commedia dell'arte*.[3] While Pierrot had initially mirrored *commedia*'s other comic servants, more commonly known as *zanni*, he had slowly evolved in France into a more morose, lovesick figure in the nineteenth century under the influence of the Romantics. Jean-Gaspard Deburau's

Romantic Pierrot (1796–1846) is often accredited with this transition. Under Deburau, Pierrot came to be regarded as a gentler, much more sensitive figure, but one still capable of mischief and slapstick humour. Writing of Deburau's Pierrot, novelist George Sands once noted:

> He is not gluttonous, but fond of food. Instead of being debauched, he is gracious… . He is not devious, he is irreverent and funny, neither is he angry, because he is reasonable, and when he administers his impressive kick in the seat of the pants, he has the impartiality of an enlightened judge and the grace of a Marquis. (quoted in Nye, 2014, p. 110)

While Sands saw the reworked Pierrot as a civilized marquis, early nineteenth-century French critic Jules Janin read Pierrot as a representative of the will of people in post-Revolutionary France (ibid., p. 109). Such was the figure's versatility. It was his ability to stand in for multiple personalities – e.g. member of the bourgeoisie and proletarian, or slapstick clown and tragic victim – that made him attractive to the Bohemians. As Julian Brigstock has pointed out, it was the way the figure reflected the Bohemians' 'persecuted but joyous' outlook on life that made him ripe for appropriation (2012, p. 226). This outlook was reflected in their art, which often drew on irony and buffoonery as a strategy for creative resistance. The image of the Pierrot-as-Bohemian (and, indeed, Bohemian-as-Pierrot) was further entrenched by illustrator Adolphe Willette's famous Pierrot cartoons for the Chat Noir's weekly magazine, *Le Chat Noir*, which first appeared in January 1882 (Segal, 1987, p. 1). One of the major adaptations Willette made to the Pierrot figure was in his visage: amending the figure's traditional oversized white tunic and coned hat for a sleeker black costume, more appropriate, visually, for parodying the bourgeoisie. High-spirited and mischievous, Pierrot's comic high jinks in Willette's cartoons are usually rewarded with abuse, 'ignored and sacrificed to the bourgeois god of money', as Brigstock puts it (2012, p. 227). In this way, even Willette's Pierrot of the late nineteenth century could be seen to stand in for the working classes – working tirelessly on behalf of an ultimately ambivalent and disinterested bourgeoisie.

It was in this aesthetic context that Salis's Chat Noir existed. Artists from both the Hydropathes and the Incoherents were, from the start of his cabaret, the core clientele, although the club quickly drew other Parisian artists as well as curious members of the bourgeoisie. Early programmes tended to resemble those of the earlier Hydropathe meetings, with poetry recitations, readings and songs making up the bulk of the programme. One of the most popular features of the early cabaret was the chanson, a type of popular French folk song that can be traced back to the late middle ages. Known for depicting everyday concerns, the chanson's revival in the nineteenth century coincided with the emergence of the working class and Naturalism in art. Like the naturalists, the *chansonniers*, i.e. the singers of chansons, were particularly interested in depicting the (often grim) realities of contemporary life. Consequently, the revived chanson of the period became known as *chanson réaliste* (Sweeney, 2001, p. 23). While they are now usually associated with female singers, such as Fréhel and Edith Piaf, in the early years of the cabaret it was the male singers for which the *chanson réaliste* were known. Aristide Bruant (1851–1925), Jules Jouy (1855–1897) and Maurice Mac-Nab (1856–1889), in particular, were some of the most popular *chansonniers* of the period – and all three performed at the Chat Noir at some point in their careers. Many *chansonniers* adopted a vocal style that reflected the form's preoccupation with social concerns. Segal, for instance, describes Mac-Nab as possessing a 'hoarse out-of-tune voice that was compared to that of a seal with a cold', while Bruant's voice was 'cutting and metallic' (1987, pp. 40, 54). The aim, of course, was not to make classically beautiful music, but to capture, through their performance, the experience and dreams of the urban disenfranchised.

As well as chansons, the Chat Noir was also known for its *Ombres Chinoises* (Chinese shadows), or shadow shows. One evening, during one of Jouy's chanson performances, the painter Henri Rivière dimmed the lights and, from behind a cloth stretched over the small proscenium on the Chat Noir's puppet stage, manipulated cardboard cut-outs in front of a light, creating a series of silhouettes that coincided with the lyrics to Jouy's song (Houchen, 2003, p. 182). The puppet theatre soon became the Chat Noir's principal attraction. Up until Rivière's intervention with the tablecloth, the Chat Noir had accommodated, mainly, Guignol shows.[4] The success of Rivière's performance led to further experimentation with the shadow form, which over time came to be increasingly sophisticated and technologically advanced. Rivière replaced the rudimentary cardboard silhouettes from the early performances with zinc cut-outs; coloured glass panels and mirrors were added to create scenographic effects; and a more vibrant oxy-hydrogen flame allowed for greater variety in the sharpness of the shadows projected. The use of photomechanical printing, a specialty of the Hydropathes and the Incoherents, enabled Rivière to produce images with even greater detail and clarity (Matsuda, 2001, p. 194).

In many ways, the technological developments of the Chat Noir's shadow theatre signalled the ultimate union of a folk performance form with the capabilities of modern, industrial society. Owing to its marginal status as non-serious popular culture, the shadow form was an ideal vehicle for offering a playful modernist critique of contemporary culture and bourgeois values – in much the same way as the poetry, songs and paintings of the Hydropathes and Incoherents had done. In practice, there were two principal varieties of shadow show produced at the Chat Noir. The first, perhaps unsurprisingly, were satirical and humorous pieces of which Henry Somm's *The Elephant* is indicative. In it, an African man pulling a long rope over his shoulder enters from one side of the screen. The rope is taut, indicating that the man is pulling something. As he works his way across, and eventually off, the screen, the rope continues to lengthen. After a time in which nothing but a knot in the rope is seen, an elephant slowly emerges. Once the elephant reaches the centre of the screen, it pauses, slowly sits down and defecates; it then resumes its journey and departs.[5] In the final moments of the piece, a flower sprouts out of the elephant's waste and the lights dim (Segal, 1987, p. 69). As well as prefiguring the later Dadaist motto 'Art is shit', *The Elephant* mischievously articulates the avant-garde belief in the possibilities and inherent tensions of the modern urban landscape: that beauty might be born from misery. And while it may have been regarded as controversial to some audiences, the performance became one the cabaret's most popular and was performed over 4000 times at the Chat Noir before its closure in 1897 (Cate, 1996, p. 57).

As well as humorous shadow performances, the Chat Noir also specialized in lyrical pieces that drew on spiritual, historic and patriotic themes. Caran D'Ache's *L'Epopée* (*The Epic*), for instance, spectacularly depicted the history of the Napoleonic wars in fifty tableaux. Audiences were mesmerized by the technical proficiency of the recreated battles. Scenes depicting the former Emperor drove some to fits of patriotic fervour, with one spectator later recounting that upon seeing images of Napoleon preparing for battle the audience responded by shouting 'Long live the Emperor!' so powerfully that the 'windows of the room trembled' (Segal, 1986, p. 71). Rivière and composer Georges Gragerolle's *Le Marche à l'étoile* (*Journey to the Star*), first performed in 1890, is a representative of a more spiritualist work. The piece is a nearly ten-minute long procession featuring people from different backgrounds, including shepherds, soldiers and slaves, following a radiant star announcing the birth of Christ. The show ends in a scene of worship and celebration. While not as radical as the satiric pieces, *Le*

Marche à l'étoile depicts a coming together of humanity for a common cause, and thus could be seen as promoting the Bohemians' utopian social vision.

By the end of the nineteenth century and the early part of the twentieth, cabarets similar to the Chat Noir popped up all over Europe, with most European capital cities hosting one or more venues by the end of the First World War.[6] Many of these spaces shared the Chat Noir's anti-bourgeois sentiment and tendency towards aesthetic experimentation that would, over time, come to define the early avant-garde. In Paris, the critical and playful attitude nurtured through the Chat Noir would, by the end of the century, see work carrying forth those ideals produced outside the safety of the cabaret in traditional theatre spaces. Alfred Jarry's infamous *Ubu Roi*, first performed at the Théâtre de l'Œuvre in Paris in December 1896 is a good example of this. Conceived as a Guignol show but performed by actors in masks, *Ubu* is essentially a grotesque parody of Shakespeare's *Macbeth*. As well as its application of popular puppet forms, the piece further upended 'high'/bourgeois theatre convention at the time by utilizing a crudely drawn backdrop and found props and objects to make up the set – a significant contrast to the elaborate stage sets associated with melodrama or Naturalism. Famously, the audience rioted during the first performance and the play was subsequently banned. However, two years later when Jarry revived his play as an actual puppet show, it ran for sixty-four performances and was considered to be a success (Schechter, 2003, p. 35). This appears to suggest that Parisian audiences and critics were willing to tolerate the unconventional, so long as it was safely confined to marginal and ultimately non-serious forms. The same could be said of the cabarets. While some members of the bourgeoisie enjoyed them as novelties, taking pleasure in the ridicule they received at the hands of Bohemian artists and the 'performances' they paid to see, the cabaret's marginal status, paired with its public reputation for being odd, made it relatively harmless.

Meyerhold and the Russian Avant-Garde

Although cabaret would not make it to Russia until 1908, the critical attitude towards bourgeois theatre was already appearing on stage at the start of the twentieth century. As I mentioned in Chapter 2, revolutionary feeling certainly existed within the country in the late nineteenth and early twentieth century, ultimately leading to the overthrow of

their autocratic government. While people had to be careful express-
ing their political views of the autocratic state in the earliest years of
the century, artists had some freedom to demonstrate their dissatisfaction with established aesthetic conventions. Once again, Naturalism
became the target for the most scorn. In the Russian context, the
naturalist theatre had developed under the watchful and inventive
eye of Konstantin Stanislavski (1863–1938), whose actor-training
techniques and productions at the Moscow Art Theatre (MAT) had
firmly established it as a high art form. Even though he had been
an actor at the MAT, Vsevolod Meyerhold (1874–1940) was one of
the many artists who had become critical of Naturalism, believing it
overburdened audiences with too many details. The exhaustive detail,
when combined with the audience's separation from the action due to
the convention of the 'fourth wall', caused them, Meyerhold believed,
'to adopt an ambivalent attitude' towards the performance they were
watching (Meyerhold, 1988b, p. 139). His frustration with Naturalism
contributed to his decision to leave the MAT in 1902. From then on,
Meyerhold worked to uncover new theatrical strategies, some of which,
as discussed in Chapter 2, were bluntly political. At points throughout
his career, Meyerhold's work can be connected to a range of historical
avant-garde movements, notably symbolism, cultural retrospectivism,
Futurism and Constructivism.

Early on in his search for an alternative stage language to Naturalism,
Meyerhold had come across traditional popular theatre forms, which
he began to integrate into his practice. A precedent for this had already
been established by the puppet plays of the Belgian symbolist Maurice
Maeterlinck, whose work hugely influenced Meyerhold. An avid reader
of German philosopher Arthur Schopenhauer's writings on human will,
Maeterlinck believed the theatre should 'throw light upon the existence
of the soul' (1909, p. 98).[7] His exploration of the spiritual manifested
in a series of plays for marionettes, which he thought to be ideal vehicles for demonstrating fate's control over mankind. These included
Interiors (1890) and *The Death of Tintagiles* (1894). Meyerhold would
later direct *The Death of Tintagiles* at the Moscow Art Theatre Studio
in 1905, replacing the marionettes with actors who were instructed to
perform as if they were marionettes. As this suggests, Meyerhold was
less interested in the mechanized object than in the mechanics of the
corporeal body. The popular forms he turned to in order to develop
his practice, notably *commedia dell'arte*, circus, clowning and Russian
fairground – which are all intensively physical – are testament to this.[8]
The slapstick comic archetypes of the *commedia dell'arte* were regarded

as particularly useful because, as C. Moody has pointed out about Meyerhold's practice, they proved a suitable 'contrast to the individual psychological portrayals on the stage of the Moscow Arts Theatre. The strolling player's continuous communion with his audience was an answer to the problem of breaking down the division between actors and audience' (1978, p. 860). These popular forms would significantly shape Meyerhold's practice, forming not only a key element of his visual style but also part of the foundation of his performer training method, Biomechanics, which he would refine throughout the 1910s and 1920s.[9]

As well as being antithetical to Naturalism and helping break down the barriers between performer and audience, for Meyerhold the appeal of popular forms such as *commedia dell'arte* rested in their ability to oscillate easily between the comic and the tragic. He believed such contrasts, when brought together, could create an effect he called the grotesque. For Meyerhold, the grotesque was generated by 'the conflict between form and content', which could be used to distort the outward appearance of real life 'to the point where it ceases to be natural' (1988b, p. 141).

In his search for a physical language that could achieve this synthesis, Meyerhold would merge the abstract expressiveness of the avant-garde with the physicality and iconography of the popular theatre. The outcome of this synthesis was a challenging, absurd (anti-realistic) aesthetic, which effectively served as an invitation for spectators to decipher its meaning, thus facilitating a more active form of spectatorship. His production of Alexander Blok's play *The Puppet Show*, which he directed on several occasions between 1906 and 1914, is a useful example of this.[10] The play, a parody of symbolist theatre, depicts a love triangle between *commedia*'s Columbina, Pierrot and Harlequin. Instead of their traditional comedic function, the figures are rendered more sombrely, sharing a preoccupation with the existential concerns more typical of symbolist drama. Many of the play's more serious scenes are juxtaposed with dances and interruptions by a chorus of clowns, the effect of which is often more disorientating and surreal than comic. In a scene between a pair of lovers, a clown is struck on the head with a sword, causing cranberry juice to pour from his skull. In another scene, Harlequin, seeking to be freed from the constraints of a world of 'mournful visions' in which 'no one knows how to love', attempts to end his life by jumping through a window, only to discover it is a prop and that his world is artificial (Blok, 1950, p. 321). The effort to expose the artifice of such theatrical illusions as the prop window and clowns is compounded by frequent interruptions from the Author, who begs the audience to forgive the absurdity they see before them. The Author claims to have written a naturalistic play, not a puppet show, and that the production was being hijacked by a bunch of clowns (ibid., p. 315).

The self-reflexivity, absurdity and blatant mixing of high and low forms within *The Puppet Show* shares similarities with the avant-garde artists discussed earlier. While Blok classified the play as a lyrical drama, which he defined as 'drama in which the experience of an individual soul, its doubts, passions, failures, falls, merely happen to be presented in dramatic form' (ibid., p. 309), it is often regarded as a symbolist satire, with the comic types playfully undermining the excessive existential philosophizing that characterized many symbolist plays. This is punctuated by the presence of the Author, a caricature of the symbolist poet who takes himself and his work too seriously.

But while it is critical, the play does not rely on the popular *commedia* characters for its humour or its critique of symbolist excess. None of the *commedia* figures, as they are written, carry its traditional comic associations. Their traditional mischievousness and playfulness is replaced with soul searching and pining. In fact, much of the play's humour is to be found in its modernist self-reflexivity, which is most clearly articulated through the figure of the Author, whose interruptions and pleas with the audience to forgive the intrusion of the comic figures into his serious modern work are playfully metatheatrical. It is the production's deliberate upending of traditions and expectations, as well as the conflation of contrasting forms – in this case the popular comic iconography of the *commedia dell'arte*, with the altogether much more serious, lyrical text – that achieves Meyerhold's 'synthesis of opposites', and thus generating the grotesque. In his essay *The Fairground Booth*, Meyerhold explains that the use of the *commedia* characters would also

> force the spectators to recognize the actor's performance as pure play-acting. And every time the actors lead the spectators too far in the land of make-believe he immediately resorts to some unexpected [...] [aside] to remind them that what is being performed is only *a play*. (Meyerhold, 1988b, p. 127)

By openly calling attention to its construction in this way, the work invites the audience to contemplate its meanings not through its similarities to real life but through its differences as a piece of playful art. This mix of elite and popular forms in *The Puppet Show* also creates aesthetic contrasts that work to destabilize any widely held assumptions audiences may have about high and low culture. These mock the seriousness and abstraction of the lyric by giving voice to it through superficial comic stereotypes, and by lending the popular a sophistication and expressiveness not usually found in its traditional contexts. In this way, the mix of forms was not only intended to help expand the possibilities of symbolist performance and facilitate new kinds of spectatorship, but also to critique the limitations of elite and popular forms of representation.

Futurism

For Filippo Tomasso Marinetti, the Italian poet, literary agent and founder of Futurism, the future of art rested not in traditions of the past but in the energy and technologies of the present. In his founding manifesto for Futurism, which was published in the French daily newspaper *La Figaro* on 20 February 1909, Marinetti not only denounced the past but also argued that its records, housed in libraries, museums and academies, ought to be destroyed (1971b, p. 42). His manifesto rejected traditional notions of aesthetic beauty in place of the modern beauty of industrialization and speed, which he exemplified as 'a racing car whose hood is adorned with great pipes, like serpents of explosive breath' (ibid., p. 41). Perhaps the most controversial aspect of the manifesto, which even Marinetti indicated was intended to be 'violently upsetting', was its glorification of war (ibid., p. 42). For the Futurists, war was the 'the world's only hygiene', clearing it not only of the relics of the past but the unnecessary waste of the present (ibid.). As Günter Berghaus observes, the aim of the Futurists was to 'obliterate the contemplative, intellectual concept of culture and bring about a total and permanent revolution in all spheres of human existence' (2005, p. 31). Other movements tended to grapple with the social, aesthetic and political challenges of modernity by attempting to develop representational strategies that might more closely reflect it. But the Futurists sought to provoke a cultural revolution by disseminating deliberately adversarial theories and controversial works of art intended to shock. The aim, as Berghaus points out, was a 'transformation of life in both its physiological and psychological aspects, [...] especially of the social and cultural political conditions in the modern metropolis' (1998, p. 59). Thus, Futurism was not intended to be just a cultural revolution; it was intended to completely revolutionize modern life.

In addition to their numerous manifestos, Marinetti and members of his circle also used the theatre to disseminate their ideas. A sort of hybrid of the literary salon, cabaret and public lecture, the Futurist *serata*, which means 'entertainment', were evenings coordinated by Marinetti in which Futurist manifestos would be recited, and literary and musical works realizing those manifestos would be performed. For Marinetti, what distinguished the *serata* from other artistic meetings was its politics. It was, in his view, 'a political meeting with an artistic format' (Berghaus, 2005, p. 33). While this might sound genteel and civilized, *serata* tended to be the exact opposite. Having developed an absurd manner of delivery, consisting of vocal and physical distortion, designed to irritate and provoke, the Futurist's evenings were characterized by strong reactions from its audiences.[11] Boos, shouting and vegetables hurled at the stage were not uncommon. Such a hostile reaction was, of course, the point. Marinetti's 1911 manifesto 'The Pleasure of Being Booed' explains that to be applauded is to be of 'average intelligence' and demonstrates something that is '*mediocre, dull, regurgitated, or too well digested*' (italics in original, 1971c, p. 115). As the manifesto makes clear, artists should '*despise the audience*' (ibid., p. 113).

In addition to 'The Pleasure of Being Booed', the other manifesto that articulates the Futurists concerns and hopes for the theatre is 'The Variety Theatre', first published in 1913. Like the other avant-garde artists discussed, Marinetti believed the mainstream theatre to be woefully inadequate for modern society. Calling it 'a finicking, slow, analytic, and diluted theatre worthy [...] of the age of the oil lamp', in keeping with the Futurist ideology he rejected the existing theatre and the traditions of the past (Marinetti, 1971d, p. 116). He did, however, see tremendous potential in the popular variety theatre owing to, among other things, its immediacy, swiftness and willingness to please audiences. He was also attracted to its low-art status, which would certainly contribute to its ability to provoke and shock traditionalists and high-art connoisseurs. In terms of form, the variety theatre possessed what Marinetti referred to as the 'Futurist marvellous', which allowed it to present 'powerful caricatures', 'delicious, impalpable ironies' and 'the whole gamut of stupidity, doltishness, and absurdity [...] pushing the intelligence to the very border of madness' (ibid., p. 117). The Futurists proposed to exploit the 'marvellous' in the variety theatre by exploding its elements, 'completely destroy[ing] all logic' in the process (ibid., p. 120).

Many of Marinetti's proposals for amending the variety theatre for Futurism were based on the element of surprise. This included defamiliarizing its popular elements, such as dying the chanteuses' arms, legs and hair strange colours, as well as disrupting their songs with revolutionary speeches. Classic plays were not prohibited from the Futurist stage, but if used they would need to be comically rearranged, condensed and possibly performed all at once and as quickly as possible. Similarly, it was recommended that if classical music was to be used, it should be performed backwards. Further surprises might include tying the actors up in sacks or soaping the floorboards to make them slip and fall, which suggests something of an attempt at harnessing the comic potential of slapstick violence. Surprises might also be found in the auditorium. The manifesto makes several suggestions as to how to surprise audiences: glue them to their seats; sell more than one ticket per seat so that altercations between ticketholders might break out; or make them itch and sneeze by sprinkling itching powder in the auditorium. The anticipated outcome of these proposals was a high-energy spectacle of chaos and absurdity, for which the variety theatre, owing to its loose form, was an all-too-willing receptacle.

Futurists were also fascinated by mechanization– not only in the possibilities of the mechanized human body, but also through the use of puppets and objects in performance. This was both an extension of Marinetti's own unique performance style as well as the Futurist's fascination with modern machines and technologies. The underlying principles of mechanized performance appear in Marinetti's essay 'Dynamic and Synoptic Declamation', first published in 1916. In it, he describes his approach to declamation, which consisted of distorted, dehumanized voice and facial expressions, geometrical and typographical gestures, and the frequent use of objects like hammers and electric bells to punctuate the performance with 'abstract onomatopoeias and different onomatopoetic harmonies' (Marinetti, 1971a, p. 144). 'In all ways,' Marinetti writes, the declaimer should be 'imitating motors and their rhythms (without worrying about understanding)' (ibid., p. 145).

The first official declamation that realized this particular manifesto occurred in Rome in March 1914 with a programme consisting of Francesco Cangiullo's *Piedigrotta*, featuring Marinetti, Cangiullo and a troupe of six little people. Marinetti describes the performance:

> Every so often the author leapt to the piano, in alternation with my declaiming of his words-in-freedom. The room was lit by red lamps that doubled the dynamism of the [...] backdrop [...]. The audience greeted the appearance of the procession of the dwarfs with frenzied applause, this troupe who bristled with fantastic hairdos of vellum paper and who circled around me as I declaimed. (ibid., 146)

Outside of declamations, the ideas about mechanization were being put into practice through other means. Gilbert Clavel and Fortunato Depero's *Plastic Dances* (1918), for instance, replaced humans with puppets. The performance's five sketches featured puppets of various forms and sizes, including the larger-than-human sized 'Great Savage'. The Great Savage had a trap door in its stomach that when opened revealed mini, dancing savages. Both humans and objects were utilized in Alexei Kruchenykh's Futurist opera *Victory Over the Sun*, performed in St Petersburg in 1913.[12] The production consisted of a cubist set and complementary costumes of geometric and abstract shapes. Recalling the production, Kruchenykh would describe how the 'costumes trans-formed the human anatomy, and the actors moved, held and directed by the rhythm dictated by the artist and the director' (quoted in Goldberg, 2001, p. 36) in a manner that Goldberg has called 'puppet-like' (ibid.). Combined, the performers and set were regarded as exten-sions of one another, as though a cubist painting had been brought to life. While there is here a conscious appropriation of the puppet for use in performance, it is important to recognize that puppetry as a popular art form held little appeal for most Futurists. Rather, it was an aware-ness of the puppet-as-machine and, more broadly, the implications of embodied machine-like choreographies that meshed well with the Futurist ideology.

The Bauhaus

The aesthetic influences of the popular theatre can also be found in work produced at the interdisciplinary art and design school Bauhaus in Germany throughout the 1920s. Led by architect Walter Gropius, the Bauhaus was formed through the unification of the Academy of Fine Arts and the School of Arts and Crafts in the central German city of Weimar in 1919 (Whitford, 1984, p. 29). The merging of two, previously separate, arts training traditions – the fine arts (including portraiture, painting, and sculpture) and crafts (e.g. pottery and textile design and production) – was intended to, as the founding manifesto made clear, rescue artists and craftspeople from isolation and to promote unity and collaboration in the arts and arts industries (Gropius, 1919). In doing so, Gropius wrote, the Bauhaus would endeavour to 'create a new guild of craftsmen free of the divisive class pretentions that [...] raise a prideful barrier between craftsmen and artists' (ibid.). Traditional studios were replaced by workshops overseen by professional artists and craftsmen, known as Masters of Form and Workshop Masters, respectively (Whitford, 1984, p. 30). While students, known as apprentices upon entry, later becoming journeymen once they had passed guilds' exams, were to be instructed by the masters, the aim was that the Bauhaus would function as an egalitarian community working together to bring practical, modern aesthetic changes to real world design and architecture. As Gropius would later note, the Bauhaus community 'had to become vital participants of the modern world, seeking a new synthesis of art and modern technology' (1961, p. 7).

Like the Futurists, Gropius placed emphasis on the modern, although, unlike Marinetti and his followers, this was not done on anarchic political grounds or to upset bourgeois sensibilities deliberately; that happened regardless.[13] While Gropius and many members of the Bauhaus staff and student body held left-wing political views, Gropius insisted that the school was apolitical and he discouraged those involved with the school from mixing politics and art (Forgács, 1995, p. 40).[14] The reason for this was that Gropius was trying to protect the Bauhaus from becoming involved in partisan political issues which could affect its funding from the state (Whitford, 1984, p. 38). Despite this, the school's aesthetics, heavily influenced by Expressionism and Constructivism, which, as discussed in Chapters 2 and 3, were both tightly enmeshed in communist politics, suggested otherwise to conservative critics and members of the public.[15] As a result of its perceived political affiliations and the public's distaste for the Bohemian character of many of its students, the Bauhaus was never given the opportunity to stay in one location for very long. In 1924 the school relocated to the northern city of Dessau, where it would thrive in a purpose-built building designed by Gropius. Following Gropius's resignation from the school in 1928, the openly socialist architect Hannes Meyer was appointed as his successor. Under Meyer, the Bauhaus became more overtly political (ibid., p. 190). Politics were not only added to the curriculum, but Meyer encouraged students to discuss and debate political views with one another in the school – both of which had been prohibited under Gropius. As Gropius had predicted and sought to avoid, the Bauhaus's foray into politics was quickly seized upon by the school's enemies and became fuel for fierce attacks against it. Meyer was subsequently forced to resign and the school's communist students were asked to leave (ibid., p. 191). His replacement, Mies van der Rohe, appointed in 1930, sought to overturn the school's bad press, but had little success. In 1932 the school was forced to relocate to Berlin, where the Nazis, who had been distrustful of the school for some time, closed it down a year later.

While the Bauhaus had been established to bring together the fine arts and crafts with a focus on professional, industrial production, it also had a theatre workshop. Whitford points out that while a theatre workshop may sound out of place in a school focused on craft and design, being an interdisciplinary medium, the theatre comfortably aligned with the school's ethos, making it much more than a 'fringe activity', and a 'vital part of the school, providing instruction in movement, costume- and set-design and construction' (1984, p. 83). Initially, the expressionist theatre director Lothan Schreyer (1886–1966) led the theatre workshop. Melissa Trimingham describes Schreyer's work as 'solemn, almost religious in its overtones, using costume and masks marked with esoteric symbols and Christian imagery' (2007, p. 13).[16] His work and approach do not appear to have been popular at the Bauhaus, and he would leave the school following his production of *Moonplay* in 1923, which the staff and students are said to have found 'incomprehensible' (Whitford, 1984, p. 85). Painter, sculptor and occasional theatre-maker and designer Oskar Schlemmer (1888–1943), who had been teaching mural painting, sculpture and life drawing at the Bauhaus since 1921, took over control of the theatre workshop after Schreyer's departure.[17] In place of Schreyer's solemn and pseudo-religious work, Schlemmer brought with him a much more colourful aesthetic constructed, at least in part, by the fusion of popular theatre forms, modern dance and modernist geometric abstraction.

As an artist, Schlemmer was preoccupied with abstraction, the human form, space and the relationship between these elements. The theatre, in particular, proved to be an ideal medium for him to experiment with these areas. Some of the ideas central to these investigations were outlined in his seminal writing for theatre, an essay entitled 'Man and Art Figure', published in 1925. In the essay, Schlemmer claimed that that the 'history of the theatre is the history of the transfiguration of the human form' (1961, p. 17). In the twentieth century, Schlemmer recognized three 'emblems' that could affect this transformation. The first emblem was abstraction, which functioned, he noted, 'to disconnect components from an existing or persisting whole', to elevate them absurdly, or to achieve 'generalization and summation' (ibid.). The second emblem he identified was mechanization, which he argued had '[lay] claim to every sphere of life and art' in the modern period (ibid.). While he regarded mechanization as a ubiquitous feature of post-industrial society, Schlemmer saw it as useful in demonstrating what, in fact, could not be mechanized (such as nature or the human body). The final emblem Schlemmer identified was technology, which he believed gave society both the promise of, and the potential to realize, its 'boldest fantasies' (ibid.).

The human transformations that Schlemmer created in his work were produced through an awareness of, and often an application of, these emblems. This was usually realized through the use of abstract, geometric, full-body costumes and masks that transformed the performer into an animator of architecture and/or a marionette. In this, Schlemmer was influenced by Romantic poet and dramatist Heinrich von Kleist's essay 'On the Marionette Theatre' (1810), which makes the point that marionettes, owing to the way in which they are operated (from above, resulting in perfect alignment) and their lack of self-consciousness, are more graceful performers than humans.[18] Equally as influential was Edward Gordon Craig's theory of the *Über-marionette*, which takes Kleist's idea further and suggests replacing human actors – who compromise the theatrical illusion with their flaws – with super puppets in performance.[19] For Schlemmer, the human body, encased in a costume-cum-puppet, but still present, could achieve something akin to Kleist and Craig's ideas. The bringing together of the puppet – the abstract, artificial and mechanical human figure – with the human operator, which is natural and non-mechanical (in the industrial or technological sense) may result in experiencing, Schlemmer believed, 'an intensification of their peculiar natures', as well as the opening up of '[e]ndless perspectives [...] from the supernatural to the nonsensical, from the sublime to the comic' (1961, p. 29). While Schlemmer's emphasis on mechanization and technology as 'emblems' may suggest that his investigations into the mechanization of human forms share some connection to the Futurists discussed earlier, Juliet Koss sees the Bauhaus puppets as explorations of abstraction and human subjectivity. Drawing on Schlemmer's words, Koss writes: 'Conflating "naïveté and reflection, naturalness and artificiality" [...] they playfully embody a model of human subjectivity that reflect[ed] the instability of their era' (2003, p. 724). While Schlemmer's influences may very well have been the increasingly mechanical and technological society in which he lived, neither his performances nor his writings suggest the same kind of commitment to machines as earlier avant-garde artists.

Schlemmer primarily saw the puppet as a means by which to explore the human form within the aesthetic and spatial codes of modernism, fusing, as Trimingham notes, 'the organic human body (the operator) with the "purity" of a puppet' (2007, p. 106). This is most clearly represented in *The Triadic Ballet* (1922–1923). The performance, developed between 1912 and 1922, featured three performers, one female and two male, in abstract full-body costumes made of padded cloth and papier mâché, moving in elaborate choreographies based on ballet, folk dance and the movements of mechanized dolls and toys.[20] The colours of the backdrop dictated the mood, aesthetic and tempo of each dance in the three-part performance. In the first part, described by Schlemmer as 'a gay burlesque', the backdrop consisted of full-length lemon-yellow curtains (1961, p. 34). The figures in this part, including a ballerina who appears to be formed from plastic (tutu and all) and a brightly coloured diver with a ropey, tentacled skirt suspended from his cylindrical shoulders, was intended to be humorous, falling into Schlemmer's aesthetic categorization of popular entertainment (Trimingham, 2007, p. 86).[21] The choreography of this section was toy-like and humorous: the ballerina's movements were robotic and mechanical, while the diver lumbered and hopped around the stage, occasionally twirling so that his tentacles would fly about. The second part, which Schlemmer described as 'ceremonious and solemn', was set against a rose-coloured stage (1961, p. 34). The costumes for this section were as elaborate as the first, but the choreographies were less toy-like and mechanical, relying much more on ballet and folk forms of dance. The final section, set on an all-black stage with black, white and metallic costumes (so as to attract the light), was intended to be a 'mystical fantasy' and an exploration of the metaphysical (ibid.). Across all parts, twelve dances were performed in eighteen different costumes.

The Triadic Ballet was, as Trimingham notes, Schlemmer's most valued artistic output. 'To him,' she writes, 'it was his most complete attempt to fuse motion and material form' (Trimingham, 2007, p. 86). It also established a template of sorts that would form the basis for much of the Bauhaus theatre workshop's work, which included the use of popular forms as aesthetic and conceptual influences. The 'puppet', as either abstracted human figure or as animated objects and architecture, was especially prevalent. For Kurt Schmidt's *Mechanical Ballet* (1923), for instance, the performers animated a collection of colourful shapes – squares, rectangles and other geometric forms – against a black background, giving the appearance of a moving abstract picture. The crude, grotesque marionettes Schmidt designed and built for *The Adventures of the Little Hunchback* (1923) offers another, perhaps more faithful, example of puppetry being used in Bauhaus work. But other popular forms were also drawn upon at the school. Schlemmer's *Figural Cabinet* (1923), for instance, was based on a fairground shooting gallery, and consisted of a collage of abstract faces, signs, pendulums, and wheels that buzzed, whizzed and moved about the stage (Schlemmer,

1961, p. 40). In Xanti Schawinsky's abstract pantomime *Circus* (1924), the artist, then a student at the Bauhaus, drew inspiration from the traditional circus that he rendered in an abstract, geometrical style. The performance consisted of series of independent scenes, including a young woman performing acrobatic tricks on a painted wood horse and a lion-taming act, in which the tamer (played by Schawinsky), in a costume made of cones, tubes and circles, sets out to tame the 'Great Monster'. The following year, he directed the ballet-pantomime *Feminine Repetition*, a piece which featured a tap dancer (once again, Schawinsky), an automatic tap machine and a 'mechanized row of cut out Tiller Girls'[22] all moving to gramophone recordings of Duke Ellington and Louis Armstrong music. Schawinsky later characterized the performance as an experiment in 'cabaret, clownery, the ridiculous, jazz, dance, rhythm, kitsch, mechanization, impromptu, color and dimensional space' (Schawinsky, 1971a, p. 36).

As these examples demonstrate, the influence of various forms of popular theatre at the Bauhaus was considerable. There are, I believe, several reasons for this. On a superficial level, it could be argued that popular forms offered Bauhaus artists a varied palette of colours, shapes and textures. The circus, fairground shooting gallery or puppet show, with their characteristic flashiness, sense of humour and use of primary colours, were congruent with the broader modernist aesthetic of the period (evidenced, for instance, in the paintings of Pablo Picasso and Wassily Kandinsky, himself a Bauhaus master). Puppets, as discussed, held a particular attraction to those working on the Bauhaus stage, as they provided a useful practical means to explore mechanization, the movement of the human form and the relationship between form and stage space. They were also popular with many Bauhaus students, who found them entertaining; puppet shows were subsequently a regular feature of the school's social life. As a student, Felix Klee, son of painter and Bauhaus master Paul Klee, is known to have developed a series of these, which typically satirized artistic trends or parodied Bauhaus faculty for the amusement of staff and fellow students (Klee, 2006, pp. 40–41). The form may very well have been convenient for those seeking a means by which to practically test their aesthetic ideas.

It is likely that the appropriation of popular theatre forms also occurred at the Bauhaus theatre workshop because the artists working there were not concerned by the politics of their low cultural status. While there are references in Schlemmer's writing to 'naïve' popular entertainment (1961, p. 18), in his theorization of the stage, he conceived of a continuum between popular entertainment, theatre and religious performance. In a diagram appearing in his essay 'Man and Art Figure', he is careful to demonstrate the linkages and overlaps between performance forms, with popular forms bordering and overlapping with scripted drama, and scripted drama bordering and overlapping into religious performance.[23] The implication of this seems to be that Schlemmer not only regarded popular performance forms as legitimate modes of performance, but a valuable and fundamental thread in the history of the theatre.[24] Another indicator of the progressive attitudes towards popular forms at the Bauhaus rests, I believe, in its overriding ethos. Seeking to unify two artistic traditions, the elitist fine arts and the vocational crafts, and to eliminate any perceived hierarchy between them suggests a progressive attitude towards art which seeks to downplay, or ignore, the historical cultural prejudices which gave rise to the popular as an aesthetic category. Unlike many of the other avant-garde artists examined in this chapter, the decision to work with popular forms at the Bauhaus had little to do with irritating the bourgeoisie or anarchically challenging cultural prejudice. Instead, popular forms seem have been drawn upon at the Bauhaus because they were conceived of as legitimate tools for aesthetic experimentation.

Conclusions

The decade of the 1930s was an intensely difficult time owing to the severe economic depression and sustained political tensions in Central and Eastern Europe. Artistic experimentation still persisted, although the social and aesthetic conservatism shared by certain governments, notably those of Germany and the Soviet Union, led to increasing limitations on artistic expression and what they regarded to be 'degenerative art'. During these challenging times, many artists fled to the United States, seeking both aesthetic and political freedom. The locus of avant-garde activity soon shifted to New York, where groups of close-knit immigrant communities would continue to experiment and develop new work. Outside of New York, the influence of the European avant-garde can be most clearly seen at Black Mountain College, the progressive liberal arts college established outside Asheville, North Carolina in 1933 by John Andrew Rice. Upon setting up the school, he hired the painter Josef Albers and his textile artist wife, Anni, to join the college's faculty. Both had decade-long connections with the Bauhaus. Within two years, another Bauhaus alumnus, Xanti Schawinsky, joined the faculty as head of stage studies, bringing his experience of Schlemmer's theatre workshop with him. His production *Spectodrama: Play, Life, Illusion* (1937) is demonstrative of how he put Bauhaus ideas into practice at the college. Played out in thirty-two scenes, the performance was a detailed study in the interplay of light, sound and movement. Performers and other materials, including large movable flats, giant puppets and long sheets of paper, interacted in a carefully set out kaleidoscopic choreography. Schawinsky developed only one further performance, *Danse Macabre*, before accepting an invitation in 1938 to join the New Bauhaus, set up by Bauhaus master László Moholy-Nagy, in Chicago (Duberman, 2009, p. 89). Unfortunately, the contracts for this appointment fell through and Schawinsky moved to New York City instead, where he worked as a designer, illustrator and teacher (Koss, 2014, pp. 28–29). Black Mountain College would, however, continue to be an important outlet for avant-garde performance in the United States until its closure in 1957.

Taking into account the histories of the early avant-garde presented here, one can see that the popular theatre played a role in helping to forge new aesthetic strategies for the modern age. At a time when artists were becoming increasingly suspect of realistic modes, the popular, which typically announces its artifice quite clearly through its costumes, masks, movement or manufacture (e.g. puppets), provided an ideal alternative on which to draw. The possibilities of the fusion of popular with the unpopular forms were numerous, from the generation of the grotesque in Meyerhold's work, intended to destabilize the familiar, breakdown illusion and promote a more active, engaged spectatorship, to destroying logic and infuriating the bourgeoisie, as the Futurists did. With Schlemmer, the puppet and its wider architectural and technological capabilities made it an ideal tool for interdisciplinary aesthetic experimentation, bringing together his and his students' work as designers, painters, sculptors and performers. As Whitford has pointed out, through his experiments, fusing popular with more high art forms like ballet, Schlemmer 'aimed for nothing less than a complete renewal of the [theatre] (1984, p. 86).

Crucially, these avant-garde artists promoted a relaxation of high and low art divisions, and demonstrated the aesthetic possibilities of merging forms from across the cultural spectrum. As the century progressed and modernism gave way to postmodernism, such experimentation would become even more commonplace. This progression, and the ways the popular continued to be drawn upon in the second half of the twentieth century, will be explored in Part II.

Part II
Contemporary Resistance

7 Post-War Popular Theatre

In the aftermath of the Second World War, the Soviet Union and the United States emerged as the two most powerful forces in world politics. While they had both fought as allies, the two countries, as representatives of two very different economic and political systems, were incompatible with one another on a fundamental, ideological level. By the end of the 1940s, this incompatibility had led to the onset of the Cold War, an ideological war for influence and power over other nations that would last until the dissolution of the Soviet Union in 1991. The latter half of the twentieth century was thus overshadowed by the performances of power of these two nations, including the construction of the Berlin Wall; the Korean, Vietnam and Afghan wars; and the Cuban Missile Crisis. As well as this, citizens of the world had to endure, depending on where they lived, sustained anti-communist and anti-capitalist propaganda, and live under the constant threat of nuclear warfare.

A radical popular theatre like that produced by workers in the 1920s and 1930s was not immediately forthcoming after the war. There were, of course, notable pockets of activity that seemed to bridge the pre- and post-war periods. Ewan MacColl and Joan Littlewood's Theatre Union, for instance, which had lapsed in 1940, resumed their work together in 1945 under the new banner Theatre Workshop. As Theatre Workshop, the group retained its agitprop politics, and aspects of its style, but expanded its repertoire to include a wider range of dramatic texts, from Molière to Shakespeare, which Littlewood sought to make politically meaningful, as well as works of the group's own devising. Dario Fo and his wife and artistic collaborator Franca Rame also bridge these periods. With the Fo-Rame Company, established in the late 1950s, they set an important precedent for creating playful, anarchic post-war popular theatre by drawing upon *commedia*, variety theatre and *guillare*[1] traditions.[2] But the fundamental problem was that there was no move-ment or coherent political vision from which a popular theatre could materialize. Part of this was connected to the onset of the Cold War. To be communist or even too left wing in the West could be equated to being sympathetic with the Soviet Union. This was especially true in the United States during the period of the Red Scare (1947–1957), where the federal government tried to smoke out and punish commu-nists. This played out in its worst form under McCarthyism, in which hundreds of Americans accused of being communist were imprisoned, while many more lost their jobs, owing to the social stigma that accom-panied such allegations. In this context, where being identified as a radical, or even thinking radically, could result in social ostracization or imprisonment, it is little wonder a more visible radical community did not emerge. Historian Katherine Sibley, drawing on the words of socialist Irving Howe, makes the point that the very public persecutions of McCarthyism 'helped to destroy whatever possibilities there might have been for a resurgence of serious radicalism in America' (Howe in Sibley, 1998, p. 10). She points out that this aggressively authoritar-ian behaviour ironically mirrored the Soviet government's, which the United States, with its promises of democracy and 'freedom', sought to define itself against (ibid., p. 10).

But the stalling of radicalism in the West was not entirely the fault of the United States. Much blame can, and should, be placed on the Soviet Union. After the October Revolution and throughout the 1920s, the Soviet Union was the aspiration for most communists. The popular theatre of the 1920 and 1930s looked to the Soviet Union not only for aesthetic guidance but also as the model of social change it could offer up to its audiences. The Soviet Union's many crises during these years, including economic collapse, famine and Stalin's deadly purges, were easily dismissed by Western communists as either the teething problems of a new state or the exaggerated tales of Western propagandists. The Cold War, however, presented a new set of issues for Western communists to negotiate, especially Stalin's apparent imperial aspirations which had been signalled by his decision to make Soviet satellites of countries conquered from the Germans in the war.[3] But the most damning indictment of Stalin's regime would come from one of his successors, Nikita S. Khrushchev (1894–1971). In February 1956, three years after Stalin's death, at the Twentieth Congress of the Soviet Communist Party, Khrushchev delivered a secret speech condemning Stalin's rule and making clear the full scale of his crimes. News of the speech hit the West within days, and in June a copy was released by the

CIA to *The New York Times*. There were riots in the Eastern bloc and disillusionment for radicals in the West. On hearing the news, many people, including French writer Jean-Paul Sartre, broke from their respective communist parties. As historian Staughton Lynd remarked, 'these events put an end to the hegemony of Soviet communism in the world radical movement' (1969, p. 65).

Without this anchor, radicalism and the popular theatre that served it floated aimlessly for much of the 1950s. Certainly there were radical theatres, but these belonged largely to the avant-garde. Towards the end of the decade, there were signs that a new radicalism was being fashioned, which, in part, revolved around the idea of extracting Marxism and the possibilities of Marxist theory from the problematic, bureaucratic communism of the Soviet Union. Two journals established in Britain – the *Universities and Left Review* and *The New Reasoner* – signalled this move. By 1960, the two had merged to form *New Left Review*, and with it the revised (or, at the time, *revising*) conception of radicalism – the idea of a *New Left* – had its name. In contrast with the Old Left, the New rejected scholasticism and the tendency of earlier theorists and bureaucratic communists to reify Marx's theories and insist upon singular interpretations of his ideas. Marxism needed to be unburdened of its past if it was going to be useful in constructing the future. In the words of Howard Zinn, one of the principal theorists of the New Left:

> If the New Left is wise, it will take from Marxism not all the exact propositions about the world that Marx and Engels lived in [...], but its approach, which demands constant redefinitions of theory in the light of immediate reality and insistence on *action* as a way of both testing and reworking theory. (1968, p. 360)

Capitalism and its wider effects continued to be a concern under the New Left. The working class was still very much a part of the conversation, although the scope of the radical project of the 1960s was much more diverse and included other inequalities, including gender, race and sexual orientation. Fundamentally, the aim was to secure genuine freedom for all, not the illusion of freedom offered under the current system, a system they referred to as corporate liberalism – which can generally be understood as a capitalist ideology which privileges the interests of corporations and big business over those of the people. Under corporate liberalism, the people's dissent is tolerated so long as the power structures that give business its power are not affected. Thus, the idea of freedom is maintained, but it is a chimera. This was the concern of Herbert Marcuse's book *One-Dimensional Man* (1964) (see Chapter 1). He writes: 'The totalitarian tendencies of the [corporate liberal] society render the traditional ways and means of protest ineffective – perhaps even dangerous because they preserve the illusion of popular sovereignty' (1964, p. 260). The New Left wished to replace these tendencies with a culture of participation in which men and women from all backgrounds would be involved in decision-making in every aspect of social life, from work to governance. This was more widely referred to as participatory democracy. On a more general level, this was a call to action – an invitation to become involved in changing society.

Despite concerns over efficacy, this was typically realized through protests, forms of civil disobedience and the popular theatre (which can sometimes be both protest and civil disobedience). In order to be effective, it was believed that these activities would need to be able to disrupt what Guy Debord had identified as the 'society of the spectacle' (Debord, 1992). Debord's work suggests that under advanced capitalism, human relationships are now mediated by images of commodities, dictating to people not only what they need in their lives but also how to live them. Such a system pacifies consumers, preventing them from engaging in meaningful human action. As Baz Kershaw has observed, effective popular performances and protest would seek to disrupt this spectacle by 'expos[ing] the systems of domination and stimulate a revolution through which popular desire for freedom would be satisfied' (Kershaw, 1999, p. 93). In the case of the popular theatre, it could seek to disrupt the society of the spectacle with spectacles of its own devising.

Popular theatre also had other benefits that were congruent with New Left politics, including the ability to occupy public spaces, such as city streets or parks, and to attract the attention of large numbers of people. The radical possibilities of popular theatres that operate in this manner are most often theorized through Mikhail Bakhtin's concept of the carnivalesque. Developed through a close reading of Medieval French writer François Rabelais's work, Bakhtin's *Rabelais and His World* theorizes the possibilities of the carnival as a space that cultivates revolutionary thinking. During periods of carnival, he observes, social hierarchies were allowed to be upended, allowing peasants to rehearse power role-playing as kings, while kings would temporarily take on the role of peasants. While it would be easy to dismiss carnival celebrations as frivolous moments of celebration in the medieval calendar, Bakhtin sees considerable radical potential in this reversal of the social order. As he notes, 'For thousands of years the people have used these festive comic images to express their criticism, their deep distrust of official truth, and their highest hopes and aspirations' (Bakhtin, 1984, p. 296). The occupation of public space as performance space and the positioning within it giant puppets, slapstick political satire or grand, ceremonial pageants by popular theatre-makers can be seen as a carnivalesque disruption of the everyday, drawing people together to critique systems of power and rehearse possibilities for change.

The political climate of the 1960s, including the revision of Leftist political ideas and radicalism, facilitated the development of new forms of popular theatre. While anti-capitalist, worker-focused performance remained a staple of the form, theatres of popular protest emerged on behalf of other causes, becoming an important auxiliary to the civil rights, feminist, gay rights and peace movements of the 1960s and 1970s. Finding ways to insert one's politics into the public's everyday frame of reference, and to have attention brought to causes through the growing media industries,[4] was a priority for many and this is reflected in the bolder aesthetic choices made by these theatre groups. In this chapter, I will look at some of these theatres, their causes and the way they constructed their work.

Puppets, *Commedia* and Pageantry: Key Models

In the United States, the San Francisco Mime Troupe and the Bread and Puppet Theatre were the leading companies of the popular theatre that emerged in the 1960s. While the companies would eventually become more widely known for their performances in public spaces, they both began as indoor experimental theatres, playing for audiences who shared an interest in avant-garde aesthetics. As the 1960s progressed, both companies found themselves seeking ways to engage audiences about the political concerns of the day. For the Mime Troupe, it was *commedia dell'arte* that brought its work out of the studio and into San Francisco public parks. The form allowed the company to map its corporeal training into its developing political consciousness in ways that proved popular with city residents and young people. For the Bread and Puppet Theatre, it was the war in Vietnam (1954–1975) that would prove central to its transition from an experimental puppet theatre to committed popular theatre.[5] Starting in 1964, the company started creating giant puppets for anti-war marches in New York City streets. Over time, these would develop into large-scale outdoor performances on issues ranging from inner-city poverty to nuclear disarmament. In this section, I will take a closer look at the practices of these two companies and the way their work developed in and beyond the 1960s, paying particular attention to the issues outlined in the previous section.

The San Francisco Mime Troupe

In 1959, following a period of training in Paris with famed corporeal mime Etienne Decroux, R.G. Davis moved to San Francisco and took up a position as an assistant director at Herbert Blau and Jules Irving's San Francisco Actor's Workshop. Later that year, he set up what was initially called the R.G. Davis Mime Troupe with performers from the Actor's Workshop. Unlike their later work, the performances that make up the company's early history were more experimental, reflecting the aesthetic influences of the local avant-garde scene. *Mime and Words* (1959), the company's first piece, is indicative of this. It was, according to Davis, a 'Grotowski-style poor theatre' production, focusing heavily on corporeal movement (1975, p. 20). This was followed by *11th Hour Mime Show* (1960), *Purgatory* (1961) and productions of Beckett's *Act without Words II* (1961) and *Krapp's Last Tape* (1961). Other works, like *Events I* (1961) and *Events II* (1963), which Davis describes as performances by 'insane people who were struggling to present all of the world in one hour', reflected his and the company's interest in other emerging arts practices, particularly Allan Kaprow's Happenings and Anna Halprin's dance events (ibid.). Another characteristic of these early works is that they contained little, if any, dialogue. In keeping with the modern mime tradition, they were largely silent, with the exception of music.[6]

In 1961 Davis and the company began practically exploring the *commedia dell'arte*. Their research into the form would result in the company's first outdoor performance, *The Dowry*, which was performed in Golden Gate Park in 1962. The *commedia* form gave the company a way of working that merged Davis's corporeal interest and training with a vocal, comic form that possessed considerable public appeal. It became clear to the company early on in their exploration of the form that it was easily adaptable for articulating their political views. Joan Holden's adaptation of Carlo Goldoni's 1751 anti-war play *L'Amant Militaire* (1967) is perhaps the clearest example of this.[7] Set in

the sixteenth century, the play's plot revolves around Spanish intervention into an Italian civil war. Holden's version was designed to offer a
satirical critique of the involvement of the United States in Vietnam.
To ensure that audiences made the connection between the play's historical setting and the present, a rolling commentary by the puppet
Punch, who was stationed off the stage, was added. As well as helping
to establish its performance style, *commedia* also gave the company its
scenography – a raised platform with a painted backdrop, which they
have retained ever since. This transition from corporeal mime to physical popular theatre marks not only a shift in the company's politics but
also in the company's attitude towards mime. Although they would
retain the word in their title, it would be used to signal the non-silent
practices of ancient Greek mime, an early popular theatre that presented domestic, everyday concerns and characters in an exaggerated,
comic manner.

Seeking to enhance their connection with American audiences, the
troupe looked to expand their repertoire of performance forms. While
the *commedia dell'arte* had allowed them to develop a physical, comic
style that had proven successful, they began to look for more indigenous forms that would resonate more strongly with local audiences.
In the 1970s, the group began a range of experiments with melodra-
mas, film noir, spy thrillers, superhero adventures, musical comedies
and cartoon epics. Like *commedia*, many of these forms rely on broad
stock characters based on stereotypes, comic rapport, spectacle and
distinct physicality and movement to appeal to audiences. The danger,
of course, in dealing with forms with a historical tendency towards
stereotype is the perpetuation of the negative aspects of those types.
Rather than denying the stereotype or the oppressive histories of some
of the forms they selected to perform, the company developed a way
to make the form work for their politics without radically re-authoring
them. A good, early example of this appears in *A Minstrel Show, or Civil
Rights in a Cracker Barrel*, which was first performed in 1965. Through
the minstrel show format – a form widely popular in the United States
in the nineteenth century constructed out of racist stereotypes of
black people – the company sought to weigh in on the Civil Rights
Movement.

A Minstrel Show consisted of a cast of seven: six blackface minstrels,
made up of three black and three white performers (whose racial identities were not revealed to the audience) and a white interlocutor. Rather
than focusing exclusively on the issue of intolerance, the performance
attacks white liberal hypocrisy and the apathy of the black bourgeoisie

(San Francisco Mime Troupe, 1966). Songs and scenes lifted from old minstrel shows were combined with new ones devised by the company, including a simulated sex scene between an interracial couple, and a white cop shooting and killing a black teenager. Laying racism from two racial perspectives – black and white – into an already racist form was intended to explode the issue, forcing, in a deliberately shocking way, an audience to confront not only blatantly bigoted attitudes towards race, but the more casual, or even repressed, forms of racism held by individuals who would deny being racist at all. As Davis would later remark: 'we had to exacerbate the deepest racist notions of the audience, even those who thought they were not racist' (quoted in Mason, 2005, p. 27). The company therefore magnifies, sometimes to grotesque extremes, the problematic aspects of some of the stereotypes found within the forms they use in order to counteract their potentially damaging effects.

Throughout the 1960s the company became more imbedded in the developing counter-culture movement. As early as 1963 Davis had already started to identify aspects of their work as 'guerrilla theatre', an anarchic theatre that aims to 'teach, direct towards change, be an example of change' (1975, p. 149). In the late 1960s, the troupe began using 'gutter puppets' in some of their works as a guerrilla tactic. These puppets, which ranged from more traditional hand puppets to nine-foot-tall effigies, would operate outside the frame of the performance, often attacking its content and calling for more revolutionary solutions to conflicts. In the brief sketch *Meter Maid* (1968), the gutter puppets taught audiences how to avoid paying to park their cars by inserting bottle caps instead of coins into parking meters. In *Telephone* (1970) the puppets taught audiences how to avoid paying for long-distance phone calls by diverting bills to major corporations. While many of their works during this period called for solutions to undermine capitalist hegemony, the gutter puppets represent some of their most direct calls to action.

Developing politically committed performances from popular theatre forms may help ensure performances possess popular appeal, but doing so can also be seen as ideologically misguided since it draws on forms that have often made the transition from popular to mass culture.[8] This is especially true of performances designed to be critical of capitalism. The Mime Troupe's work is indicative of this problem, although over the years the company appears to have found ways – aesthetic and dramaturgical – to militate against this. Aesthetically, the company's performances often possess a deliberate DIY quality to them. They are performed loudly (necessarily so, being outdoors), in an over-the-top manner and often with a hint of amateurism. The way the performance seems to resist commodification, therefore, is by establishing itself aesthetically in opposition to the polished, commercial mass-culture industry. This extends to their dramaturgy: characters may be recognizable types, but the comic intent of the type is usually allied with the group's politics, as can be seen with the company's use of minstrelsy. The familiar plot will be peppered with critical commentary and other forms of disruption designed to poke holes in its construction and the systems of power that such a form may seem, through its circulation as a mass-culture text, to represent. Doing so facilitates a kind of disidentification for audiences, a process which Jose Muñoz has described as 'a mode of recycling or re-forming an object that has already been invested with powerful energy' (1999, p. 39). The process of disidentification is ultimately a transformative one: identifying the original in the reformed object may undermine the values inherent in the original and reveal a new perspective on it.

The company's *FactPerson* tetralogy from the 1980s is indicative of this. In these plays, the company openly manipulates the familiar superhero narrative advanced through comic books, popular Hollywood films and television. The first FactPerson was a disgruntled waitress named Rita Book, who is gifted by the Spirit of Information with the superhuman power of knowing *everything*. As FactPerson, Rita fights against opponents of communism, Cold War scaremongers and supporters of President Ronald Reagan's economic policies, more popularly known as 'Reaganomics'. In the play's final scene, she goes to battle with Milton Friedman, the architect behind Reaganomics, in a TV debate and wins. Here, a working-class female is used to disidentify the superhero figure and the industries such a figure represents. The superhero figure is disidentified further in these works by having intellectual rather than physical superhuman strengths, thus reconfiguring the values advanced by the traditional superhero narrative. At the same time, the performance uses the cultural power bound up with the superhero to empower working-class women, who are typically under-represented in popular culture texts. Later, in *Factwino Meets the Moral Majority* (1981), *Factwino vs. Armageddonman* (1982), and *Factwino: The Opera* (1985), further disidentificatory mechanisms are in place as the hero role is taken over by a homeless, black alcoholic man named Sedro F. Wooley. As these examples demonstrate, the company are not simply recirculating popular mass-culture texts, they are appropriating and rewriting them to give voice to those who are not just misrepresented in such texts, but who are marginalized and left out of public conversations on important issues. Like the treatment of stereotypes discussed earlier, the distortion of well-known forms and cultural narratives in the work of the company facilitates a more critical evaluation of the familiar, or what we accept to be normal, fostering a more critical attitude towards the issues explored in performance.

The Bread and Puppet Theatre

When Peter Schumann and his wife, Elka, emigrated from Germany to New York City in 1961, he was a dancer and choreographer looking for opportunities to continue a career he had started in Munich in the late 1950s. He quickly inserted himself into the city's avant-garde scene, observing the composition classes of Robert Dunn, working, for a short time, with Yvonne Rainer, Richard Levine and Simone Forti, and becoming acquainted with Julian Beck and Judith Malina of the Living Theatre (Brecht, 1988, p. 64). Despite moderate success with his masked dance piece *Totentanz*, performed with the Alchemy Players in 1962, he soon abandoned dance in favour of sculpture and puppetry, which he had also nurtured interests in growing up. While Schumann is perhaps best known now for his outdoor performances involving giant puppets and masks, his early puppet shows were produced on a much smaller scale and often indoors. Also a skilled baker, Schumann started serving freshly baked sourdough rye bread at his performances. His rationale for this was simple: 'For a long time, the theatre arts have been separated from the stomach. Theatre as entertainment was meant for the skin. Bread was meant for the stomach. Theatre is more like bread, it is a necessity' (quoted in Erven, 1988, p. 56). The company's name stems from this belief and the continued practice of serving bread to audiences following a performance.

Schumann appears to have become politically engaged through two channels. The first was through his encounters with disadvantaged areas of New York City. Living with his family in Manhattan's Lower East Side, he had first-hand experience of the poverty that millions of city residents faced. In response to this, he began developing plays about issues like rat infestations, high rents and poor-quality housing for, and sometimes with, those communities (Erven, 1988, p. 54). This was not allied to a particular political belief, but out of a concern for his community. The second influence was the Living Theatre, who Schumann had a close working relationship with in the early 1960s.

Schumann's first foray into political activism would come as part of the Living Theatre's World Wide Strike for Peace, in February 1962, when members of the Alchemy Players marched wearing death masks Schumann had constructed for *Totentanz* (Brecht, 1988, p. 490). By the mid-1960s, Schumann and the company were a regular presence in the New York City peace movement, performing with life-sized and larger-than-life-sized puppets and masked performers to protest the war in Vietnam. Despite working in a spectacular mode, Schumann's approach, and his activism, were much gentler than that of early agit-prop or the Mime Troupe. Instead, his work has striven to be more ritualistic, poetic and visually profound.

This approach is perhaps best exemplified by *Fire* (1966). The performance was Schumann's response to American air raids in Vietnam and was dedicated to Alice Henry, Roger LePort and Norman Morrison, who had burned themselves to death in protest of the war (Erven, 1988, p. 54). Taking the form of a silent vigil, *Fire*, barring a few instances of music, the repeated sound of a bell (to signal the beginning of each scene), and any accidental sounds, was played in near silence. The protagonists consisted of a chorus of approximately twenty masked Vietnamese women, some played by human performers, others by mannequins, with puppet hands and long, black cowls. Divided into nine parts and structured according to days of the week, the audience was shown short vignettes that traced the effects of war on the women.

The performance began in a gentle, peaceful manner. Following the first bell, the curtain parted to reveal the women seated and looking out at the audience. A placard indicates that it is Monday. After a few moments, the women begin to whisper to one another and the curtain is pulled closed. As the week progresses, the days and images become darker as war works its way into the community. On Thursday, the women's quiet daily routines are disrupted by the appearance of a man completely entangled in ropes, which the women endeavour to free him from. On Friday the curtains part to reveal a scene of mourning: the man lies motionless in a cot as the women look over him. Before the curtain closes, they slowly draw a sheet over his face. Saturday's scene punctuates death's presence in the community: the curtain parts to reveal the women standing frozen in fear as a piercing, metallic noise blasts through the space. Above their heads, a lone theatre light swings violently while an indiscernible but 'large, demonically ungainly, snuffling creature flops among their feet' (Dennison, 1970, pp. 39–41). In the final scene, two Western figures, masked but with bare, human arms and wearing blue jeans, enter and place cinderblocks and wire around an elderly Vietnamese woman dressed in white. Encaged, the woman proceeds to tape herself to the floor with red tape, an act symbolically representing the act of lighting herself on fire. As George Dennison described it:

> With deliberate movements – movements at once practical, prosaic, and ceremonious – she tears long strips of the tape and fastens them on her robe near her feet. The red strips become numerous, and move higher, beginning to entwine her and hamper her movements. One wrist is immobilized against her chest, but the fingers still tear and fasten the strips. The strips cross her mouth, and her cheeks, and finally lie across her eyes. She folds in upon herself and topples forward, sagging heavily against the fence. (1970, p. 42)

The Vietnamese women in *Fire* would later reappear in many of the company's street performances between 1964 and 1967, becoming haunting representations of the war as well as iconic images of the anti-war movement. In a demonstration on 26 March 1966, for instance, they appeared as 'prisoners of war' and were subsequently tied together and marched down Fifth Avenue in Manhattan. They were accompanied by figures in skull masks banging drums, and a ten-foot-long airplane, resembling a shark, swooped down occasionally to frighten them.[9] They appeared again in May of that year. Dressed in white, they were marched in front of a casket bearing the words 'American Dead 4000 – Vietnamese Dead 1,300,000' (Brecht, 1988, p. 525). The women hummed as they marched and distributed flowers to onlookers (ibid.). Both marches made a striking visual statement, and were subsequently picked up by the media. One commentator noted, 'The impact was such that the rest of the marchers, all those thousands might just as well have stayed home' (quoted in Brecht, 1988, p. 520).

Performances produced by the Bread and Puppet Theatre may best be described as a popular puppet theatre of mixed means – which would be true of the company's work in the street, in theatre spaces, or on the company's thirty-acre farm in Glover, Vermont, where they have been based since 1974.[10] The puppets, which have varied from traditional hand puppets to fifteen-foot-high giants, have been constructed from papier mâché and wire, broom handles, large wooden dowels, scraps of recycled fabric, as well as clay and celastic, a fabric infused with plastic that is faster and more stable to work with than paper (Brecht, 1988, p. 136). It is fundamentally a poor theatre constructed largely of sustainable materials that can be easily, and cheaply, acquired. Schumann sculpted the moulds for the masks and puppets in a grotesquely distorted manner that would, over time, become recognized as the company's visual style. The performances have tended to be ceremonial in style (as the discussion of *Fire* demonstrates), with slowed gestures and movement, ritual-like music performed by live musicians, and some spoken language (often from a narrator). The outcome is not a polished spectacle, but often a crude aesthetic that, like the Mime Troupe's, borders on being amateurish. Françoise Kourilsky sees this as a kind of '"de-construction", or reversal' of the logic of the popular forms the company selects to work with (1974, p. 109). For Stefan Brecht, the deliberate 'avoidance of prettiness' in the work is designed to alienate 'the ceremony of the performance' (1988, p. 288). He writes:

> [it] makes the point that it is not there for its own sake, but is something gotten up and invented as part of a transaction between the performers and the audience by which the latter is to be put in touch with ultimate realities, with the realities of their lives outside of the performance. (ibid., p. 288)

So while it is ceremonial in style, the work does not wish its audiences to become lost in spectacle. There is more than a hint of Brechtian thinking in this approach, which Schumann acknowledges (Kourilsky, 1974, p. 108). Still, the politics are quite different. While Schumann, like Brecht, is concerned with the forces of capitalism, his work does not seek to provoke audiences to action. Neither is he particularly concerned with the efficacy of his methods. Instead, it is much more about bringing people together and inviting them, through the work, to see the world around them differently.

While the Bread and Puppet Theatre's body of work over the last fifty years is diverse, it is possible to identify within it some common features. In general, the company's output is quite different to that of the Mime Troupe and other groups discussed in this book. Whereas the Mime Troupe has developed a style of political satire that draws on often comic and musical popular forms, utilizing stereotypical characters in a politically driven narrative, the Bread and Puppet Theatre's work cannot be said to adhere to any particular popular puppet tradition. Schumann acknowledges a number of influences, including Kasperle, Bunraku and Sicilian marionettes,[11] although the puppets themselves are as much a product of his imagination, his skill as a sculptor and the materials he has to hand when he makes them. While the work is developed to offer a political statement, it often does so visually and through the use of allegory, as opposed to the more direct, verbal methods of the Mime Troupe. The puppets and masked performers in Bread and Puppet shows are not so much characters in the twentieth-century realistic sense, but figures demonstrating concepts, themes or ideas – or, as Stefan Brecht states, they are 'conceptualizations of aspects of social and of moral existence' (1988, p. 117).

While story is important in the company's work, it is not necessarily privileged in the development process. As Schumann confirms, 'we don't start with [a story]. We are starting from forms – pure musical and movement ideas – and then we proceed slowly to something that, we feel, becomes understandable, becomes communicable' (quoted in Kourilsky, 1974, p. 105). Few scripts have been produced in advance – instead, they are usually worked out between Schumann and the performers during the rehearsal process. As a visual theatre, however, the very notion of a script can be misleading. The process shares perhaps more in common with choreography, where one sequence of images and movements give way to others, and so forth. Dialogue or narration may then be laid over these in order to help improve the communication. Borrowing from the work of theorist Michael Kirby, Kourilsky points out the similarities between the structure of the company's performances and the circus or Happenings, where compartmentalized theatrical units are brought together to form a whole (1974, pp. 106–107). A good sense of this can be gained by looking at the few plays published by the company. The texts, which contain hand-drawn illustrations by Schumann, much more closely resemble comic books than traditional plays. With usually little in way of text, the illustrations are essential in understanding what is to be staged.[12]

Unlike many of the pre-war popular theatres that typically maintained a tight focus on the cause of the worker, both the San Francisco Mime Troupe and the Bread and Puppet Theatre have placed their practices into the service of many causes. While their work may have attracted attention in the 1960s for its treatment of national and international political events, such as civil rights (the Mime Troupe) and the Vietnam War (both), both companies have also made it a priority to address the concerns of the communities they are a part of. As well as the Bread and Puppet Theatre's early community work in New York, once the company moved to rural Vermont, they made an effort to integrate into and support their new community, eventually becoming, as Erven points out, 'an ineffaceable element of Vermont life' (1988, p. 55). This included participating in community parades and celebrations, as well as hosting summer performances on the Bread and

Puppet farm, free for all to attend. The San Francisco Mime Troupe has also become an outspoken advocate for San Francisco residents, taking up causes including urban redevelopment and housing prices (*Hotel Universe*, 1977; *City for Sale*, 1999; *Ripple Effect*, 2014), local political corruption (*Coast City Confidential*, 1995), and the city's hippy, radical past (*Ripped Van Winkle*, 1988). Feminism, gay rights and the environment, among other issues, have also been addressed through the work of these companies.[13]

Post-War Popular Theatre in Europe

The revolutionary atmosphere created by a series of nearly spontaneous uprisings in Europe, the United States and Mexico in 1968 – the product of a complex network of political movements, baby boomer dissatisfaction, heavy-handed government actions and the circulation of images of unrest via the television – is largely responsible for the burgeoning of popular theatre internationally in the second half of the twentieth century. Sensing, perhaps, some similarities to the revolutionary spirit of early generations of theatre-makers, some groups, including London's Agitprop Street Players (re-named Red Ladder in 1971), formed in the summer of 1968, revived the agitprop form from earlier workers' theatres to develop performances about modern working-class concerns, including housing prices, industrial relations and women's rights. Armed with a red ladder and few other props and costumes, the group developed mobile theatre pieces that could be easily transported to wherever the work was needed, from tenant meetings to political demonstrations. Welfare State International, which was founded by John Fox in December 1968, was directly influenced by the Bread and Puppet Theatre.[14] While Welfare State was, like Red Ladder, a theatre of limited means, their work was aesthetically more spectacular. Borrowing Schumann's more allegorical approach, the company constructed elaborate performances and celebrations with communities around issues affecting them. *The Raising of the Titanic* (1983), for instance, was a performance-cum-community celebration which culminated in the extracting of the famous ship – or, a metal framework designed to look like part of it – from London's Limehouse Basin, a disadvantaged area that was undergoing significant regeneration at the time. Other companies, which existed before 1968, would become radicalized by the revolutionary moment. French company Le Théâtre Populaire de Lorraine, for instance, founded by Jacques Kraemer in 1963 to stage well-known plays for rural audiences, radically rethought its work in light of the social and political unrest in May 1968. Abandoning its largely classical repertoire, it began developing original work about the Lorraine region. One of the first, and most successful, was a comic burlesque entitled *Splendeur et misère de Minette, la bonne Lorraine* (*Splendour and Misery of Minette, the Girl from Lorraine*). Loosely modelled on Brecht's *The Resistible Rise of Arturo Ui*, the play looked at the effects of the iron mining and steel industries on local people. As well as larger works like *Minette*, the company toured what they called *spectacles d'intervention*, shorter, more mobile satirical pieces, which allowed them to develop a closer relationship with audiences in the region (Erven, 1988, p. 67).

As these examples show, locality and community were hugely important to popular theatre-makers during this period, and the search for the ideal popular audience became a central concern for many. This could – and often did – result in theatre companies relocating from larger cities to areas where they believed their work held particular resonance. For instance, Red Ladder, after nearly a decade performing in London and touring the country with its worker-focused plays, chose to relocate to Leeds, where the company felt there was a much more identifiable working-class base (Mason, 2013). Claude Alranq's Théâtre de la Rue (Theatre on the Street), initially an agitprop troupe based in Lyon, France and founded in 1968, relocated to southern France in 1970 in order to make work for and with regional audiences. Translating its name into Occitan, Lo Teatre de La Carriera, the company began developing plays about regional concerns in the French and Occitan languages, drawing on popular traditions, folktales and other local customs. Like the San Francisco Mime Troupe and the Bread and Puppet Theatre, the company's works range from shorter political sketches, which were especially prevalent from 1968 to 1970, to full-scale productions of original plays written by Alranq and the company. Many of these were based on interviews and surveys the company conducted with local people. As D.M. Church has pointed out, the company's work shares much with Brecht, with songs, caricatured characters and simple, non-realistic sets used to break down the illusion and produce something akin to the *Verfremdungseffekt* (1985, p. 68). The company's aesthetic and political ambitions are perhaps best exemplified by *La Postorale de Fos* (*The Pastoral Play of Fos*), which was written and performed in 1975. For this play, the company used the structure of a Provençal pastoral play, an indigenous popular form typically associated with representations of the nativity, as well as local myths and legends, to discuss the effects of industrialization in the Occitan. The work retained an underlying socialist critique, but its emphasis shifted away from global or even national concerns to local ones. The company notes that the use of the traditional pastoral play to explore the issue of industrialization was designed to immerse audiences into their history in a way that might demonstrate the impact these industries were having, not just on the regional economy but on the environment and the local culture as well.[15]

The question of audience was also central to the work of John McGrath and his two companies, 7:84 England and 7:84 Scotland, formed in 1971 and 1973, respectively.[16] In *A Good Night Out* (1981), his seminal text on popular theatre, McGrath stressed directness and locality as being fundamental for a theatre to establish a meaningful relationship with working-class audiences. McGrath's interpretation of directness was to speak plainly and in terms that working-class people understand. While this may seem crudely didactic to the politically sophisticated, McGrath believed this was not the case for working-class people who interpreted such directness 'as self-evident – truths being stated publicly, socially, in an entertaining way' (1981, p. 54). For his work with 7:84, McGrath conceived of localism as a dialogic process, where regular exchanges between communities and the theatre-makers could take place, which was then fed into the performance. Local also meant taking theatre into spaces where it was believed working-class people were regularly entertained and felt comfortable, such as pubs and community halls, as opposed to conventional theatres that were ideologically oppositional to working-class values. The goal of developing performances in this manner was not about indoctrinating and proselytizing, but about 'help[ing] people to a greater awareness of their situation and their potential' (McGrath in MacLennan, 1990, p. 46). Nadine Holdsworth has suggested this strategy aimed to create something of a workers' club that 'would nourish group identification, commonality, and cultural/political affirmation' (1997, p. 34). Identification was also central to this, and for it to work effectively the community/audience had to believe the performers identified with them and were working fundamentally in their best interests. This locality and developed sense of identification and camaraderie was especially apparent in the work of 7:84 Scotland from its inception, and would become more central to 7:84 England's strategy around the mid-1970s. By the end of the decade, 7:84 England was targeting around forty communities in London, the Midlands and the North, which they tried to perform for twice a year (McGrath, 1990, p. 18).

In this respect, the company worked to cultivate stronger relationships with specific working-class communities, who identified as such, instead of trying to appeal to some generic conception of a 'working-class' audience.

McGrath's *The Cheviot, The Stag and the Black, Black Oil,* performed by 7:84 Scotland in 1974, offers an example of the company's strategy at work. The play traces a history of oppression in Scotland, drawing parallels between the horrors of the Scottish Clearances and the British government's managing of the country's oil revenues in the twentieth century. It was devised by the company with McGrath, incorporating his nearly fifteen years' worth of research on the Clearances and their aftermath, as well as views collected through discussions with Scottish people.[17] The play was developed using the form of a ceilidh, a native form involving folksongs, storytelling and dancing. The form allowed the company to weave stories about the Clearances – historical accounts, as well as interpretative commentary by the company – together with classic Scottish songs (some sung in Gaelic), new songs used to advance the narrative and dances.

In 1973, *The Cheviot* toured over fifty locations in Scotland, playing mostly in village halls and community centres. In most locations, the performance was followed by a dance with music provided by the company's musicians. This feature was especially important to McGrath, who saw it as making the performance more of an event (i.e. 'a good night out') for local people (MacLennan, 1990, p. 46). As well as this, efforts were made to articulate the performers' unity with the audience before and during the performance. This relied on the performers' engaging with the audience as themselves, not characters, from the moment of their arrival until they left the venue (Kershaw, 1992, p. 156).

Welfare State International's work was also reliant on locality and cultivating strong bonds with their audiences. This was typically realized by involving people from the local community directly in the making of its work. According to Fox, the aim of involving participants was to help give them 'some control over their lives by accessing their creative potential and by taking to the streets together' (2002, p. 34). This creativity might be realized through the construction and parading of a lantern, as nearly 10,000 people did for *Glasgow All Lit Up* (1991), a processional performance involving nearly 250 educational and community groups and culminating in a spectacular community celebration (Fox, 2002, p. 130), or through learning to tell stories as part of a celebration of one's community, as was the case with *Bay Tales*

(2005), a project involving storytelling workshops with people from the Morecombe Bay area. While the company certainly produced work that argued its radical political position much more forcibly, these more politically discreet projects gave participants an opportunity to collaborate and create with others in a way that resembles the kind of inclusive, fairer politics and society that Fox and Welfare State International aspired to in their practice. In the case of both 7:84 and Welfare State International, the decision to involve local people in the performance, or indeed in its making, was a deliberate strategy to establish a closer bond between the audience and the company and to make their politics more palatable for them.

Like the Mime Troupe and Bread and Puppet Theatre, many of the popular theatres that emerged during this period engaged with much more than just working class politics and often used their practices to attend to other forms of social and economic injustice. Le Théâtre Populaire de Lorraine, for instance, while using their work to comment on regional industrial development, also looked at the highly contested issue of immigration and racist attitudes towards migrant workers in Lorraine. In *Les Immigrés* (1972), the company satirized French bourgeois attitudes towards migrants through a series of satiric, ironic sketches that drew a historical link between the African slave trade in the sixteenth and seventeenth centuries and the present treatment of migrant workers. The aim of the play, as Erven points out, was to promote solidarity between local working-class people and the 'oppressed foreign laborers' (1988, p. 70). The first performance of 7:84 England, *Trees in the Wind* (1971), investigated attitudes towards Marxism alongside three feminist perspectives – bourgeois, socialist and radical – which were represented by three strong-willed female characters. In particular, the play was interested in exploring the contradictions often found between political theory and its practical deployment in the real world. In the end, individualism – and concern over one's individual, daily circumstances – is identified as the biggest barrier to social action and the reason why, ultimately, people do not always practice what they preach. Lo Teatre de La Carriera would also turn their attention to feminism in the late 1970s and early 1980s, devising a number of plays about women in the Occitan, including *Seasons of a Woman* (1979) and *The Mirror of Days* (1980). In shifting focus, the company uncovered tensions between many of the popular traditions in which they had worked, such as carnival and *commedia dell'arte*, and feminist politics. Essentially, they came to regard such forms as not only traditionally male dominated, but also fundamentally misogynist (Lo Teatre de la Carriera, 1980, p. 7).[18] While popular elements, including songs, dances and comedy, were retained, the company's feminist plays were driven much more by the stories of the women interviewed and were, consequently, intended to be serious and empowering. Red Ladder's *Strike While the Iron Is Hot* (1974) also represented an aesthetic and stylistic departure for what had been up to that point a predominantly agitprop company. The play grew out of the frustration of the company's female members that Red Ladder did not address issues affecting women enough in their performances (Aston, 1995, p. 75). Loosely based on Brecht's *The Mother*, *Strike While the Iron is Hot* depicts a woman trying to find balance between her roles as mother, wife and union activist. The play shows that such a balance can only be reached when domestic responsibilities, such as raising children and minding the home, are shared evenly with one's spouse.

Other Popular Theatres

As well as established theatre groups taking up what they saw as politically related causes, there also emerged a number of popular theatres for specific rights-driven movements. In the United States, the practice of a popular theatre working as an auxiliary to a rights movement had started in 1963 with the establishment of the Free Southern Theatre (FST) in Jackson, Mississippi. Composed of professional and amateur actors, the FST's aim was to take theatre to black communities. As well as cultural enlightenment, the company's founders, Doris Derby, John O'Neal and Gil Moses, who had come to the south as student activists through the Congress for Rights Equality and the Student Nonviolence Coordinating Committee to participate in the Civil Rights Movement, thought that the theatre could advance the cause of black liberation and function as a critical tool to encourage black people to review and reflect upon their historical oppression (Fabre, 1983, p. 55). Initially the company produced plays by white authors, including Beckett, Genet and Brecht,[19] but after the first year of touring and relocating to New Orleans, they adopted a policy of performing plays by and about southern blacks. One strand of the company's work consisted of running workshops with local people, who would be invited to devise performances that reflected their experiences. One of the performances that emerged from the workshop was *Where Is the Blood?* (1972), a documentary play about antebellum slavery, formed from a number of historical documents, including autobiographies, newspaper reports and legal documents, and organized into a dramatic montage. O'Neal was also responsible for several of the plays produced. His *When the Opportunity Scratches, Itch It* (1974), for instance, offered a satirical look at contemporary black politics by drawing on a range of black stereotypes, and controversially demonstrating the corruption of the church, which, in the play, shared an alliance with big business. Throughout the 1970s, the group continued to experiment with different forms in the search for better, more effective ways of representing the values and experiences of their community. However, funding issues seriously compromised the company's work, preventing it from expanding its workshop provision across the south. The company officially disbanded in 1980.

Starting in 1969, the Gay Liberation movement would also see the development of several important popular theatre groups. The London Gay Liberation Front's (GLF) Action Theatre Workshop, formed soon after the organization's founding in 1971, became an innovative workshop for creating eye-catching public disturbances, referred to as 'zaps', which were designed to raise awareness of the GLF's cause.[20] Member Peter Tatchell recalls that the group 'mocked and ridiculed homophobes with wicked satire, which made many hard-faced straight people laugh and realize the stupidity of bigotry' (2009). In a brief article in the London GLF's Gay Pride Week Programme for 1973 entitled 'What is Action?' it was explained that

> Meaningful action [...] is whatever increases confidence, the autonomy, the initiative, the participation, the solidarity, the equalitarian tendencies and the self-activity of the masses and whatever assists in their demystification. (Gay Liberation Front, 1973)

One of the most successful London GLF actions was planned in response to the Festival of Light in 1971. The Nationwide Festival of Light was a morality movement established in 1970 by Peter and Janet Hill, two British Christian missionaries. It was designed as a response to the sexual permissiveness that the Hills believed pervaded British society at the time. The movement rapidly grew with the support of churches and religious celebrities around the country, including social reformer Mary Whitehouse and rock star Cliff Richard. The festival consisted of a series of localized events, including bonfires and public sermons, culminating in two major events in London on 25 September in which an estimated half a million people were believed to be in attendance. A zap was organized by the Action Street Theatre group to coincide with the official launch of the Festival at Central Hall, Westminster, on 9 September.

The 'script' distributed to GLF demonstrators offered quite precise instructions. Participants were instructed to dress conservatively and not draw attention to themselves. As the event was to feature a series of performed actions, members were instructed to wait for the room to settle before initiating the next assault. The demonstrations began subtly, with GLF members applauding longer than necessary. This was followed by interruptions by people in costumes, including nun's habits, who proceeded to jeer and dance through the Hall. Security staff roughly and forcibly removed them. Once the Hall had calmed, white mice were released, causing a stir among the speakers; soon after, two men dressed as conservative old ladies unfurled a banner that read 'Cliff for Queen'. Pornography disguised as religious literature was circulated to members of the audience and a kiss-in was initiated, after which the electricity in the hall was cut. The final performance given was by demonstrators dressed as Ku Klux Klan members, where the key religious messages of the Festival were delivered to the audience in their full, harsh reality (Robinson, 2007, p. 72).

Outside of the movement itself, one of the more important gay-focused popular theatres in Britain was Gay Sweatshop. Gay Sweatshop grew out of the activist arts organization Inter-Arts, which, in 1973, began staging feminist plays at the Almost Free Theatre in London. In 1974, Inter-Arts put out a call for plays about gay issues with a view to setting up a gay theatre company. Later that year, Gay Sweatshop was formed. The company's first season at the Almost Free Theatre in 1975, entitled 'Homosexual Acts', consisted of lunchtime performances of plays by Robert Patrick, Lawrence Collinson and Alan Wakeman. In the same year, the group was invited to prepare a play for the Campaign for Homosexual Equality conference in Sheffield. Drawing on the personal experiences of the members of the company and the book *With Downcast Gays: Aspects of Homosexual Self-Oppression* by Andrew Hodges and David Hutte, the company collectively devised the agitprop *Mr X*. The play traces the history of an individual, known simply as Mr X, coming to terms with his sexuality in light of sustained discrimination from oppressive social institutions, including school, the church, work, the media and the gay scene itself. The title, *Mr X*, refers to the idea of the 'anonymous homosexual', a popular idea at the time used to discuss closeted gay people who were too ashamed and/or afraid to reveal their sexualities or identities to friends, families or employers. Those active in the movement generally saw them as a barrier to gay liberation. At the end of the play, Mr X has an epiphany and stands in front of the audience and comes out. No longer Mr X, but the actor playing the role, the performer announces his own name and sexuality to the audience. Jill Poesner's *Any Woman Can*, written in 1974 and toured by Gay Sweatshop between 1975 and 1977, shares a similar directness. Written in a testimonial style, Poesner's autobiographical play traces her journey from bullied teenager to a young adult trying to understand the politics of queer relationships. Throughout the play, the protagonist addresses the audience directly in an attempt to establish a personal connection, and also to put a human face on her sexuality. In this regard, both plays sought to humanize the debate about sexual orientation and to encourage others to come out and join the growing ranks of out gay people.

While there was certainly no shortage of LGBT-focused theatres to emerge in the United States in the 1970s and early 1980s, the WOW Café in New York has proven to be one of the most influential and longest lasting. WOW began its life as the Women's One World Festival, which was organized by Peggy Shaw, Lois Weaver, Pamela Camhe and Jordy Mark in 1980 and again in 1981. Following on from the success of the festival, the organizers opened the WOW Café in March 1982 in a storefront on East 11th Street in New York's East Village, later moving to a former factory on East 4th Street, where it remains today. Since its inception, the WOW Café sought to empower and give voice to women through performance. Weekly variety nights, open to all and at no financial cost to the performer, allowed anyone with a desire to perform the opportunity to do so. Owing to the café's radical feminist politics, its open-to-all-women membership policy, and its lack of resources, performances have tended to be anarchic, playful and what Kate Davy has described as 'unapologetically amateur' but 'heartfelt' (2011, p. 2). This politically charged but welcoming environment has proven an effective launch pad for the careers of many important feminist and/or lesbian theatre practitioners, including playwrights Holly Hughes and Lisa Kron, and companies Five Lesbian Brothers and Split Britches. Of these, Split Britches, in particular, seems to embody the spirit of the WOW Café. Formed by Peggy Shaw, Lois Weaver and Deb Margolin in 1982, Split Britches' work has often drawn upon the personalities and personal experiences of its core members – Weaver, a femme lesbian; Shaw, a butch lesbian; and Margolin, a Jewish heterosexual – and conflated these with parodies of popular culture texts, current events, myths and other materials. Their approach, as Dolan points out, is based on a complete rejection of 'realism and its domestic concerns', and the playful defacing of 'dominant culture's conventional forms' (2010, p. 32). Like other groups discussed in this chapter, Split Britches' aesthetic is low-fi and DIY, with thrift store costumes, found props and handmade sets. Sue-Ellen Case, in her study of the company's work, discusses the linkages to be found between their 'poor theatre' aesthetic and popular theatre traditions of the past, comparing their work to *commedia dell'arte* players in a market square, or turn-of-the-century nightclub sketches or vaudeville acts (1996, p. 3). The company's performances have included *Split Britches* (1982), which offered a look at the lives of three of Weaver's female ancestors living in rural isolation in the 1930s; the working class farce *Upwardly Mobile Home* (1984), which re-imagines the economically prosperous 1980s as a time of economic hardship; and *Belle Reprieve* (1991), a collaboration with British drag troupe Bloolips, which remakes Tennessee Williams's *A Streetcar Named Desire,* humorously interrogating gender stereotypes, homophobia in the 1940s and the subtexts of Williams's play. Their personable, intelligent performances, alongside others at WOW, were responsible for drawing a regular and committed crowd to the café. As Davy remarks, the popularity of this work, particularly in the years immediately after WOW's founding, was a

> by-product of an ecstatic moment in which a group of women came together in a rush to make theatre and to unleash desires that had been too long reined in: the desire for voice, imagination, and sex free from censure and the strictures of gender and race. (2011, p. 2)

In this regard, the work of WOW and Split Britches operates as a popular women's and lesbian theatre not only because they draw on popular culture resources, but because they have spoken to and for a diverse community of women at an important time in their history – and they continue to pursue those conversations with audiences now over thirty years later. While Margolin, Shaw and Weaver have not produced work as a trio since the 1990s, Shaw and Weaver continue to operate under the Split Britches heading, with both solo shows and joint projects. While the tone and texture of their work has changed as the women have aged, it is still principally concerned with women's issues, butch-femme gender types, theatricality and femininity in the twenty-first century.

Legacies and Final Thoughts

In the last two decades of the last century, the popular theatre was hit by financial and political crises. The financial obstacles were always there. Many groups, including the Mime Troupe and Bread and Puppet Theatre, sustained themselves largely from audience donations, revenue from touring and grant funding from state and national sources. The objective was not, as their work made clear, to make a profit. In Britain and other places in Europe, many companies benefited from state support in the form of annual grants or one-off commissions for particular projects. In Britain in the 1980s, under Prime Minister Margaret Thatcher's Conservative government, the Arts Council, which had sustained many popular theatres, pursued a radically different approach to funding, one which placed emphasis on self-sufficiency and entrepreneurship – values that were antithetical to many of the these groups. 7:84 England lost its funding in 1984, and ceased working later that year. Many companies followed, while those that remained worked furiously to adapt in order satisfy the new funding agenda. Red Ladder, for instance, shifted its work away from socialist politics to focus on young people, directing its work at 'youth clubs and social welfare organizations' (Pal, 2010, p. 58). McGrath saw the Arts Council's actions as an attempt to censor art, discredit alternative political positions and taint the legacies of radical theatre practice. He lamented in his book about the crisis, *The Bone Won't Break*, that by the end of the eighties, the combined efforts of Thatcher's Tory government, their Arts Council and the right-wing media had made terms like socialism and working class sound 'pre-historic' (McGrath, 1990, p. 20). Politically, Thatcher gave radical companies a brilliant target, but they had effectively been neutered by the new funding arrangements. The revamped Cold War rhetoric of Thatcher and President Ronald Reagan's governments certainly contributed to the public's revived suspicion of the Left. This was compounded by the collapse of communism across Eastern Europe and Russia between 1989 and 1991. While the end of decades of political suppression by bureaucratic communist regimes was certainly worth celebrating, the distorted Marxism used to rationalize the regimes within those countries remained largely unchallenged. In the battle for ideas played out during the Cold War, the Left is generally regarded to have lost; in the public's mind, the free-market Right won.

Not all of the popular theatres disappeared, of course. Of the ones mentioned in this chapter, the Bread and Puppet Theatre, the San Francisco Mime Troupe, Le Théâtre Populaire de Lorraine (now known as NEST – Centre Dramatique National de Thionville-Lorraine),[21] WOW Café, Split Britches and Red Ladder are still operating. 7:84 Scotland outlived its English counterpart by nearly twenty-five years, disbanding in 2008 owing to changes in funding. Welfare State International officially ended in March 2006 with *Longline: The Carnival Opera*, a spectacular piece involving live music, puppets and projections inside a circus tent in Ulverston, England. While the company's funding had not been removed, Fox had started to feel that their creativity was being compromised because they had become a 'goal-orientated corporate institution' (2005). Fox and his wife, Sue Gill, now invest their creative energies in Dead Good Guides, a company that works with artists and interested others to make art, rites of passage ceremonies and site-specific performances. Lo Teatre de La Carriera and Gay Sweatshop disbanded in 1986 and 1997, respectively. Both ended owing to financial difficulties.

The San Francisco Mime Troupe and the Bread and Puppet Theatre have proven to be the most consistent of the post-war popular theatre survivors, not just in terms of their aesthetic and dramaturgical styles but also their politics. The Mime Troupe's 2015 show, *Freedomland*, waded into the issue of police violence against African Americans, recently brought to light by the shootings of Michael Brown in Ferguson, Missouri and Freddie Gray in Baltimore, Maryland, resulting in significant social unrest and riots in those areas in 2014 and 2015. The Bread and Puppet Theatre continues to develop work on its farm in Vermont and to tour nationally.

Currently, Red Ladder's fate is uncertain. In the late 1990s, the company collaborated with Theatre in the Mill, Bradford to set up the Asian Theatre School, a youth theatre programme under the direction of Madani Younis that evolved into a highly successful producer of new work. The venture proved incredibly successful and, in 2008, it became Freedom Studios, independent of Red Ladder. Since 2006, the company has seen a radical shift back to the Left under artistic director Rod Dixon. Under his direction, the company has produced a number of politically charged new works, several of these by Boff Whalley, a member of the anarchist alternative rock group Chumbawumba. These include *Sex & Docks & Rock 'n' Roll* (2010), which took a nostalgic look back at the 1960 Liverpool dockworkers and seafarer's strike, and *Big Society* (2012), a musical that used the framework of an Edwardian music hall variety show to comment on the Conservative–Liberal Democrat coalition government in Britain at the time. Speaking to Dixon ahead of the performance, he acknowledged the popular dimension of the work and what he hoped it might achieve:

With *Big Society* we took a different approach: we wanted to create a good night out and see what happened. So, the ideas are pretty obvious: everyone hates the coalition government. But surely it's better to celebrate our commonality by laughing at the coalition, to celebrating our collective dislike. (2012)

In 2014, Red Ladder saw all of its funding withdrawn by the Arts Council. At the time of writing, an Internet campaign run through the company's website and Twitter accounts has been established to help solicit donations from the public.

The global economic recession of 2008, which is still being felt in many parts of the world, has contributed to a revived interest in popular theatre. The People's Puppets of Occupy Wall Street, a theatrical offshoot of the Occupy Movement, for instance, have made regular appearances at New York City protest events and parades with their large-scale puppets, including a solemn Lady Liberty, a Monopoly man capitalist and dollar-sign serpents. The work is certainly visually striking, but unlike Schumann's, it is direct, uncomplicated and less ceremonial. Since the energy of the Occupy Movement has faded, the group has sought to ally their work with other noble causes, including the oil industry, fracking and high healthcare costs in the United States. In the UK, the most sustained recent activity, and the most innovative, has come from Theatre Uncut, a group formed in 2010 by Hannah Price and Emma Callander. The premise for the work is simple: playwrights from anywhere in the world can submit a script about a political topic to them (for which the authors are paid), which Theatre Uncut makes available through its website for anyone to perform for free for a period of time. In just four years, Theatre Uncut plays have been performed by over 6000 people in twenty-five countries (Callander & Price, 2012). While many of their plays do receive professional productions, the fundamental project here is about making political texts available to theatre groups who need them. As we have seen throughout this book, the sourcing of quality texts has been one of the greatest problems (if not *the* greatest problem) for many modern popular theatres. Free, accessible and constantly evolving to reflect contemporary political concerns from around the world, Theatre Uncut might have uncovered a new, sustainable model of popular theatre for the global age.

8 The Popular in Postmodern and Contemporary Performance

In Chapter 6 it was explained that what characterized the work of the modernists and the associated avant-gardes was a concern with representing the chaos of modern life. For some modernists, it was a frustration with the capitalist production of mass culture and the perceived levelling down of cultural standards that became a central concern of their work. For avant-garde artists, it was the politics and aesthetic preferences of the bourgeoisie, the perpetuation of high and low art categories and the privileging of popular forms and other artistic traditions of the past that would produce the politically and aesthetically resistant practices for which they are now well known. After the Second World War, the political and cultural prejudices that had motivated much of the work of both camps gradually became less pronounced. Experiments conducted with form – such as the musical compositions and performances of John Cage, or the mixed-mode Happenings of Allan Kaprow – were not done necessarily to politically critique or shock the bourgeoisie, as work produced earlier in the century had done. Instead, they were intended to advance alternative discourses about the construction and make-up of particular art forms. This is not to say that the work was unpolitical or that it could be positioned outside of issues relating to class – inevitably any art which works against an acknowledged set of traditions cannot escape class conflict as they are firmly embedded in those traditions – but that the work was not offering didactic social or political messages. The radical politics became more localized to the art and to each individual who experienced it.

From the 1960s onwards this shift in aesthetic and political perspective would be felt more acutely; and the acknowledgement of this shift would come to form part of what is understood to be postmodern. It will be recalled from the last chapter that a fundamental transition occurred in the second half of the twentieth century, with emphasis shifting away from class-centred politics to politics that were much more personal. This resulted, as Kershaw has observed, in a 'new promiscuity of the political' that would see it manifest 'into almost every nook and cranny of culture' (1999, p. 16). While some of the work that emerged still possessed a commitment to challenging hegemonic systems, much of it was far more relaxed in its attitude towards class politics, preferring instead to concentrate on more localized concerns. The politics of the body, including gender, sexuality and race, as well as those prompted by new forms of media and technology, became, in some contexts, much more pressing and would subsequently become the focus of many of the performances that were made. The decline in class-focused politics would also see an easing of cultural attitudes towards popular and mass culture. This was compounded by technological developments that gave individuals more access to and control over the mass culture they consumed, notably in the form of television, video and music players, computers and the Internet. It was inevitable, given the significant presence of mass and popular culture in almost every aspect of human life, that it would become a crucial material for performance-making in the latter half of the twentieth century, and continues to be so at the present time.

This chapter broadly considers the political and cultural shifts associated with postmodernism and will demonstrate how these paved the way for a further relaxing of the divisions between low and high art. These conditions, I argue, allowed for greater slippages to occur between these once oppositional art forms, enabling 'low' popular culture to be integrated into 'high' art and, reciprocally, high art to influence the popular. The direction of these 'slippages' forms the two main parts of the chapter. In the first part, I will consider the ways in which popular culture has affected what would have historically been labelled 'high' art performances. I explore this from several angles: risk to the human body, participation and accessibility, and through the deliberate distortion of popular forms. These issues are explored through examples ranging from the solo-based performance art of the 1970s to contemporary devising ensembles. In the chapter's second part, I consider how some of the aesthetic features often associated with postmodernism have influenced popular performance. My analysis focuses particularly upon contemporary puppetry and the circus and how certain practitioners of these forms have adopted complex dramaturgical and aesthetic strategies that bear similarities to the practices discussed in Part I. The final section of the chapter unites some of the key threads from the two major parts and offers a discussion of the wider possibilities – social, political and aesthetic – of postmodernism's embracing of the popular.

Postmodernism: Key Critical Contexts

The shift from modernism to postmodernism is typically thought to be the consequence of the expansion of capitalism after the Second World War. Marxist theorist Ernest Mandel identifies this as post-industrial capitalism, which refers to the spread of capitalism globally.[1] This period of capitalism is characterized by the rapid development of technology and the significant increase in the number of products that could be bought and sold in the post-war period. While manufacturing technologies had made the mass production and distribution of agriculture or textiles possible in the earlier stage of capitalist development, modern developments have made it possible to mass-produce practically anything, from art to ideas. Given its prevalence in practically all aspects of human life, it is now considered impossible to completely disentangle oneself from this system. Consequently, as Fredric Jameson has pointed out, taking a critical position against postmodern culture or the global capital developments that have made it possible are difficult because critical distance is effectively eliminated (1984, p. 87). Many of the theatre practices considered in this chapter try to grapple with this knowledge, and seek to find aesthetic strategies that simultaneously foreground this impossibility while still attempting to critique its influence and power.

While the economic changes that brought about postmodernism can be dated back to the Second World War, it would not be until the 1960s that the cultural changes would start to be recognized by artists and critics. One of the earliest to do so was theorist Susan Sontag who wrote in 1965 about what she saw as the 'new sensibility' of modern culture, which she believed was rooted in the new experiences of contemporary life brought on by new technologies, the accelerated production of new commodities, and the speed of everything from travel to image production (e.g. film) (2009 [1965], p. 296). One of the key side effects of this phenomenon was, Sontag points out, the 'abandonment of the Matthew Arnold idea of culture' and the weakening of 'high' and 'low' art categories (ibid., p. 302). It will be recalled from Chapter 1 that Arnold was one of the first in a string of cultural critics who agitated against the levelling down of cultural standards by mass-culture production. With high and low art now participating in the same global marketplace, such discriminating categories have lost their value. As a consequence, there have been greater exchanges and crossovers between the two. One can see this particularly with Pop Art, which first emerged in the mid-1950s. Artists associated with Pop Art, including Jasper Johns, Roy Lichtenstein and Andy Warhol, incorporated aspects of popular culture, including cartoons, advertisements and commercial products, into their work. Though Pop Art was destined for the art gallery, technically making it high art, affordable Pop Art prints were widely available and found their way into people's homes and offices, making it popular culture as well. On the reverse, there are many instances of high art being taken up by popular culture under postmodernity. Take, for instance, the example of composer Carl Orff's 'O Fortuna' from *Carmina Burana*, which has been popularized through its use on reality television shows like *The X Factor*. This does not change the status of Orff's masterpiece from high art to low, rather, as with Pop Art, the current cultural environment allows it to slip between those categories as its users need.

One final area worth exploring in the present context is Baudrillard's concept of the simulacrum and the important questions it raises about representation and perceptions of reality in the postmodern era. In his book *Simulations*, he argues that in contemporary culture reality and meaning are replaced by signs, more specifically the simulacrum, which he defines as: 'the generation of models of a real without origin or reality: a hyper-real' (Baudrillard, 2009, p. 409). Owing to the prevalence of the simulacrum in a society where, as discussed, everything from cultural artefacts to ideas may be reproduced and sold as commodities, individuals are no longer able to differentiate between the real and the copy. As he explains, 'It is no longer a question of imitation, nor of reduplication, nor even of parody. It is rather a question of substituting signs of the real for the real itself. Never again will the real have to be produced' (2009, p. 410). A useful example of this phenomenon provided by Storey is of CDs and films (2006, p. 133). It would be difficult to argue in either of these cases that one owned or had seen 'the original', as both are constructed with the assistance of reproductive technologies specifically for the purpose of being copied. The broader implications of Baudrillard's theory are that people measure the perceived reality of real-life events and construct their own realities through their experience of simulations. Here, one might consider comparisons made between life-like depictions of war, such as the opening sequence in Steven Spielberg's 1998 film *Saving Private Ryan*, with real images of war shown on cable news channels. The latter, usually shot at a distance by journalists with poorer-quality equipment, may not align with the more 'ideal' images taken from the Hollywood film. One subsequently regards the less attractive version (still, inevitably a copy) as less real than the representation. Connected to this, someone's life may become hyperreal when, for instance, they try to emulate the look of celebrities, describe the personalities of their friends or acquaintances as being like those of fictional characters from television shows or set out to recreate the layout or decoration of a room in photographs uploaded to Pinterest. More recently, the hyperreal is most abundantly found on social networking platforms. Think of the ways, for instance, some people manufacture particular looks and poses in personal photographs ('selfies') to (re)present particular (perhaps desired) aspects of their personalities for their virtual audience. It would appear that the more infiltrated our lives become with technology, the more hyperreal our lives are.

Postmodernism is the consequence of technological and economic developments that became prevalent in the second half of the twentieth century and continue up until the present time. The wider effects of a more interconnected, global economy have led to regular intercultural exchanges of products, ideas, values and cultural practices. The individual in this system is left negotiating a dizzying array of products and images from around the globe. Of this phenomenon, Jean-François Lyotard famously observed: 'one listens to reggae, watches a western, eats McDonald's food for lunch and local cuisine for dinner, wears Paris perfume in Tokyo and "retro" clothes in Hong Kong' (1984 [1979], p. 76). In many cases, these products eventually lose their cultural distinctiveness and take on universal generality. The development of computer technologies and the Internet have only further compounded this. People now have almost immediate access to cultures outside their own; and, of course, these encounters are mediated not only through the computerized digital technologies that now dominate contemporary life, but also the advertisers that also inhabit those spaces. According to theorist Guy Debord (discussed in Chapter 7), contemporary life is a 'society of the spectacle' in which human lives are mediated, and their actions sometimes determined, by images of commodities (1992). As I write this I am conscious of the cool glow of the illuminated Apple logo on my laptop reflecting back at me from the window opposite. Even in the critical space of scholarly writing I am not only reliant upon mass-produced technology, I am haunted at all times by its branding.

While there is no definitive postmodern aesthetic that emerges out of this system, certain characteristics of art developed under it have been identified. One that has already been discussed is the rejection of high and low art categories. Postmodern arts practices are more likely to work across the cultural matrix and draw freely on traditions of the past and present, working, at times, as a pastiche constructed of several forms. Realism, as a literary and theatrical genre, continues to be challenged owing to its recognized artificiality. Consequently, the work is more likely to be self-reflexive and call attention to its constructedness rather than seek to disguise it. Narrative, as a system for organizing and framing stories, is regarded to be equally problematic. Like realism, it is seen as unnatural and misleading. This, combined with its free appropriation of other art forms and traditions more often than not results in more fragmented, disordered structures in which the spectator is left to pull the pieces together and make sense of it for themselves. In the theatre, this has broader implications for traditional notions of character too, which had already started to be contested under modernism and the avant-garde. Rather than fully embodying characters, the simple but powerful presence of the performers, maintaining their own personal identities, was regarded to be more politically progressive. In a similar way, the authority of the author or playwright would also be challenged. This was most clearly signalled in Roland Barthes's essay 'The Death of the Author' (1977 [1968]), in which he argues that the author can no longer be regarded as the fixer of meanings in a text; rather, they are mediators who organize language for the reader to decipher. It is as commonplace now for a theatre company to collectively devise their performance through rehearsal as it is to see single-authored plays.

While it is possible to identify these characteristics in a great number of performances since the 1960s, they should not be regarded as composing a comprehensive or stable poetics of postmodern or contemporary performance practices. Given postmodernism's openness to form and content, it is impossible to define it precisely or attribute to it a stable set of characteristics and features. Neither should the term postmodern be regarded as constituting a distinct genre of contemporary performance. It is, at best, a term used to harness performances that share some of the features set out above together and fall, historically, into the period under discussion.

Part 1: Connecting with the Popular

Participation, Accessibility, Risk

In Chapter 6 I discussed how the body for the avant-garde artist was a site for challenging social norms and aesthetic standards and traditions, as well as for articulating one's radical politics (cf. Marinetti). This was also the case for many artists working in the United States in the 1960s and 1970s, who began incorporating live human subjects – most often themselves – into their art as a form of aesthetic challenge and political critique of the commercialism of the modern art industry. Unlike traditional art objects, such as paintings or sculptures, works involving a live human subject could not easily be reproduced or sold, and were thus seen as resistant to commercial forces. Some artists compounded this anti-capitalist critique by conceiving of projects that involved the participation of spectators, in which they were given instructions or tasks to execute, resulting in the making of an ephemeral experience-cum-performance that in its totality was considered to be the work of art. This played out in many forms and with varying degrees of extremity. In Yoko Ono's *Cut Piece* (1964), for instance, spectators were instructed to cut off the passive artist's clothing with a pair of scissors. For Marina Abramovic's *Rhythm 0* (1974), participants were invited to pleasure or torture the artist for a designated period of time with a range of objects, including a rose, a feather, a scalpel and a loaded gun.[2] In works like these, which have been variously referred to as conceptual art, body art, performance art or live art,[3] spectators were able to freely participate in the making of the work, even if there were very real dangers to the artists for granting such freedom.

While performances like Ono's and Abramovic's are distinctly *unpopular*, I would suggest that the move to the use of the familiar – primarily in the form of the vulnerable human body – and the reliance on spectator participation share certain connections with the popular that distinguish them from earlier works of 'high art'. In particular, participation, a central component of popular forms, is found here in literal, physical ways, bringing spectators together through a shared arts experience and lending the performances a democratic sensibility.

This is aided by the use of familiar tools, e.g. human bodies, a feather, a pair of scissors, and the refusal of the artists to transform themselves into characters, preferring instead of offer spectators their 'raw, physical presence', as Auslander puts it, unmitigated by any fiction or artifice (1989, p. 119). The work therefore places emphasis on human-to-human contact, where the spectator and the performer share equal footing. The collaborative element of the performance might therefore be read as a politically progressive gesture, promoting the practice and value of collective creation.[4] While inevitably such works still operate fundamentally according to the logic of Bourdieu's 'pure aesthetic' (see Chapter 1), the more democratic design of such practices shares connections with popular forms.

There are other connections to the popular found within body-based performance art practices that are worth pursuing. The element of risk for the performer, for instance, bears similarities to centuries of dangerous popular entertainments, such as tightrope walking, knife throwing or lion taming, where the perceived risk to the performer's life contributes to its attractiveness for audiences. Risk, of course, is utilized rather differently between popular entertainments and performance art practices. As entertainment, risk provides a context for obtaining a spectator's interest and helping to forge a connection between the performer and the audience, in much the same way that a narrative contextualizes characters whom audiences subsequently come to empathize with in a drama. If audiences were unable to participate in the work in this way – that is, to become genuinely concerned for the performer – then the act would not work. Given the important role risk plays in the success of the act, then, every effort is made to maximize its effects: suspenseful music might be played, for instance, or the performer might pretend to make a minor mistake, drawing audiences to the edge of their seats and more anxiously into the act. Risk in performance art practices like Abramovic's, on the other hand, has historically been more conceptually driven, rooted in a desire to resist cultural commodification, raise questions about acceptable aesthetic tools and materials, and to test the pain thresholds and physical limitations of the human body. In popular entertainments, risk is ultimately militated against by the virtuosity and skill of the performer: the aim is to complete the act unharmed. In performance art, however, the promise of the risk is often fulfilled. It is because of this that live artists have historically resisted sensationalizing risks with theatrical effects, as such effects could make spectators question the authenticity of the harmed body and potentially minimize the impact of the performance. Still, this kind of performance retains an invitation for spectators to participate. Kathy O'Dell has conceived of this form of participation as a 'masochistic bond between the performers and the audience', brought on by an attraction to witnessing the body in pain and the willingness of the performer to satisfy those needs as well as their own artistic impulses (1998, p. 2). Aesthetically and formalistically, the two performance modes could not be further apart, and yet they share certain features, notably the deploying of risk and the need for human participation.

Risk remains a crucial tool in contemporary performance and live art practices, although attitudes towards popular culture and theatricality are now typically more relaxed. British artist Richard DeDomenici's humorous, socially engaged works have involved the artist placing himself in potentially dangerous situations in public spaces. In *Cable-Tie* (2004), DeDomenici walked through the city of Chicago with a clear plastic bag over his head with his hands bound behind him with nylon cable ties. The performance was a protest against the US military's method for detaining combatants, which was stopped following the Abu Ghraib scandal (which coincidentally broke within days of DeDomenici's performance). In his more playful piece *Unattended Baggage* (2005–), the artist is enclosed in a large suitcase and positioned in busy public areas in major cities. Holes cut into the bottom of the suitcase for his feet and legs allow the suitcase to move, giving it a humorous puppet-like appearance. With this performance, the aim was to playfully undermine the unattended baggage regulations of many public spaces introduced after the September 11 attacks. In both cases, the risks to the artist are very real. Walking through a busy American city with a plastic bag over one's head and no easy means of removing it comes with the very real danger of suffocation or walking unaware into busy traffic. Contorting one's body in order to fit inside a suitcase comes with similar dangers, made worse by the complete lack of visibility. As videos of these pieces show, responses by the public who encounter DeDomenici during these performances are mixed. In the case of *Cable-Tie*, DeDomenici is repeatedly stopped by the police who claim to be concerned for his well-being, although their hostile reactions suggest they are irritated by his actions, failing to grasp that they are part of a performance and may have symbolic significance (despite the fact he repeatedly tells them so) (DeDomenici, 2007). Unsuspecting spectators for *Unattended Baggage* in Berlin in 2009 regard DeDomenici's walking suitcase with ambivalence, laughter and confusion (DeDomenici, 2010). DeDomenici expects the mixed and often confused reactions from unsuspecting spectators. The ultimate aim, the artist admits, is to 'create the kind of uncertainty that leads to possibility' (DeDomenici, 2012). In this regard, the artist's choice to perform in public, non-theatre spaces for the unsuspecting audiences is fundamental to the broader aims of his art.

Australian live artist Tristan Meecham also works with risk in performance in order to engage audiences with what he describes as his 'playful yet subversive politic' (Johnstone & Meecham, 2013). Meecham's performances stem from his shared interest in conceptually driven performance art practices, community arts and theatrical spectacle, and the tensions created by working across these historically antithetical fields (2014). These tensions exist in *Fun Run* (2010–), a durational performance in which Meecham runs a full marathon on a treadmill while an army of community groups, which have included cheerleaders, marching bands and dance groups, perform around him.[5] The performance was conceived as an exploration of the risk of physical failure associated with endurance sports like long-distance running, with Meecham being particularly attracted to images of 'marathon runners going over the line and their bodies going into meltdown'(2014). While he has undertaken some training for each performance, he has only done so moderately in order to preserve its risk element. Indeed, as Meecham has pointed out, if spectators considered him to be a proficient runner and athlete, their engagement with the work would be very different (ibid.). Whereas, his visible physical struggles to execute his set task works to draw spectators into the spectacle, where their empathy for Meecham's challenge transforms them into cheerleaders and eventual celebrants of his success. *Fun Run* marks the first part of a trilogy of works that Meecham refers to as 'The Coming Out Trilogy',[6] which serves as a public celebration of his sexuality. It is here where the work's gentle but subversive politic can be found. Although the performance does not explicitly announce its sexual politics, some spectators may find themselves part of an inclusive, queer celebration without ever knowing it – which Meecham believes gives the performance its power (ibid.).

Outside of risk, it is also possible to find connections to the popular in the level of accessibility that can be found in some contemporary performances. This is especially true of the confessional solo performances that emerged in the 1970s and have since become a staple contemporary performance mode. Such work usually consists of a solo performer delivering a direct-address monologue regarding personal experiences, political views or philosophies to an audience. The form has its roots in storytelling, but there are numerous instances throughout theatre history of solo, character-driven performances. The modern version of the form can be found in the lecture and monologue performances of the nineteenth and early twentieth centuries, made popular by Mark Twain and Ruth Draper.[7] A re-emergence of solo performance occurred in the mid-twentieth century with the development of variety television programmes, including *The Carol Burnett Show* (1967–1978), *Laugh In* (1968–1973), and *Saturday Night Live* (1975–present), which would popularize the comic character monologue. Artists like Julia Heyward saw the monologue form as a way of reintroducing narrative and emotion into conceptual art practice (Whitney Museum of American Art, 2013). Still critical of the idea of character, however, many artists choosing to work with the form, including Heyward, elected to perform material based on their own personal experiences. *Shake Daddy Shake* (1976), for instance, was about Heyward's father, a southern Presbyterian minister suffering from palsy. In particular, the performance offered a history of his right arm, from its significance in his role as a minister (shaking parishioners' hands) to its eventual paralysis as a result of his illness. While taking on her father's southern dialect, idiom and aspects of his degenerative condition, Heyward remained present in the work. With the performer standing on a small, raised turntable in a neutral, dark outfit covering most of her body, excluding her head, right arm and shoulder, there were no other visual signifiers to contribute to the illusion that Heyward was attempting to fully embody a character based on her father. By constructing the performance out of personal material and in a format familiar to many audience members, Heyward made the work easier to relate to than some of the solo artists that preceded her.

Merging the aesthetic minimalism of late 1970s performance art practices with more traditional character acting, Eric Bogosian's performances showcased American male stereotypes in a manner designed to expose their ridiculous, vulgar and often violent excesses. Bogosian began his career performing as a character called Ricky Paul, a crass variety show–style entertainer from a bygone era with an inappropriate sense of humour. Bogosian performed Ricky Paul in New York City cabarets and clubs alongside other performance artists – which he has admitted he felt more at home with than with traditional theatre-makers (Bogosian & Sussler, 1994, p. 30). In the 1980s Bogosian turned his attention to full-scale productions and developed a series of solo shows consisting of monologues for a diverse range of male characters. The first of these, *Men Inside* (1981), considered machoism and prevalent masculine stereotypes with characters including a small boy whose desire to be just like his father (successful, heterosexual and racist), transforms him into a stuttering, seizuring mess, and a cowboy who celebrates shooting, speeding and drinking to violent excess. By the early 1990s, Bogosian's work had become mainstream, with performances like *Sex, Drugs, Rock & Roll* (1991), a show which reflects on masculinity and greed in the Reagan era, garnering significant critical and commercial success.

Heyward, Bogosian and many of their contemporaries have been categorized by Goldberg has being part of the 'media generation' (2001, p. 190). Of this generation of artists, she writes:

> Raised on twenty-four-hour television and a cultural diet of B movies and 'rock 'n roll', [these artists] interpreted the old cry to break down barriers between life and art to be a matter of breaking down barriers between art and the media, also expressed as a conflict between high and low art. (ibid.)

The influence of media on these artists can be seen in a number of ways, including the presence of television monitors, computers, projectors, and popular culture references (music, film and television clips, for instance) and stereotypes (usually appearing in the aforementioned media) in their work. As the media's presence in society has increased since the 1960s, so has its prevalence on stage. Indeed, it is now increasingly rare to find a performance that does not engage with media – as either technology or cultural artefact – in some form or another.

Our cultural and individual interconnectedness to the media and popular culture is a central concern of Hawaiian-born British artist Stacy Makishi. Playing with the boundaries between fact and fiction, Makishi's performances weave together experiences from her life with those of fictional characters borrowed from film and television. In *The Making of Bull: The True Story* (2011), Makishi draws upon the Coen brothers' 1996 film *Fargo* which professes to be based on a true story (when, in fact, it is not)[8] in order to challenge audiences to determine what, in her own confessional performance, might be true. The performance incorporates sequences from the film, conflating them with Makishi's personal anecdotes and observations. At points, the film and Makishi seem interconnected, which is played out in slapstick-style physical sequences in which Makishi both quotes and exaggerates physical gestures she borrows from actors in the film. Technology is used to amplify, repeat, fast-forward and rewind sequences of the film, which

Makishi physically imitates as well, allowing for a double commentary on the way that media operates in our lives. Makishi takes this idea further in *Falsettos* (2013), in which she explores her experience of menopause and her changing awareness of time through the fictional figure Tony Soprano, the damaged anti-hero from the popular HBO series *The Sopranos*. As with *Bull*, *Falsettos* conflates Makishi's own outlook and experiences (this time apparently all true) with mediated content. The effect is endearing, playful and, as Makishi admits, 'absurd' (in Damian, 2013). Of her use of popular culture, Makishi has observed she feels it is an effective way to 'challenge people's perceptions' of the familiar, as well as an accessible means to explore issues like 'danger, violence, love, sexuality and age' (ibid.).

The accessibility and personal quality of the work discussed so far often allows it to slide between performative categories. Bogosian, for instance, is widely recognized as a stand-up comedian, although he identifies more as an actor and performance artist. Makishi began her performance career as a stand-up comedian, but after meeting Lois Weaver and Peggy Shaw of Split Britches (discussed in Chapter 7) in Hawaii in the early 1990s, she felt her talents would be better placed in an arts context. Soon afterward, she moved to London and began to develop her interdisciplinary live art practice (Kleiman & Makishi, 2011). Such distinctions once disclosed as much about one's politics as they did about one's artistic practice; but today, when the categorical distinctions between low and high art are increasingly unclear, such categories carry less weight.

Unmaking Popular Forms

In the discussion of Baudrillard earlier, it was noted that under the conditions of modern capitalist production, representation and what it means to *re*produce more generally are called into question. This is due not only to questions of reproducibility, but also because of concerns about the ways in which these have historically served to reinforce power, privilege certain forms of knowledge and fix aesthetic forms which close off interpretation and meaning-making. One of the regular ways this challenge is posed in contemporary performance is through appropriation and re-presentation which allows the limitations of the appropriated form, and aesthetic representation more generally, to be exposed and critiqued. As literary theorist Linda Hutcheon has observed:

Reappropriating existing representations that are effective precisely
because they are loaded with pre-existing meaning and putting them
into new and ironic contexts is a typical form of postmodern com-
plicitious critique: while exploiting the power of familiar images, it also
de-naturalises them, makes visible the concealed mechanisms which
work to make them seem transparent, and brings to the fore their
politics, that is to say, the interests in which they operate and the power
they wield. (1989, p. 44)

Outside the genre of realism, forms of popular entertainment have
widely been appropriated for the purpose of postmodern deconstruc-
tion and critique. There are a number of reasons why the popular has
lent itself so productively to this task. Prizing virtuosity and accomplishment, the success of an act of popular entertainment depends on
the masterful completion of a special skill, from acting a convincing
character to juggling, in a way that seems to mirror the gloss and
high sheen of cultural products produced for mass consumption. To
this extent, many forms of popular entertainment may be regarded as
embodiments of the capitalist logic. There is also the problem of the
kinds of representations that popular forms themselves have mastered
in order to appeal to mass audiences. Surveying the history of popular
entertainment, one finds an extensive array of ethically dubious representations of minority groups (e.g. blackface minstrelsy) and social
types (the vixen or shrew) designed in accordance with the views and
prejudices of 'the masses', which in the West have historically been
white and patriarchal. Mass views are incorporated to ensure broad
appeal and secure the financial success of the act (at the expense of
re-inforced prejudices and compromised social progress). Beyond this,
certain generic popular icons, such as the clown, magician or marionette, set up specific expectations for an audience that entertainment
will be forthcoming – thus demonstrating how culturally fixed certain
kinds of representations have become. All of these features also point
to the implicit contract involved in spectatorship, one which is not
exclusive to popular entertainment but certainly underscores it: that
people go to the theatre, pay their money, and, in exchange, they are
entertained. The popular, therefore, is rife with features that make it
attractive for postmodern critique, and it has been extensively appropriated and re-presented in ways that deliberately reconfigure these
traditional impulses. In some cases, the forms are emptied of their
contents and deconstructed in order to expose their mechanics, as well
as the expectations and ideologies, implicitly or explicitly, promoted
through them.

Many of these issues are apparent in the work of UK-based theatre company Forced Entertainment. Formed in 1984 by a group of graduates from the University of Exeter,[9] the company's work, as their name suggests, is concerned with the conventions and cultural expectations of theatre, particularly those elements of artifice and pretence that are intended to work on spectators in certain ways. Central to this is a preoccupation with the labour of actors in the live performance situation, and what they are expected to do to fulfil the demands of the theatre/spectator contract, that is, to be entertaining. Writing about their practice, theatre practitioner and scholar Sara Jane Bailes characterizes the company's work as: 'a sustained attempt to foreground the labor that performance demands of the performer in order to withstand or "cope" with the overly charged live-ness of the harrowing on-stage moment' (2011, p. 69). The company has sought to expose this labour in many ways, but most often by deliberately performing 'badly' in a consciously metatheatrical way: a performer's tears are produced by splashing their face with pints of water (*Bloody Mess*, 2004), or the dying man's guts, spilled out in his lap, are nothing more than tinned pasta (*Showtime*, 1996). While the company have devised performances from a wide range of sources – questions, props, stories, specific locations, built settings – elements of the popular are frequently appropriated and re-presented in their work. Indeed, as the company's artistic director Tim Etchells has acknowledged, half their main influences come from art and theatre and the other half from popular entertainment (in Trueman, 2008).

Performances including *Quizoola* (1996) and *First Night* (2001) offer examples of how aspects of popular entertainment feature in the company's work. In *Quizoola*, two performers in clown make-up, but otherwise ordinary clothing, sit in wooden chairs encircled by a ring of carnival lights and take turns quizzing one other at random from a list of approximately 2000 questions. Above their heads, a sign announcing 'Quizoola!' glows in red neon letters. In this performance, which, in various incarnations has lasted between six and twenty-four hours, the popular is signalled most clearly through the clown-face, the neon sign and the carnival lights. But the performers consciously resist each of these signs and the expectations they set up. For instance, while appearing in clown-face, the performers are otherwise themselves, answering questions in a manner that anyone might do if they were pulled inside the circle before an audience: awkwardly, playfully, sometimes self-consciously. As the performance runs its course, and the performers wear down, their ability to 'perform', even as slightly enhanced versions of themselves, becomes challenging. Barriers drop, cognitive filters relax and the answers become more delirious, more sincere and freer. While some of the exchanges between the performers are funny, there is not a conscious or rehearsed attempt at provoking laughter in the way that a clown does. The expectations established by the scenographic elements, such as the neon sign and the carnival lights, are equally unfulfilled. Their incorporation, like the clown-face, is ironically juxtaposed with the reality of the performance situation: two people asking each other questions over an extended period of time. This idea is taken further in *First Night* (2001), a grotesque variety show consisting of familiar acts – mindreading, magic, ventriloquism, etc. – but in a nightmarish form. Dressed respectively in cheap suits, short sequined dresses, high-heels and with faces excessively bronzed and stretched into big, toothy grins, the eight performers stare wide-eyed at the audience in a manner that is both desperate and confrontational. Instead of entertaining us, the performers bore, scare and confront the audience. The traditional acts are distinctly unvirtuous and consciously displeasing: the ventriloquist uses a real person instead of a dummy; dance routines appear awkward and under-rehearsed. During the 'mind-reading act', performer Cathy Naden points to individual members of the audience and announces how they are going to die. The effect is so unsettling that many audience members leave. In this case, the performance explodes the conventions of the popular iconography it utilizes, taking the aim to please to shocking and ridiculous extremes. In place of the polish and high-gloss of traditional showbiz, the audience faces something messier, scarier and more confrontational – in many ways the antithesis of what the popular theatre traditionally sets out to do.

Similar uses of the popular can be found in the work of Australian performance collective Brown Council. Formed in 2007 by Francis Barrett, Kate Blackmore, Kelly Doley and Diana Smith – all of whom studied art at the University of New South Wales in Sydney – the collective's work is concerned with what it means to perform, both on stage and socially, and the act of spectating. Endurance performance and body art practices, like those mentioned earlier, have held particular appeal for the company and have provided a 'framework' within which they feel they can develop their work (Brown Council, 2014). The collective is also indebted to popular forms, including stand-up comedy, spectacle and pantomime, which they consciously appropriate and re-present in their practice. The mixing of 'low' and 'high' art forms in this way, the group acknowledges, allows them 'to parody the stereotype of the 'male artist genius' and to open up an alternative space for [their] own [feminist] practice to be considered' (ibid.). The group's use of predominantly comic modes of popular culture is also deliberate, allowing them to 'challenge the well-worn cliché that women, especially feminists, can't be funny and to antagonize the seriousness of "high" art forms including early performance art' (ibid.).

As with Forced Entertainment's work, Brown Council tends to ironically upend the popular conventions they draw upon. This is perhaps most clearly demonstrated in their performance *A Comedy* (2010–2012), a durational performance designed to explore not only what it means to laugh and provoke laughter, but also, and more fundamentally, the politics and ethics of spectatorship and aesthetic participation. The performance, which Brown Council have referred to as an 'endurance spectacular', centred around five classic comic forms or gags: stand-up comedy, performing magic tricks, the dancing monkey act, performing slapstick routines and taking a cream pie in the face (Brown Council, 2014). A large white box with 'COMEDY' spelled out in capital letters suspended at the rear of the performance space told the audience what to expect, and tomatoes – those symbols of performative failure and audience dissatisfaction – marked out the playing area. With tall, handmade paper cones atop their heads, recalling the image of the classic 'dunce' or fool, the performers took turns executing each act as chosen by the audience. The acts themselves are almost humorously under-whelming and usually humiliating: the 'magic act' consists of a performer making bananas 'appear' out of their trousers and 'disappear' by eating them; in the slapstick act, two performers slap one another repeatedly for a period of time. In the 'dancing monkey' act, a performer danced for the audience in exchange for donations of pocket change. As each of these simple but exposing acts is repeated and endured by each performer over the four-hour period, the darker aspects of the act and humour are uncovered. One can eat *too* many bananas and be slapped too many times. What begins as cheerful and good-natured becomes violent and cruel the more times the acts are repeated.

The durational and repetitive elements of the performance were designed to prompt the audience to reflect on their agency and their own role in tolerating, or actively participating in, what effectively constitutes forms of (albeit invited) abuse on the performers. If this were not clear enough, at the end of each hour the performers blindfolded themselves and stood in dimmed lights in the middle of the performance space. With an unspoken invitation given, many audience members chose to pelt the performers with the tomatoes that lined the performance space. The questionable ethics of spectatorship and the uneven distribution of power in the room at that moment were fully revealed by spectators enacting (further) abuse on the performers through a simulated firing line. For Brown Council, allowing the audience to freely engage with the work in a direct way was important, even if violence and humiliation were the outcomes. Building these choices discreetly into the work alongside other forms of participation (i.e. choosing the acts), a 'tension' was produced between the spectacle of entertainment and the spectacle of endurance. This was picked up on by curator Anneke Jaspers who, in an article for Australian live art journal *Runway*, observes: 'At this point the friction between viewing pleasure and discomfort, and between obedience and empowerment, took a more confronting turn. Even in refusing to act, viewers were complicit in [the performers'] degradation and in fulfilling the work's critique' (2011, p. 16). It is Brown Council's hope that this tension will provoke 'audiences to consider the politics of spectatorship and highlight the disparity in how [they] understand and exercise agency' (Brown Council, 2014).

In the cases of both Forced Entertainment and Brown Council there is a deliberate subversion of the conventions of popular entertainment forms and the expectations audiences hold about the way they are supposed to work. In contrast to the virtuosity and accomplishment required of the forms' 'successful' performance, their re-presentation in these contexts is decidedly un-virtuosic. In her book *Performance Theatre and the Poetics of Failure*, Sara Jane Bailes refers to this as 'radical amateurism', a deliberate aesthetic strategy, of which she writes:

> Amateurism emerges through a highly developed but intentionally 'poor' delivery style, an affect in performance that they have honed in order to derail stage conventions, the ambitions of dramatic integrity, and the process of spectatorship to often spectacular effect from within the structure and rules of the 'traditional' theatre event. (2011, p. 56)

This amateurism, or failure to meet an acknowledged standard, is not accidental, but a deliberate subversion of the conventions one associates with or ascribes to the forms. Bailes theorizes this kind of failure through slapstick comedy and punk rock music. In slapstick, it is the failure to execute a typically mundane task that presents opportunities for humour. Punk, formed as an anti-establishment genre in the mid-1970s, provided a more anarchic and political entry into failure; as Bailes observes '[t]he approach and style of playing [Punk] are aggressively antithetical to established mainstream values of harmony, continuity, and social stability' (ibid., 51). In both cases, failure is not to be regarded as something accidental or as a mistake, but operates as part of the fundamental logic of the forms – therefore their 'successful' performance is reliant on their in-built failings. In a similar way, the re-presentation of the popular in ways that contradict their origins in these contexts is a strategy designed in part to critique traditions, representation and capitalist production. Writing about Forced Entertainment's work, Bailes observes:

> [their] performances provide a vital challenge to the understanding of what it means to be good at something and widen our comprehension of the aesthetic commodity and its (mal)functioning properties [...] Such labour – for it is definitively *work* – threatens to make hostages of us all until we learn to see differently. (ibid., p. 109)

In resisting the aesthetic conventions of the commercial theatre or, indeed, of the popular forms appropriated and re-presented, the work may increase our awareness of the failure of the larger systems that govern our world and our lives. In this sense, as Bailes argues, we may also regard failure as a hopeful strategy; if we can 'valorize the potentiality of disappointment', we might start to see the impression of another world take shape among the chaos (ibid., p. 56).

Although resistant to popular virtuosity, the desperation, awkwardness and failure built into some of these acts can appeal to us in other ways, perhaps because they are more relatable to our everyday experiences (and our own failures) than the circus clown or the bronze-faced showbiz entertainer. This was recognized by theatre critic Lyn Gardner who, in her review for *First Night* for *The Guardian*, noted '[h]ow fascinating these fragile, glittering, tottering creatures remain, even when we have seen behind the pancake and sequins, and how we recognize our own vulnerable, embarrassed humanity in them' (2001). In *A Comedy* there is the deliberate failure of the acts and the audience's reaction to the performers to consider. For Brown Council, as with Ono's *Cut Piece* discussed earlier, allowing the audience to freely engage with the work in a direct way was important, even if violence was one of the outcomes. In fact, in the moments where violence was sometimes chosen by spectators resides the work's most promising political potential. As the company explain: 'It was in these moments that direct agency was given to the audience to anonymously humiliate and potentially hurt us or not to participate' (Brown Council, 2014). It is here where the aforementioned tension between the spectacles of entertainment and endurance is located. It is Brown Council's hope that this tension will provoke 'audiences to consider the politics of spectatorship and highlight the disparity in how [they] understand and exercise agency' (ibid.). Thus their performed failure and the violence they subject themselves to are seen as potentially politically efficacious. It is perhaps in this tension that we also find what Bailes recognizes as hope: 'a different image of a different world' (2011, p. 62).

Part 2: Popular Forms Rejuvenated

So far I have concentrated on the role popular forms have played in the development of postmodern and contemporary theatre practices. In this final section, I will consider contemporary performances that have been more faithful to the origins and functionality of popular forms. In keeping with the subject of this chapter, however, I will concentrate on works which also share postmodern characteristics; so while the popular form remains intact, its traditional impulses, its aesthetic and narrative strategies, in particular, more closely resemble the experimental practices laid out in the sections above. As this section will show, a critique of contemporary experience and aesthetic traditions need not necessarily be opposed to theatrical illusion, virtuosity or narrative. Indeed, as the distinctions between high and low art have become less pronounced, forms that were historically labelled as 'popular' owing to the traditions from which they emerged have increasingly become more experimental and challenging in their own right. Just as post-modern artists and theatre-makers have drawn on the popular in order to articulate their responses to modernism and contemporary society, the popular has equally drawn upon those artists and developed an aesthetic that is at once familiar and unconventional. In an ironic turn of events, forms traditionally thought of (by elites) as debased, ignorant and low have become sites for radical artistic innovation. This they have done by not only appropriating aesthetic forms once hostile to their existence, but by also demonstrating their own unique capabilities at critiquing the social and political systems of which they are a part, and to which they have historically been allied.

Contemporary Puppetry

Nowhere is this set of possibilities more acutely felt than in the field of contemporary puppetry. As discussed in Chapter 6, puppetry, as a concept and collection of unique forms, has proven to be particularly appealing to avant-garde and experimental artists, from Chat Noir shadow shows to the Schlemmer's theatre workshop. Polish theatre director Tadeusz Kantor (1915–1990) was one of the strongest proponents of puppetry in the twentieth century, often mixing actors with puppets on stage, or replacing the actor with puppets, throughout his career.[10] One of the legacies of Kantor's work and that of the other artists who entered into a dialogue with puppetry is that they presented formalistic challenges to the puppet forms they appropriated and, indeed, to our perceptions about the ways puppets might be used in performance. Through Kantor's work, for instance, one could see how complex questions regarding the body, materiality and existence might be articulated through a puppet frame, particularly one which allows for direct comparisons to be made between object/puppet-performer and human performer. Not only is representation challenged through these practices, but they can also be regarded as consciously confusing 'the distinction between reality and simulacrum', or in Baudrillard's terms, the real and the hyperreal (Eruli, 2012, p. 142). The sidestepping of traditional techniques by artists not always fluent in those skills also saw a relaxing of certain assumptions about the way puppets might be handled or manipulated during performance. As puppet scholar Henrik Jurkowski has observed, some of the characteristics to be found in contemporary puppetry include 'the visibility of the acting subject (the puppet manipulator) demonstrating the artificial character of puppet theatre; the return to ritual forms of theatre; the playing with elements of drama, especially time, space and characters which have undergone the process of atomization' (quoted in Francis, 2012, p. 176). Readers will note the similarities between these characteristics and those identified for contemporary performance earlier in the chapter.

These characteristics can be found in the work of London-based company Blind Summit Theatre. Formed in 1997 by Nick Barnes and Mark Down, the company has developed a reputation for innovative puppet performances. In particular, as the company's website indicates, 'they are subverting and reinventing the ancient Japanese artform of Bunraku puppetry for contemporary audiences' (Blind Summit, n.d.).[11] The company has developed an international reputation, performing across the UK, the United States and Europe.[12] The company's performance of *The Table*, first performed at the Edinburgh Festival in 2011, has proven to be one of its most popular productions, and at the time of writing (2015) it is still touring internationally. The performance is centred on Moses, a 'two-foot tall, three-man operated, Japanese bunraku-style table-top puppet with interchangeable parts' (Blind Summit Theatre, 2012). Those interchangeable parts consist of a comically large cardboard head, carved wooden hands and black leather shoes, all attached to a simple fabric body. No attempt is made, aesthetically, to make Moses look more realistic than this. At the beginning of the performance, Moses promises us an evening of 'epic' puppetry that will consist of him performing the last twelve hours of biblical Moses' life, 'in real time', on top of a rather ordinary table. But this spectacle (thankfully) never materializes. Instead, Moses becomes preoccupied with explaining how he is operated and what his life is like on his table, which, it transpires, has been his home for nearly forty years. During the performance, he shows us his favourite parts of the table; where he likes to 'sun' himself; and how many steps it takes him to get from corner to corner. Throughout, he speaks to his handlers, critiquing their efforts, and breaks down the practice of effective puppet manipulation. In doing this, he both builds and breaks down the illusion he asks audiences to participate in: it is a kind of metapuppetry whereby the success of the work is in part based on the audience acknowledging its role in the construction of the illusion. In an interview, Down acknowledges that this paradox is central to the performance: 'The more he tells you he's the puppet, the more you believe [in] him' (Anderson, 2014, p. 138). Indeed, Moses is so thoroughly convincing in legitimizing his puppet world that when a human female sits down at the table to read a book as part of the performance, the effect is jarring (which Moses points out, decrying her presence as 'dramaturgically inconsistent!'). The conflation of a puppet that so openly exploits its own construction and artifice with the unexplained physical presence of the human body seems to raise questions about our own materiality and the fragility of our human lives. It is as if Moses' existential concerns are transferred on to the body and subsequently on to us, the audience. At the same time, the work's simplicity, its tight focus on the object's constructed body, seems to invert the logic of the solo works discussed earlier. While it draws attention to materiality, it does so as constructed aesthetic material. In using the puppet body, and emphasizing it as such, it does not so much resist the commercial forces and commodification of the arts that motivated early conceptual and performance artists, but becomes a reproducible thing that could operate within that system, if that were the choice. That its parts are interchangeable, and are announced as such alongside other metatheatrical moments that remind us of the object's material and theatrical status, only further emphasizes that possibility.

Similar concerns can be found in Invisible Threads' production *Plucked* (2012), a performance that mixes puppet and animation forms to look at loneliness and abandonment. Invisible Threads was established in 2011 by Liz Walker, better known for her work with Faulty Optic, an interdisciplinary (but puppet-heavy) British theatre company that she co-directed with Gavin Glover from 1987 to 2011. *Plucked* concerns the end of a relationship and the difficulty of moving on. The performance features two haunting, skeleton-like puppets with bulging white eyes with polished, black marble centres. The puppets possess both bird and human-like qualities: they flutter and fly from one location to another, they hunt and eat worms, but the emotions they experience are distinctly human. Early in the performance, the pair meet, fall in love and set up a nest together. Soon after, they begin to raise a family. Unlike themselves, the children are non-puppet objects. The first is a miniature high chair, which cries constantly. The second is a runaway train, which runs straight off the stage at its birth, not to be seen again. The final child is a small television set on wheels. After the births, the couple's relationship begins to break down; it ends with the male partner flying off with the television, their only remaining child. Left alone, the female turns against the world, fearful of further rejection. Escaping to the woods to live in isolation, she starts to imprison all the male suitors who come to woo her. The effects of her anger are visualized through the transformation of her body into that of a black raven. In the end, she comes to recognize what her inability to move on has cost her: her youth and a happy life. It is a bittersweet ending (Walker, Kerrigan, Evans & Wright, 2012).

While decidedly more surreal, *Plucked* shares with *The Table* a visual simplicity, largely owing to its obviously handcrafted puppets and simple DIY settings. The performance not only features a synthesis of visual styles and forms – puppet theatre, shadow theatre, object theatre – but also of textual styles; while containing no dialogue, the text recalls simple folk tales, as well as the disorienting qualities of surrealism. On the practical level, once again we find exposed handlers, although in contrast to Moses, these do not interfere or engage with the puppets and objects, beyond moving them through the staging and the story. Still, their exposed presence continues to invite comparisons between the human body and the objects they manipulate to be human-like. That the puppet's 'children' turn out to be non-puppet objects, like a train or child's highchair, also raises interesting questions about materiality and fiction and the spectator's ability to re-assign the object a role other than what it should have in real life. This is a common challenge posed by contemporary object theatre, one that Brunella Eruli describes as producing a surrealist-like effect through its separation of 'form from the utilitarian function that has been assigned to the object by realist convention' (2012, p. 142). While the effect may be 'surreal' or playfully disorientating, it seems the human brain is able to synthesize disparate visual images or concepts in this way, accepting, as the fiction requires it, that the chair is no longer a chair but a child, for instance. In this regard, *Plucked* offers us a unique opportunity to interrogate representation and how one comes to understand the 'real' world around them. Puppet theatre of this kind gives audiences a chance to see other possibilities in everyday objects and things that fill their lives.

Circus Theatre

Like puppetry, the circus has been a recurring topic of this book. Many notable twentieth-century theatre artists looking to engage audiences in new ways turned to circus aesthetics. While the circus has itself undergone significant changes since the mid-eighteenth century, certain features appear to be constant, notably the inclusion of clowns and demonstrations of specialist skills or strength, such as juggling or acrobatics.[13] Up until the 1960s, animal acts were also a principal feature, but these grew less popular as the public's concern for the welfare of animals increased, leading to legislation in many countries that prohibited, or seriously restricted, the use of animals in entertainment. From the nineteenth century until the early 1970s, the principal circus mode was the tent circus, otherwise known as the 'big top', where acts were usually performed in between one and three circular playing areas, or 'rings'. Like the variety theatre or cabaret, this format allowed for a multitude of acts to be performed without the need for thematic or narrative unity. In recent years, however, the circus has been subject to considerable experimentation and renovation. Contemporary Circus, as it is broadly known, is an interdisciplinary performance form that merges certain elements of the traditional circus, most often clown acts and specialist skills, with gymnastics, dance and theatre. As Sara Selwood, Adrienne Muir and Dominic Moody have pointed out, unlike the variety format of traditional circus, Contemporary Circus typically consists of an integrated production developed around a chosen theme and/or involves some kind of narrative (1995, p. 51). Traditional circus skills, like acrobatics, trapeze or juggling, are still present, but are used to illuminate the theme or to help tell the story. Theatre-maker and circus scholar Louis Patrick Leroux has argued that this approach is designed to 'give sense – political and aesthetic – to the circus act beyond its own spectacle' (in Cruz, 2014, p. 269). While spectacle and entertainment are still very much a part of Contemporary Circus's remit, its privileging of experimentation and integrated aesthetic makes it 'more self-consciously artistic than traditional circus' (Selwood, Muir & Moody, 1995, p. 51). In this regard, Contemporary Circuses cut across the cultural matrix, seeking to retain the long-established popular status of the circus, while also working to realize more ambitious aesthetics which more closely resemble works of high art.

Perhaps the most widely recognizable Contemporary Circus is that of Montreal-based company Cirque du Soleil. Since the company's founding in 1984 – by street performers Guy Laliberté and Gilles Ste-Croix – it has created over thirty productions that synthesize circus, dance and acrobatics. Each show is crafted around invented myths or expressive themes. For instance, *Alegría*, one of its most popular touring productions, concerned a 'young girl's escape into imagination' (Cirque du Soleil, 2013), while *Kooza*, one of their more recent works, tells the story of 'a melancholy loner in search of his place in the world' (Cirque du Soleil, 2014b).[14] The skills one might expect of the traditional circus can still be found in Cirque du Soleil's performances, but they are used as plotting devices, like pit stops on the protagonist's journey, which are tethered together by spectacular visual and scenographic effects. While some critics have been critical of the company's 'over-theatricalizing', which can make their shows 'pretentious [and] imbued with a meaning [...] rarely discernible to the audience', this has not prevented them from attracting a significant international following (Peacock, 2009, p. 56). According to the company's website, over one hundred and fifty million people have seen a Cirque du Soleil performance since 1984 (Cirque du Soleil, 2014a).

The Welsh company NoFit State Circus offers a smaller-scale, but no less spectacular, model of Contemporary Circus. Founded in 1986 as a small juggling act, the company quickly grew into its first big top tent show, which toured the UK for eight years (Gamble, 2014). In the mid-1990s, the company's *Autogeddon*, based on the anti-automobile poem of the same name by Heathcote Williams, established its reputation as a maverick in the UK's circus sector. Doing away with the tent, the show was performed across several, multi-level stages in a warehouse in Cardiff. The show featured aerialist and acrobatic circus skills, alongside flaming automobile sculptures, rap music, projected video, and pyrotechnics. *Autogeddon* marked the company's first experience of working in a promenade format. Many of their most successful works to date, including *Immortal* (2004), *tabú* (2007) and *Bianco* (2013), have utilized promenade staging. In promenade, spectators are much closer to the action than in a traditional circus big top or arena theatre, which has allowed NoFit to place emphasis on the human element of the performance while still pursuing spectacular aesthetics.

In her assessment of the field, Jeni Williams acknowledges just how important the 'human' element is in the evolution of the Contemporary Circus (2005). This goes beyond the issue of human risk and the way this works to attract audiences, which was explored earlier. Williams argues that whereas the traditional circus, with its origins in the period of the Enlightenment, seemed preoccupied with human control over their environment (evidenced by the animal-taming acts, for instance), the new circus 'reflects the dislocated vision of the contemporary world, its attention shifting away from control over the natural world to questions about the limits and possibilities of the human' (ibid.). In this, the Contemporary Circus shares a similar preoccupation with the human body and its presence in performance as many of the conceptual and solo performances discussed earlier. The ways in which these 'limits and possibilities' are pursued in circus performances are, of course, unique to each company, although Williams has identified two aesthetic tendencies that may determine how the human element is approached. The first tendency can be linked to the aesthetic of commercial musicals, where audiences are impressed with spectacular scenic and visual effects, while the second is based on the human intimacies produced by the audience's close encounters with the action during immersive and site-specific performances (ibid.). Cirque du Soleil unquestionably leans to the side of commercial spectacle. In their productions, the human element is emphasized narratively and is explored with a protagonist who confronts, at each stop along their journey, a series of demonstrations of human strength and cunning from acrobats, contortionists and clowns. NoFit, on the other hand, operates between the two tendencies, creating impressive visual effects within close range of their freely roving audiences. The human element in the work is found both through the use of narrative as well as the proximity of the audience to the work and the sensations this produces in the spectators. While both companies use spectacle to impress audiences, each uses it very differently, which I would suggest also impacts spectator/human engagement. In contrast to the fantastical costumes and makeup that transforms Cirque du Soleil performers into the exotic creatures that populate their fantastical, fictional stage worlds, NoFit State's performers retain their humanness and dress like they belong in our world.

Torsos, arms and legs may be exposed so that audiences can see the performers' bodies at work (which is another way the human element is emphasized), but the clothing and other elements of the production's style are distinctly of the modern world. In this, NoFit State seeks to impress audiences by exposing, at close range, the limits and possibilities of the virtuous, undisguised human body in performance.

The limits and possibilities of the human body, as well as the 'dislocated vision' of the modern world identified by Williams are also prevalent in the work of French acrobat and director Camille Boitel.[15] Boitel's production *L'Immédiat* (*The Instant*), which premiered in 2009 featuring Boitel and a company of six other performers, staged the chaos and destruction of the modern world as a nearly hour-long slapstick sequence.[16] In the first part of the performance, a man returned to his home – a rudimentary structure located in the centre of what appears to be a trash heap – which gradually began to fall apart around him and his partner: the coat rack crumbled, a chair broke, the bookshelves fell apart, then the walls followed suit and collapsed on the performers. This initiated a domino-like effect with the rest of the junk on stage, which began to cave in on the acrobatic performers who expertly dodged, leaped and flew out of the way as needed. In subsequent parts of the performance, the performers – wearing costumes that looked as though they may have been found in a box of discarded clothing – battled the furniture, rubbish piles, gravity and themselves for control of what is clearly an uncontrollable environment.

While this performance fundamentally relied on accomplished acrobatic skills, its Beckett-like bleakness and sophistication set it apart from traditional circus aesthetics. This is in part due to the work's central investigations, which Boitel admits was catastrophe and failure (2014). In the four years it took to develop the performance, company members approached their work through numerous frames: seeking to fail at performing ordinary tasks, reading (Beckett and the philosophical works of Vladimir Jankélévitch proved especially important), and constructing props and scenery that would break apart, allowing them to test their theories practically. There was apparently not an overriding aesthetic vision at the start of rehearsals, but a critical interest in 'experimenting, transmitting, sharing – finding a way to work together' (Boitel, 2014). Boitel explains that these investigations were fundamentally about finding the 'rhythm of accident' and searching for ways this might be used to score a production (ibid.).[17] In the end, the performed 'accidents' and 'failures' that had been successfully mastered by the company became the foundation for the show.

While *L'Immédiat* is a stage show that must keep its audiences at a distance owing to the very real dangers of its collapsing set, I would suggest that its cluttered aesthetic of familiar, everyday objects and use of undisguised, human performers provides a distinctly more relatable human experience for its spectators than the highly theatrical productions of Cirque du Soleil. Although it is relatable in a way that might be called 'popular', bearing the hallmarks of participation that, as discussed, form part of the popular aesthetic, one must acknowledge that the aesthetic results of Boitel's philosophical and practical investigations into catastrophe are much more akin to those of high art. The bold colours, sequined Lycra costumes, clown noses and organ music of the traditional circus are nowhere to be found in Boitel's catastrophic world. Instead, objects and costumes of the mundane and everyday have replaced them, generating a spectacle from the unspectacular. The production also offers up an interesting parallel with the work of Forced Entertainment and Brown Council discussed earlier. Here, Boitel and his company have sought to engage with failure not only as a concept but an overriding practical and aesthetic strategy for developing their existential circus/ slapstick performance. While Boitel's work is born from a philosophical, rather than political, interest, these artists share a productive attitude towards failure and its performance-making potential.

Final Thoughts

Like many of the practices discussed in this chapter, contemporary puppetry and circus are products of the postmodern era's 'new sensibility' (to recall Sontag once more), which has levelled the cultural playing field, reducing the hierarchical, prejudicial perceptions of culture and allowing for greater exchanges between what were once regarded to be low and high art forms. In this climate, the DNA of contemporary popular theatre contains within it an eclectic range of forms and artefacts that have circulated alongside it in the capitalist system in the last century. While becoming more aesthetically complex, the puppet shows and circuses discussed here managed to retain their popular appeal by working to involve the spectator, impress them with virtuous acts and play to their tastes. Like the artists of Goldberg's 'media generation', many of today's spectators have been efficiently trained to negotiate the flurry of fragmented images and texts of daily life (emails, social media, television and the corporate advertising used across these platforms) and thus expect aesthetic approaches that capture this multiplicity.[18]

Working the other way, makers of what would have historically been classified as 'high art', which includes the work of DeDomenici and Makishi, frequently appropriate and re-present popular texts as a fundamental component of their work. Hutcheon, it may be recalled, saw appropriation in a similar way to the avant-gardes, identifying it as a postmodern strategy of critique designed to denaturalize the capitalist mechanisms of the appropriated forms (1989, p. 44). Brown Council and Forced Entertainment have certainly used popular modes critically, drawing on failure, as discussed, to unpack the problematic associations and histories of their chosen forms. However, DeDomenici's and Makishi's work seems less concerned with this. While DeDomenici's performances are politically engaged, he is less concerned with re-presenting the forms use uses than provoking critical thought about hegemonic systems altogether. His target is not necessarily the forms he draws upon, but the systems in which he and the forms, by no choice of their own, belong. Makishi freely appropriates popular culture because it is relatable to her and her audiences and she therefore recognizes it as a useful tool for communicating with them. As I explained earlier, while her work can be read as a commentary on media's impact upon modern life, her performances are not profoundly or forcefully critical or demystifying. My general impression is that, as is the case with many artists of the media generation, Makishi's work freely draws upon popular culture because it has been a consistent and valued presence in the artist's life. Contemporary artists do not always select popular forms so that they might be critiqued, but because they are familiar resources that in some ways have defined the cultural lives of the artists themselves.

Regardless of aesthetic outcome, what seems to unite the practitioners discussed in this chapter is a preoccupation with relational human experience and what it means to be human at the present time. The limits and possibilities of human beings and especially the human body seem to be a recurring theme. In Meecham's *Fun Run*, this is explored through the demanding physical challenge of a marathon. The performance celebrates human ability and success through its aesthetic of fun, transforming audiences into celebrants and cheerleaders for the artist as he works to complete the run. Human agency and success also play a significant role in the work of Forced Entertainment and Brown Council. Their work invites audiences to consider the very notion of success in performance by relying on failure as a performative strategy. Such a choice may, as Bailes has suggested, serve a radical, political function, helping contemporary spectators peer through the mystifying fog of late capitalist production and see the wider inequalities it attempts to disguise.

9 Conclusions

Power and the Popular

In the first chapter of this book I introduced some of the ways in which the word popular has been used historically and demonstrated how its myriad uses and mutations problematize straightforward attempts at defining a 'popular theatre'. One feature that seemed to be shared across popular's many definitions, however, was its relationship to power. Popular, it was argued, typically designated subordinated people in society. As a form of theatre sometimes developed by, and at other times for, these people, popular theatre will usually reflect their experiences, needs, tastes and values. At the end of Chapter 1, I noted that this had been done in three primary ways since the eighteenth century: (1) as a theatre for all, like the communal festivals theorized by Rousseau; (2) a theatre which seeks to politically intervene into issues of importance to subordinated people; and/or (3) performances intended as entertainment that seek to amuse and delight popular audiences. As the discussion has shown, each form may operate independently or may be used in conjunction with the other forms. The popular-political theatres that have been the principal focus of this book often worked across all popular forms in an attempt to engage or inform audiences more effectively.

As a social and aesthetic category that has been defined against power, the popular, and the popular theatre, is often characterized by a fundamental desire for fairness, equality and unity. Given its inherent invitation for participation, the popular theatre's strengths rest in its ability to draw people together and offer up opportunities for fun and/or for reflection upon issues of concern. The experiences provided by these performances allow communities to not only reaffirm or recalibrate their bonds, but to also define plans of action that may help them overcome issues relating to their oppression. In social and economic systems that have been constructed so as to disqualify the voices of the subordinated and to discredit their cultural preferences, such as we find with global capitalism, the popular theatre – constructed from some of those preferences – provides one of few opportunities to speak back to power. I have provided numerous examples of this phenomenon in this book – from the Workers' Theatre Movement, which worked on behalf of the working class, to Gay Sweatshop, which played an important role in the gay rights movement in Britain. Although the aesthetic and political goals of each of these theatres have varied, their main target has been consistently that of oppressive and unjust systems of power. Because their critique is effective, those in power often seek control of popular forms and the messages they seek to impart (see Chapter 1). I demonstrated in Chapters 2 and 3 through the discussion of the Soviet Union and Weimar Germany how such co-option works. So while the popular theatre emerges from the people, it can get caught in the crossfire between those people and those who dominate them. This is, in part, what Hall referred to as the 'double movement of containment and resistance', discussed in Chapter 1 (2009, p. 509). This does not make popular theatre any less effective as a resource for the subordinated, but it does mean that those who make it need to be alert to the slipperiness, hypocrisies and, crucially, the malleability of popular forms. While the flexibility of these forms certainly qualifies, in my view, as a strength – allowing forms to serve many purposes: entertainment, propaganda or as modes of critique (as in the avant-garde) – it is something popular theatre-makers must be finely attuned to, otherwise they run the risk contradicting themselves and, subsequently, undermining the aims of their performances.

As I have shown, the popular's relationship to power can trouble its political commitments. This is especially true of the popular's relationship to mass culture and the wider mass-culture industry. I have tried to tread carefully across what is a rather hazy line between the two cultural forms throughout this book. In adopting Fiske's view, that 'a homogenous, externally produced culture cannot be sold ready-made to the masses', I have sought to distinguish between cultural forms which have been adopted by the people as part of their culture and those that have not (1989, p. 23). To regard all Hollywood films or commercial musicals, for instance, as manipulative mass-cultural forms is plainly wrong. Many of these forms do become meaningful to people and constitute an essential part of their lives. But if each object of popular culture, as Fiske conceives of it, contains 'the forces of domination and opportunities to speak against them', it seems to me that the forces of domination are typically much more clearly pronounced in mass cultural texts than the critical voices of its users – which in part explains the charges against mass culture (ibid., p. 25). One might very well argue that consumers' dissent can be articulated by ticket sales, for instance; but framing dissension exclusively in financial terms only reinforces the presence and power of an oppressive economic system that ensures popular audiences remain in a position of domination. Some people, including many of the artists introduced in this book, have used the theatre to do the talking. Many of the avant-gardes' playful defacing of popular culture, for instance, suggests to me a sincere and innovative means by which to speak back to domination (see Chapter 6). The *disidentified* figures borrowed from modern popular culture texts that appear in the work of the San Francisco Mime Troupe suggests another effective strategy (Chapter 7), as do the 'failed' attempts at reproducing popular entertainment in the work of Forced Entertainment and Brown Council (Chapter 8). In unmaking, remaking, exaggerating and distorting popular forms, these companies demonstrate how to speak against the power bound up in forms that have been made into mass-consumer products. One must accept, though, that not all popular performance modes do this, neither is it always in the financial or political interest of their makers to resist hegemonic systems. This would be as true for the Broadway megamusical (in certain instances) as it would be for Soviet agitprop. While these forms are economically and aesthetically oppositional, both operate(d) as part of the hegemony of their respective cultures. Thus, one is right to question where the popular's loyalty rests in each given case, as the work's political affiliations alone may not always be a suitable indicator.

Endurances of the Popular

As Brecht once observed, 'What was popular yesterday is not today, for the people today are not what they were yesterday' (1980, p. 83). In other words, the popular changes because the people it represents and/or speaks to change. In the nineteenth century and for much of the twentieth, the working class has typically been thought of as forming the principal consumers and practitioners of popular theatre – from gritty naturalistic plays staged by the Freie Volksbühne in Berlin (Chapter 1) to communist agitprop performed on the back of a truck at a political rally (Chapters 4 and 5). The survival of groups like the Bread and Puppet Theatre, San Francisco Mime Troupe and Red Ladder suggests that on some level this is still the case, although as I mentioned in Chapter 7, their work clearly represents a trend that has been in decline since the 1980s because of reduced levels of funding and the continued identity crises of the radical Left. The decline is also due in part to the changing make-up of social systems. Statistically, the working class has shrunk since the end of the Second World War. In Britain and the United States in the 1940s and 1950s, the working class constituted the largest class in those countries, comprising between approximately 60 and 90 per cent of the population, respectively.[1] Those figures now stand at half what they were, making the working classes a minority social group. It is the middle class that now reigns in many developed nations as the dominant class. Does this trouble the popular's relationship to the working class? I do not think so. Popular, as discussed, can accommodate oppression in many forms. If one is to believe the slogan of the recent Occupy Movement – 'We are the 99%!' – which is based on data the shows that 1 per cent of the population now control the majority of the wealth,[2] then everyone barring a very small minority would constitute the dominated, popular classes. In this system, pretty much everyone could be considered a consumer of popular theatre and a maker of popular culture. This partly explains the democratization of culture discussed in Chapter 8, where historical prejudices regarding culture have eased in the postmodern era under the expansion of capitalism globally. Not only has this expansion generated the gross wealth inequality that can see 1 per cent of the population dominate the others, but it also homogenized the cultural system in such a manner that (to use old categories) low and high art can operate in tandem. In this system, those cheap and easy popular entertainments from the past, like the circus or musicals, possess a constantly shifting aesthetic and cultural status. This not only means that one can find contemporary versions of popular forms that adopt aesthetic strategies from 'high art', like those discussed at the end of Chapter 8, but also fetishized commercial entertainments, like circuses or musicals, that can charge elite prices for tickets.[3] Of course, high prices do not make these forms elitist, or 'pure' in the Bourdieuian sense, but they do demonstrate how cultural and aesthetic values have shifted significantly in the last century. The theatre itself, regardless of what is playing, is seen by many as a luxury and as a special night out. As such, the desire to be entertained is no longer a popular taboo but an expectation that most audiences hold regardless of class.

The steady decline of the working class has had a profound impact on their left-wing politics and the popular theatre more generally. As I mentioned at the end of Chapter 7, the radical Left has struggled to recover from the attacks levelled at communism in the latter years of the Cold War – attacks which significantly shaped the views of a generation of people who came to see the rhetoric of socialism as dated and, as McGrath noted, 'pre-historic' (1990, 20).[4] Increasingly, this has also been used to transform the working class itself into an outdated social category, so much so that by the late 1990s, the deputy leader of Britain's Labour Party – a historically socialist political party (see Chapter 4) – would famously announce 'we are all middle class now'.[5] While more people are middle class now than they were a century ago, this erroneous and troubling belief was used as the rationale for shifting the party's politics to the political centre in order to win elections. In doing so, the Labour Party abandoned its traditional working class base.[6] The party for the working class had essentially become, to use another outdated term, another party of the bourgeoisie.

This shift has had wider consequences. As recent research undertaken by Geoff Evans and James Tilley has indicated, the working class in Britain now identifies as being losers in a society predominantly made up of the middle classes (2015, p. 300). This has generated widespread 'political disillusionment and non-participation' (ibid., p. 298). Members of the working class that still vote tend to look for representation outside the mainstream, as they do not see their interests represented there. This has resulted in the working class shifting their support to smaller parties, such as the far-right-wing UK Independence Party (Ukip) (ibid.). A similar phenomenon has occurred in the United States, although the working class's turn to the Right there appears to have accompanied the rise of the New Left as early as the 1960s. As Jefferson Cowie has noted, the working class 'barely more than a generation out of poverty itself, [and] believ[ing] it had a world to lose' became frustrated with the many rights movements that sought to win others the same freedoms they enjoyed (2008, p. 73). This gradually resulted in the working class shifting their support from the more liberal Democratic Party, which was more sympathetic with the liberation movements, to the conservative Republican Party, which was not. This is despite the fact that income growth has historically risen for the working classes under Democratic administrations and lagged under Republican ones (Bartels, 2008, p. 30). In his book, *What's the Matter with Kansas?*, political analyst Thomas Frank explains that American working-class voters have learned to 'vote against their economic interests [in order to] defend traditional cultural values', which they believe are threatened by those on the left who advocate for social equality (2004, p. 65). There are a couple reasons for this. Firstly, the American working class has historically been more evangelical Christian, and therefore voting against their own personal interests in favour of what they believe their religion teaches is unsurprising. Secondly, and applicable to all of us, people tend to make comparisons with others in order to raise their self-esteem (Evans & Tilley, 2015, p. 300). The middle class, as the new majority class, look down upon the working class disparagingly. In the worst manifestation of this, the middle class develops negative myths about the working classes, such as that they are a strain on public services, and brands them with unpleasant names, like 'white trash' or 'chav', in order to keep them in their place.[7] The working class essentially does the same thing, but will look to do so with minority groups and social others that they perceive to be socially lower than they are – immigrants, ethnic minorities, LGBT people, etc. – in order to enhance their self-esteem.

Of course, these kinds of prejudices are not new, as this book has demonstrated. They are the same kinds of prejudices that led Arnold to write *Culture and Anarchy* in the nineteenth century and the Leavises to critique mass culture so sternly in the early twentieth. The popular has been defined and redefined on how these prejudices are set out in society. The working class's turn to right-wing parties does not disqualify them from being 'popular' in the twenty-first century. But it does mean that the kinds of interventions the popular theatre stages for and with working-class communities will need to be formalistically and politically different than those discussed in this book if it seeks to represent their interests. Practitioners interested in taking up this cause might question the benefit of returning to methods like those proposed by John McGrath and 7:84, which took into account the diversity of working-class people and sought to build relationships with communities on their own terms, or to Theatre Uncut, whose impressive collection of radical plays, distributed online, continues to grow each day (Chapter 7). But perhaps the more fundamental problem is political. The working classes no longer know political alternatives that will work to improve their social and economic conditions. If socialism were to be revived in a meaningful way in the twenty-first century, I would think it wise to seek help from the classes it was designed to support in the first place.

The spread of the Occupy Movement internationally in 2011 and 2012 demonstrates the wider frustrations with the global financial system and, I would suggest, an appetite for action on the matter of economic inequality. Unifying, committed popular theatres anchored by our collective frustration at being 'the 99%' could operate well in this context, and possibly contribute to social change in the future. While such a call inevitably sounds utopian, it is no more or less so than the popular theatres of the past century whose makers fundamentally believed that the work they produced was capable of bringing about meaningful change for the people they worked with, represented or agitated on behalf of. Without exaggeration or historical distortion, I believe it can be argued that many of these theatres, working in tandem with political campaigns and social movements, successfully managed to do that. Popular theatres at the present time would be wise to bear in mind the lessons of these theatres. In particular, practitioners should be alert to the popular theatre's unique strengths, including the malleability of its many forms, which can be easily and completely reshaped to accommodate the needs, tastes or values of their audiences; its ability to bring people together and become involved, through the popular's inherent invitation to participate; as well as its bright and playful aesthetic, which can kaleidoscopically distort capitalism's illusions so as to reveal the hidden sources of oppression. Such theatres also hold the potential to stage what a fairer future might look like, providing us with glimpses of what we could possibly achieve if we committed ourselves to working together.

Notes

Notes to Chapter 1: Introduction

1. See Althusser (1971).
2. According to the OED, 'popular culture' was first used in 1854.
3. Cecil Sharp, Mary Neal, Ralph Vaughan Williams, and A.L. Lloyd are some of the better-known advocates of the British Folk Revival (1890–1920).
4. *Natural Son* was a play by Diderot first performed in 1757.
5. During the French Revolution, many dramatists were keen to take advantage of patriotic sentiments and would quickly transform news of battles into plays within a short space of time. Germani notes how some critics felt that the sheer abundance of military plays reeked of opportunism, and many, written hastily in order to keep their work topical, were of poor quality and, consequently, poorly received (2006, p. 205).
6. The *sans-culottes* were a group of French artisans and labourers. Their name translates to 'without culottes'. Culottes were knee-breeches popular among the bourgeoisie during the period. The *sans-culottes* wore pantaloons, or full-length trousers, instead of the more fashionable culottes. See Priestland (2009, pp. 7–12) for a detailed discussion of the group and their politics.
7. Wille's view toward art was not uncommon during this period. As Raphael Samuel has pointed out, the prevailing attitude throughout much of the nineteenth century was that art should be autonomous and not be forced to take on politics (1985, p. xvii). This belief was more commonly known as *Bildung*, which refers to the process of self-cultivation or self-improvement.

Notes to Chapter 2: Popular Revolutionary Theatres I: The Soviet Union

1. Lunacharsky was also a gifted playwright and literary critic. His work included short, agitprop sketches as well as full-length plays, including the historical drama *Oliver Cromwell* (1919) and popular melodrama *The Chancellor and the Locksmith* (1921).
2. The use of circus and bridging the stage and auditorium with scenographic and performative elements became a trademark of Mayakovsky's theatre practice. See Schechter (1985, p. 85).

3. Futurist was a term broadly used to describe work that was unconventional in Russia at the time. It does not precisely equate to Filippo Tommaso Marinetti's brand of Futurism, launched in Italy in 1909, which is discussed in Chapter 6. See Braun (1995, p. 156).

4. Mamont, meaning monument, was a nickname stemming from his work on the monument plan. Vinogradov actually got his start in theatre working as an actor for Pavel Gaideburov's Mobile Popular Theatre, a group formed in 1907 that travelled around Russia performing mostly classical plays.

5. But, interestingly, as Geldern points out, the events it depicted did not happen quite as heroically as the spectacle would have audiences believe. 'The palace housed a powerless and ineffectual cabinet; it was seized a day after the Bolsheviks had taken power; and it was never really stormed' (1993, p. 2).

6. Casson notes that in 1919 the Central Committee of the Soviet Union Communist Party decreed for 'public readings of the news, illustrated with "demonstrations," illuminated by cinema and magic lantern shows, and "concert numbers" to ensure the dissemination of news and revolutionary propaganda amongst the illiterate' (2000, p. 108). This resulted in a proliferation of proletarian-focused performance throughout the 1920s.

7. Constructivism was an arts philosophy that emerged out of Russian Futurism after the Revolution. It specifically rejected the autonomy of art in favour of art with a social function, and extending the abstraction of avant-garde arts practices into design and practical functionality.

8. Petrushka is the Russian equivalent of the British hand puppet Mr. Punch.

9. Celebrated designer and painter Marc Chagall is known to have painted some of the backdrops for TEREVSAT. See Curtis (1990, p. 219).

10. Mayakovsky is known to have written some of the sketches performed by TEREVSAT.

11. Left Front of the Arts was a radical arts group made up of artists, designers, critics and writers. Its journal, *LEF*, was co-edited by writers Osip Brik and Vladimir Mayakovsky.

12. In 'Simple Advice to Participants', the Blue Blouses advise that a 'Satirical sketch – village type' is to follow the *feuilleton* (Blue Blouse, 1995 [1925]). Stourac and McCreery eliminate this entry in their discussion of the programme, presumably because of its similarities to a rural *feuilleton*.

13. Deák notes that Blue Blouse programmes would also feature 'acrobatic and physical dances', executed in pairs or collectively, typically performed to jazz music (1973, p. 37).

14. See also Blue Blouse (1995 [1925], pp. 182–183) and Deák (1973).

15. International Workers' Aid, or *Internationale Arbiter-Hilfe* (IAH) in German, was a relief organization set up by Willi Münzenberg, a member of the German Communist Party, in 1921 to amass international support for famine-stricken Russia.

Notes to Chapter 3: Popular Revolutionary Theatres II: Germany

1. The German Workers' Theatre Federation was known as Deutsche Arbeitertheater Bund. See Bradby & McCormick (1978, pp. 65–66); Willett (1988, p. 21); Bodek (1997, pp. 9–10) for further information.
2. Pre-war Expressionist plays include Carl Sternheim's *The Trousers* (1911), Georg Kaiser's *The Burghers of Calais* (1914) and Walter Hasenclever's *The Son* (1916).
3. Presber was the editor of a magazine entitled *Pages of Fun* (*Die Lustigen Blätter*), and wrote what Rorrison describes as 'humorous trivia' (see Rorrison in Piscator, 1980 [1963], p. 22). The conflation of the highbrow Goethe with the lowbrow Presber was intended to be ridiculous.
4. This was the Tribunal Theatre in Königsberg (now Kaliningrad), which Piscator set up in 1919. It was most certainly indebted to the earlier Tribüne.
5. Innes explains that Piscator chose for this theatre a collection of 'progressive plays' which had been written for the commercial theatre. Piscator came to realize that 'their visionary idealism was unsuited for political application' and 'their methods delusive by Marxist standards' (Innes, 1972, pp. 20–21).
6. According to Robert Heynen, the revue's title is a reference to *Rummelplätz*, or a fairground, which was favoured by working class youth during the period (2015, p. 538).
7. On 4 May 1886, a bomb was thrown at police during a labour demonstration in Haymarket Square in Chicago. Eleven people were killed. Eventually eight anarchists were charged and convicted for the crime; four of them were later hanged. The trial was controversial because the jury was known to be biased and little evidence could be found of the men's guilt.
8. He served his month-long military service as a medical orderly in a venereal disease clinic.
9. A good account of Valentin's influence on Brecht can be found in Schechter (1985, pp. 22–31).

Notes to Chapter 4: The Workers' Theatre Movement I: Starting Points, and Germany

1. The two parties were affiliated between 1906 and 1932, although the Independent Labour Party was more left-wing than the Labour Party. Ideological divisions would, however, lead to the two parties separating after 1932, which would see Independent Labour membership quickly decline. In the mid-1970s, the party would become Independent Labour Publications, a pressure group as opposed to a political party, and once again become affiliated with the Labour Party.

2. The Scottsboro boys were nine African-American youths who were falsely accused and tried for the rape of two white women in Alabama in 1931. The men were found guilty by three all-white juries, despite a wealth of evidence – including the redaction of the story by one of the accusers – that they did not commit the crime. After a ruling by the US Supreme Court (*Norris v Alabama*, 1935) that juries needed to be of mixed races and a further trial, charges for four of the men were dropped and the remaining five were once again found guilty.
3. Figures for the number of troupes vary between sources. Bodek draws on figures published in the *Rote Fahne* in March 1930, which shows that the ATBD had at that time 300 affiliated troupes and nearly 4000 members (1997, p. 81). Stourac and McCreery indicate that the national figure stood at around 500 troupes in 1930 (1986, p. 300).
4. *Komsomol* is the name given to the All-Union Leninist Young Communist League.
5. See Willett (1988, p. 134) for a brief discussion of Eisler's role with the company.

Notes to Chapter 5: The Workers' Theatre Movement II: Britain and the United States

1. See also Samuel and Thomas (1977, pp. 113–127).
2. *Red Stage* later became *New Red Stage*, before becoming the *WTM Monthly Bulletin*. *Red Stage* proved to be financially unsustainable (Stourac & McCreery, 1986, pp. 233–234).
3. Some of the most significant figures from the European radical theatre were in attendance at the Olympiad, including Romain Rolland and Erwin Piscator (Mally, 2003, p. 332).
4. See also Cosgrove (1985, p. 273).
5. While most workers' theatre theorists advocated for sparse scenographic elements, others saw potential in grander arrangements. In Mordecai Gorelik's essays for *Workers' Theatre*, for instance, he argues that props and costumes should not only be used, but they should be *exaggerated* in order to make for a more pronounced visual attack. See Gorelik (1932).

Notes to Chapter 6: Rejuvenation and Resistance: Popular Forms and the Avant-Garde

1. Dennis G. Loffe and Frederick H. White have defined modernism as 'the totality of the numerous aesthetic theories that emerged in the late nineteenth century' (2012, p. 10). This would include the avant-garde.
2. Not least of all for pre-dating Marcel Duchamp's *LHOOQ* (1919), which also features a distressed *Mona Lisa*.

3. Gourdeau coined the term *fumisme* to refer to the prankster-like spirit shared by many artists at the end of the nineteenth century. Michael L.J. Wilson translates the term to mean 'blowing smoke', which he uses to refer to the 'satiric inversion' of some of the work produced at the time (2001, p. 82).

4. Guignol is a French hand puppet derivative of *commedia dell'arte*'s Pulcinella. He first appeared in France in the early nineteenth century.

5. According to Cate, Salis, who would sometimes narrate the performance, referred to the elephant's faeces as 'an odiferous pearl' (1996, p. 57).

6. The first cabaret in Amsterdam opened in 1895; Barcelona, 1897; Berlin, 1901; Budapest, 1907; Moscow and St Petersburg, 1908; London, 1912; and Zurich, 1916 (Segal, 1987, pp. xiii–xiv).

7. See Schopenhauer (1969).

8. J. Douglas Clayton makes the point in his book *Pierrot In Petrograd* that Meyerhold's introduction to *commedia dell'arte* would have most likely come from the European symbolists who, especially the French, had reimagined the *commedia* form as one less crudely humorous but more Romantic. See Clayton (1993, pp. 8–10).

9. Biomechanics was Meyerhold's performer-training method consisting of sixteen physical etudes, which he believed prepared performers for all scenic movement possibilities. Generally speaking, it consists of a merging of principles borrowed from physical theatre practices like *commedia* and the circus, with the scientific management of Taylorism and innovations in reflexology available to Meyerhold at the time. See Gordon (1974).

10. *The Puppet Show* is also known as *The Fairground Booth*.

11. Berghaus explains that Marinetti specialized in a form of 'visual and gestural presentation' that caused 'altercations and agitated audiences' (2005, pp. 32–33).

12. For a detailed account of this production, see Bartlett and Dadswell (2012).

13. The Bauhaus was controversial from the beginning. Many residents in the right-leaning city of Weimar, including several of the staff from the former Academy of Fine Arts, were hostile to the Bauhaus's existence and worked to see it closed. Some of these conflicts at Weimar are explored in Éva Forgács's *The Bauhaus Idea and Bauhaus Politics* (1995, pp. 38–45).

14. Whitford notes that Gropius's politics had shifted to the left as a result of the First World War (1984, p. 31). He also assumed the role of chairman of the Working Soviet for Art, a group of left-leaning artists and intellectuals in 1919, and was a member of November Group, the renowned socialist arts group formed in Berlin in 1918 (ibid., pp. 37–38).

15. This school's Expressionist and Constructivist leanings are clearly signalled by Gropius's appointment of workshop masters. Johannes Itten (who led the school's preliminary course), Lionel Feininger, Paul Klee, Oskar Schlemmer and Wassily Kandinsky, all of whom were appointed

between 1919 and 1923, were well-known Expressionist painters. The influence of Constructivism would come with the appointments of Theo van Doesburg and László Maholy-Nagy in 1922 and 1923, respectively.

16. Descriptions of Shreyer's work suggest that his primitivism may very well share certain features with the Dadaists. See Trimingham (2007, pp. 12–13).

17. Schlemmer signed a contract with the Bauhaus in December 1920 (Whitford, 1984, p. 80).

18. See Kleist (2012, pp. 121–125).

19. See Craig (1978, pp. 37–57).

20. *The Triadic Ballet* was a collaboration between Schlemmer and dancers Albert Burger and Elsa Hötzel. They started work on the piece in Stuttgart in 1912. The first full performance was given in Stuttgart in September 1922. It was revived in 1923 for the Bauhaus exhibition (Schlemmer, 1961, p. 34).

21. This is based on a diagram Schlemmer includes with his essay 'Man and Art Figure' entitled 'Scheme for Stage, Cult and Popular Entertainment'. See Schlemmer (1961, p. 18).

22. The Tiller Girls were an all-female British dance troupe known for spectacular staging, glitzy costumes and the precision of its kick-lines.

23. See Schlemmer (1961, p. 19).

24. He certainly believed this about *commedia dell'arte*, which he uses to explain the value of costume as a means of transforming the actor (Schlemmer, 1961, p. 25).

Notes to Chapter 7: Post-War Popular Theatre

1. *Guillare* is a medieval entertainer that prospered between the tenth and fifteenth centuries. See Farrell (1989, p. 322).

2. The Fo-Rame Company was disbanded in 1968 when Fo and Rame set up Nuovo Scene, which was to operate as a communist theatre. Nuovo Scene lasted less than two years because Fo and Rame found its collective artistic and management structure problematic. Like others discussed, they became increasingly suspicious of the Communist Party's authoritarianist tendencies. This led to the creation of La Comune two years later, a theatre dedicated to the New Left ideology. With La Comune, they created some of the best known works, including *The Accidental Death of an Anarchist* and *Can't Pay? Won't Pay*. See Hood (1987) and Scuderi (1988) for more information on Fo and Rame's work.

3. The central and eastern European Soviet satellite states were Albania, Bulgaria, Czechoslovakia, East Germany, Hungary, Poland and Romania. Many of these remained under heavy Soviet influence, or outright control, until 1990.

4. The role of the media in shaping public perceptions in the 1960s should not be underestimated. By 1955, around 65 per cent of Americans owned a television set, an increase from 9 per cent only six years earlier (Spigel, 1993, p. 32). According to Stephen Cushion, by the mid-1950s, television had overtaken radio as the primary news source in America (Cushion, 2012, p. 40). A carefully crafted slogan or eye-catching spectacle could easily find its way onto the evening news and subsequently disseminate one's cause.

5. The involvement of the United States in this war heightened in 1961 and would last until 1973.

6. I make the distinction 'modern mime' here because the company's later work is more indebted to the ancient mime tradition, which was not silent.

7. L'Amant Militaire was Holden's first piece for the Mime Troupe. She would serve as the company's principal playwright until her retirement in 2000.

8. This is the view of British playwright David Edgar, who has argued that the forms' relationship with the media industry has left them so corrupted, 'they are no longer usable' (quoted in Kershaw, 1992, p. 153). Kershaw also echoes this view, noting in his discussion of the work of John McGrath and 7:84 that even when used critically, the 'ideological doubleedge' of the forms 'may reinforce the very values which they aim to subvert' (ibid., p. 154).

9. The performance is described in detail in Brecht (1988, pp. 519–522).

10. In 1970 the company would relocate to Vermont – first to take up a residency at Goddard College in Plainfield, which would last until 1974, and later to a farm near Glover (Erven, 1988, p. 54). From 1974 until 1998, the company organized Our Domestic Resurrection Circus, an annual festival of outdoor performance on the Schumann farm each summer, attracting thousands of spectators.

11. For his Kasperle background, please see S. Brecht (1988, p. 10). For Japanese Bunraku and Sicilian puppetry see Kourilsky (1974, p. 106) and S. Brecht (1988, p. 136).

12. See, for instance, The Birdcatcher in Hell (1965), This Is (1980) or The Foot (1983).

13. The Mime Troupe's work has tended to be more inclusive in terms of the issues it sets out to explore. All three of the issues listed here have been addressed through their work. The Bread and Puppet Theatre's work has not, to my knowledge, engaged overtly with feminism or gay rights, but it has frequently addressed environmental issues. So the list here is meant to be indicative, to give a sense of the scope of both companies' work; it is not applicable to both individually.

14. John Fox saw a performance of the Bread and Puppet Theatre that had been coordinated by Peter and Joan Oliver at Oval House in London in

the late 1960s. Fox acknowledges that Schumann was a significant influence on his work (Fox, 2002, pp. 9, 259).

15. See Lo Teatre de La Carriera (1975, p. 11).
16. The name 7:84 came from a headline in *The Economist* printed in 1966 that indicated that 7 per cent of the British population owned 84 per cent of the wealth.
17. The full process is outlined in the Methuen edition of the play (see McGrath, 1981).
18. For a good introduction to Lo Teatre de la Carriera's 'women's plays' see Moss (1987, pp. 551–55.
19. The company was also initially integrated, having white and black members. But in 1965, the company's racial policy changed. O'Neal would later explain that one of the reasons for this was due to the difficulty of translating black oppression/experience to white audiences and white members of the company. See O'Neal (1968, pp. 72–74).
20. The Gay Liberation Front (GLF) was formed out of the Action Committee of the Mattachine Society in New York in the wake of the Stonewall riots in 1969. Within two years, other GLF groups had been established in other major cities around the United States as well as in London. Unlike earlier homophile organizations, the GLF was revolutionist.
21. In the 1980s and 1990s, the theatre shifted its focus away from radical politics and onto youth work. It is now known for its work in schools and with young people. See http://www.nest-theatre.fr/.

Notes to Chapter 8: The Popular in Postmodern and Contemporary Performance

1. Mandel's periodization of capitalism described here is taken from his book *Late Capitalism* (1979).
2. *Rhythm 0* has become a landmark example of the extremity of participation. Within hours, the participants had cut off Abramovic's clothes, cut her flesh and drank her blood and, in the end, placed the loaded gun in her hand and aimed it at her head. Gallery staff had to intervene and declare the performance over.
3. For our purposes such distinctions are unimportant, as I am intending simply to discuss performance in a broad sense, but I feel it is important to stress that I do not believe these terms are synonymous with one another, although they clearly overlap.
4. One cannot, however, deny the sacrificial element of such works and how this potentially problematizes just how equal the collaboration is.
5. To date, *Fun Run* has been performed in Melbourne (2010), Darwin (2011) and Sydney (2013) in Australia; Ansan, South Korea (2015); and Kuopio, Finland (2015).

6. The remaining works in the trilogy include *Game Show* (2014) and *Miss Universe*, which is in development.

7. In the nineteenth century the lecture-monologue and monodrama became prominent owing to high profile performances given by the likes of Charles Dickens and Twain, as well as through variety theatre, Chautauqua and vaudeville. The work of Ruth Draper (1884–1952), renowned American diseuse of the early twentieth century, is a particularly important precursor. For more information on Draper, see Zabel (1960).

8. See Vincent (2014).

9. Members of the company currently include Tim Etchells (artistic director), Robin Arthur, Cathy Naden, Richard Lowdon, Terry O'Connor and Claire Marshall.

10. One his best known productions, *The Dead Class* (1975), for instance, mixed mannequins and actors, with the mannequins serving as youthful avatars of a class of old, dead people (played by the actors). For Kantor, the effect was a metaphor for how memory works, and the work an exploration of the Self and the Other. See Kantor (1993).

11. Bunraku is a traditional form of Japanese puppetry first developed in the late seventeenth century. It typically involves three operators who share responsibility for controlling, respectively, the puppet's head, arms and feet. Often, the handlers are dressed completely in black so as to not distract from the illusion.

12. Blind Summit designed and directed giant puppets for Danny Boyle's Opening Ceremony of the London 2012 Olympic Games. Among those they created was a 90-foot-tall Lord Voldemort puppet from J.K. Rowling's popular *Harry Potter* series.

13. While some scholars argue that the circus dates back to ancient Rome, with the construction of circuses – i.e. buildings designed for a multitude of entertainments, including chariot races and gladiatorial battles – the modern circus is typically accredited to Englishman Philip Astley, who set up the first circus in 1756. Astley's circuses focused on equestrian acts and trick horse riding. By the late nineteenth century, the big-top format had become firmly established as the principal circus mode, which would continue until the 1970s. See Peacock (2009, pp. 41–63) for a concise overview of circus history.

14. *Alegría* premiered in 1994 and toured internationally until 2013. According to the company's website, the production visited 250 cities and was witnessed by some fourteen million spectators (Cirque du Soleil, 2013).

15. Originally from Traverséres, France, Boitel got his start at the age of twelve developing small street performances with his sister, Raphäella. After a brief period at Annie Fratellini's École Nationale Du Cirque, Boilel was hired to perform in James Thiérré's production *The Junebug Symphony*, which toured internationally from 1998 to 2005. Following his stint in Thiérrée's company, Boitel began producing his own work (Boitel, 2014).

16. Several critics who reviewed *L'Immédiat* were keen to align the catastrophe it performs with the global financial crisis of 2008, reading it as a critique of (or at least a meditation on) the failings of global capitalism. Boitel can see how such interpretations have been reached, but he admitted that no attempt was made to append such a precise political meaning to the work itself. 'The work is our thinking about catastrophe and failure. I wouldn't want anyone to believe we had any specific meanings in mind [...] I would prefer to leave it open' (2014).

17. In fact, Boitel noted in our interview that the 'rhythm of the accident' is central to most of his work (2014).

18. While popular taste is evolving and will therefore be generational, a large proportion of what we might qualify as a popular audience at the present time would, I believe, meet these criteria.

Notes to Chapter 9: Conclusions

1. This data is taken from two sources. For Britain, see Evans and Tilley (2015, p. 300). For the United States, see Edsall (2012).

2. See Stiglitz (2011).

3. The average ticket price for a Broadway show in the week ending 2 August 2015 was $106.05. The top ticket price average was $258.57. See Broadway World (2015).

4. Negative views are likely to have been further shaped by the news of human rights abuses that seem to be a staple of modern communist regimes, such as China and North Korea.

5. See BBC (2007).

6. This strategy was largely successful until the economic recession of 2008, which saw their defeat in the national election in 2010.

7. This is explained particularly well in Owen Jones's book *Chavs: The Demonization of the Working Class*. See Jones (2011).

Bibliography

Abramovic, M. (n.d.) *Marina Abramovic. Rhythm 0. 1974*, http://www.moma.org/explore/multimedia/audios/190/1927, accessed 23 September 2014.

Adorno, T.W. & Horkheimer, M. (1997 [1944]) *Dialectic of Enlightenment*, trans. J. Cumming (London: Verso).

Althusser, L. (1971) *Lenin and Philosophy* (New York: Monthly Review Press).

Anderson, E.A. (2014) '"It's New Eyes We're Trying to Create": Speaking with Blind Summit's Mark Down', in *Theatre Topics*, 24 (2), pp. 137–144.

Arnold, M. (2009 [1869]) 'Culture and Anarchy', in J. Storey (ed.) *Cultural Theory and Popular Culture: A Reader*, 4th edn (Harlow, UK: Pearson Longman), pp. 6–11.

Aston, E. (1995) *An Introduction to Feminism and Theatre* (London: Routledge).

Auslander, P. (1989) 'Going with the Flow: Performance Art and Mass Culture', in *The Drama Review*, 33 (2), pp. 119–136.

Bailes, S.J. (2011) *Performance Theatre and the Poetics of Failure* (London and New York: Routledge).

Bakhtin, M. (1984) *Rabelais and His World* (Bloomington: University of Indiana Press).

Barnett, D. (2014) *Brecht in Practice* (London: Bloomsbury).

Bartels, L.M. (2008) *Unequal Democracy: The Political Economy of the Gilded Age.* (Princeton, NJ: Princeton University Press).

Barth, J. (1984) 'The Literature of Replenishment', in *The Friday Book: Essays and Other Non-Fiction* (London: The John Hopkins Press), pp. 193–206.

Barthes, R. (1977 [1968]) 'The Death of the Author', in *Image Music Text*, trans. S. Heath, (London: Fontanta Press), pp. 142–148.

Bartlett, R. & Dadswell, S. (2012) *Victory Over the Sun: The World's First Futurist Opera* (Exeter: University of Exeter Press).

Baudrillard, J. (2009) 'The Precession of Simulacra', in J. Storey (ed.) *Cultural Theory and Popular Culture: A Reader* (Harlow, UK: Pearson Longman), pp. 409–415.

BBC (2007) 'Profile: John Prescott', *BBC News*, http://news.bbc.co.uk/1/hi/uk_politics/6636565, accessed 11 August 2014.

Berghaus, G. (1998) *Italian Futurist Theatre 1909–1944* (Oxford: Clarendon Press).

_____ (2005) *Avant-Garde Performance: Live Events and Electronic Technologies* (Basingstoke: Palgrave Macmillan).

Blind Summit (2012) *The Table*, dir. M. Down. Soho Theatre, London. 14 January 2012.

Blind Summit (n.d.) 'About Blind Summit', http://www.blindsummit.com/ aboutBST.htm, accessed 23 August 2012.

Blok, A. (1950) 'The Puppet Show', in *The Slavonic and East European Review*, 28 (71), pp. 309–322.

Blue Blouse (1995 [1925]) 'Simple Advice to Participants', in R. Drain (ed.), *Twentieth Century Theatre: A Sourcebook* (London: Routledge), pp. 181–183.

Bodek, R. (1997) *Proletarian Performance in Weimar Berlin: Agitprop, Chorus, and Brecht* (Columbia, SC: Camden House).

Bogosian, E. & Sussler, B. (1994) 'Eric Bogosian', in *BOMB*, 48, pp. 30–35.

Boitel, C. (2014) 'Camille Boitel interviewed by J. Price', trans. A. Satgé, London, 14 November 2014.

Bonney, J. (2000) *Extreme Exposure: An Anthology of Solo Performance Texts from the Twentieth Century* (New York: Theatre Communications Group).

Bourdieu, P. (1984) *Distinction: A Social Critique of the Judgement of Taste*, trans. R. Nice (London and New York: Routledge).

Boyes, G. (2010) *The Imagined Village: Culture, Ideology and the English Folk Revival.* (Leeds: No Masters Co-operative Limited).

Bradby, D., James, L. & Sharratt, B. (1980) *Performance and Politics in Popular Drama* (Cambridge: Cambridge University Press).

Bradby, D. & McCormick, J. (1978) *People's Theatres* (London: Croom Helm).

Braun, E. (1995) *Meyerhold: A Revolution in Theatre* (London: Methuen).

Brecht, B. (1964a) 'A Short Organum for Theatre', in J. Willett (ed.) *Brecht on Theatre* (London: Methuen), pp. 179–205.

_____ (1964b) 'On Gestic Music', in J. Willett (ed.) *Brecht on Theatre* (London: Methuen Drama), pp. 104–106.

_____ (1964c) 'Short Description of a New Technique of Acting which Produces an Alienation Effect', in J. Willett (ed.) *Brecht on Theatre* (London: Methuen Drama), pp. 136–147.

_____ (1964d) 'Theatre for Pleasure or Theatre for Instruction', in J. Willett (ed.) *Brecht on Theatre* (London: Methuen Drama), pp. 69–77.

_____ (1980) 'Against Georg Lukács', in R. Taylor (ed.) *Aesthetics and Politics* (London: Verso), pp. 68–85.

_____ (2003) 'Theory of Pedagogies', in T. Kuhn & S. Giles (eds.) *Brecht on Art and Politics*, trans. L. Bradley, S. Giles & T. Kuhn (London: Methuen), pp. 88–89.

Brecht, S. (1988) *The Bread and Puppet Theatre*, Vol. I (New York: Methuen).

Breitzer, S.R. (2011) 'Race, Immigration, and Contested Americanness: Black Nativism and the American Labor Movement, 1880–1930', in *Race/Ethnicity: Multidisciplinary Global Contexts*, 4 (2), pp. 269–283.

Brigstock, J. (2012) 'Defiant Laughter: Humour and the aesthetics of place in late 19th century Montmartre', in *Cultural Geographies*, 19 (2), pp. 217–235.

Broadway World (2015) 'Broadway Grosses – Week Ending 8/2/2015', http://www.broadwayworld.com/grosses.cfm?sortby=topticket&orderby=desc, accessed 9 August 2015.

Brook, P. (1968) *The Empty Space* (Cambridge, MA: Athenaeum).

Brown Council (2014) 'Brown Council interviewed by J. Price', email correspondence, 18 August 2014.

Browne, E.M. (1953) 'The British Drama League', in *Educational Theatre Journal*, October, pp. 203–206.

Bulson, E. (2013) 'Modernisms High and Low', in J.M. Rabaté (ed.) *A Handbook of Modernist Studies* (Chichester: Wiley-Blackwell), pp. 55–73.

Bürger, P. (1984) *Theory of the Avant-Garde*, trans. M. Shaw (Minneapolis, MN: University of Minnesota Press).

Calandra, D. (2003) 'Karl Valentin and Bertolt Brecht', in J. Schechter (ed.) *Popular Theatre: A Sourcebook* (London and New York: Routledge), pp. 189–201.

Callander, E. & Price, H. (2012) 'Theatre Uncut: Our Story', http://www.theatreuncut.com/our-story, accessed 14 March 2014.

Case, S.E. (1996) *Split Britches* (London: Routledge).

Cate, P.D. (1996) 'The Spirit of Montmartre', in P.D. Cate & M. Shaw (eds.) *The Spirit of Montmartre: Cabarets, Humor and the Avant-Garde* (New Brunswick, NJ: Rutgers University Press), pp. 1–92.

Casson, J.W. (2000) 'Living Newspaper: Theatre and Therapy', in *The Drama Review*, 44 (2), pp. 107–122.

Church, D. (1985) 'Activist Theatre in Minority Agricultural Milieux: California's El Teatro Campesino and Provence's Lo Teatre de la Carriera', in P.M. Hopkins & W.M. Aycock (eds.) *Myths and Realities of Contemporary French Theatre: Comparative Views* (Lubbock, TX: Texas Tech Press), pp. 57–70.

Cirque du Soleil (2013) 'Press Release: Cirque due Soleil Return to Spain with *Alegria*', http://www.cirquedusoleil.com/en/press/2013/alegria-in-spain-general-on-sale.aspx, accessed 14 June 2013.

Cirque du Soleil (2014a) 'About Us: At a glance', http://www.cirquedusoleil.com/en/home/about-us/at-a-glance.aspx, accessed 22 October 2014.

Cirque du Soleil (2014b) '*Kooza*: About the Show', http://www.cirquedusoleil.com/en/shows/kooza/show/about.aspx, accessed 13 October 2014.

Clayton, J.D. (1993) *Pierrot in Petrograd: Commedia Dell'Arte/Balagan in Twentieth-Century Russian Theatre and Drama* (Montreal: McGill-Queens University Press).

Cosgrove, S. (1980) 'Prolet-Buehne: Agit-prop in America', in D. Bradby, L. James & B. Sharratt (eds.) *Performance and Politics in Popular Drama* (Cambridge: Cambridge University Press), pp. 201–212.

———— (1985) 'From Shock Troupe to Group Theatre', in R. Samuel, E. MacColl & S. Cosgrove (eds.) *Theatres of the Left 1880–1935: Workers' Theatre Movements in Britain and America* (London: Routledge and Kegan Paul), pp. 259–279.

Cowie, J. (2008) 'Introduction: The Conservative Turn in Postwar United States Working-Class History', in *International Labor and Working-Class History*, 74, pp. 70–75.

Craig, E.G. (1978) 'The Actor and the Über-Marionette', in *Gordon Craig on Movement and Dance* (London: Dance Books), pp. 37–57.

Cros, C. (1987) 'The Song of the "Salt Herring"' in H.B. Segal, *Turn-of-the-century Cabaret*, trans. A. Allais (New York: Columbia University Press), p. 9.

Cruz, C.A. (2014) 'Contemporary Circus Dramaturgy: An Interview with Louis Patrick Leroux', in *Theatre Topics*, 24 (3), pp. 269–273.

Curtis, J. (1990) 'Down with the Foxtrot! Concepts of Satire in the Soviet Theatre in the 1920s', in R. Russell & A. Barratt (eds.) *Russian Theatre in the Age of Modernism* (Basingstoke: Palgrave Macmillan), pp. 219–235.

Cushion, S. (2012) *Television Journalism* (London: Sage Publications).

Damian, D. (2013) 'An Interview with Stacy Makishi', *Exeunt Magazine*, http://www.exeuntmagazine.com/features/an-interview-with-stacy-makishi/, accessed 31 August 2014.

Davies, C. (2000) *The Volksbühne Movement: A History* (Amsterdam: Harwood Academic Publishers).

_____ (2013) *The Plays of Ernst Toller: A Revaluation* (London: Routledge).

Davis, R. (1975) *The San Francisco Mime Troupe: The First Ten Years* (Palo Alto, CA: Rampart Press).

Davy, K. (2011) *Lady Dicks and Lesbian Brothers: Staging the Unimaginable at the WOW Café Theatre* (Ann Arbor, MI: University of Michigan Press).

Deák, F. (1973) 'Blue Blouse', in *The Drama Review*, 17 (1), pp. 35–46.

_____ (1975) 'Russian Mass Spectacles', in *The Drama Review*, 19 (2), pp. 7–22.

Debord, G. (1992) *Society of the Spectacle* (London: Rebel Press).

DeDomenici, R. (2007) *Cable-Tie*, http://www.youtube.com/watch?v=Q3t1gU7YCFg, accessed 5 January 2012.

_____ (2010) *DeDomenici: Unattended Baggage Berlin*, http://www.youtube.com/watch?v=ycYISc1bENk, accessed 5 January 2012.

_____ (2012) *Popaganda*, dir. R. DeDomenici, The Basement, Brighton, 11 October 2012.

Dennison, G. (1970) 'Fire', in *The Drama Review*, 14 (3), pp. 36–43.

Diderot, D. (2011 [1757]) *Revue Secousse*, http://www.revue-secousse.fr/Secousse-04/Auxdepens/Sks04-Diderot-Fils_naturel.pdf, accessed 23 July 2013.

Dixon, R. (2012) 'Red Ladder's Rod Dixon interviewed by J. Price', Leeds, UK, 3 February 2012.

Dolan, J. (2010) *Theatre & Sexuality* (Basingstoke: Palgrave Macmillan).

Drain, R. (1995) 'Blue Blouse', in R. Drain (ed.), *Twentieth-Century Theatre: A Sourcebook* (London: Routledge), p. 183.

Duberman, M. (2009) *Black Mountain: An Exploration in Community* (Evanston: Northwestern University Press).

Edsall, T. (2012) 'Canaries in the Coal Mine', *The New York Times*, http://campaignstops.blogs.nytimes.com/2012/06/17/canaries-in-the-coal-mine/?_r=0, accessed 23 July 2015.

Eisenstein, S (1995 [1923]) 'The Montage of Attractions', in R. Drain (ed.) *Twentieth-Century Theatre: A Sourcebook* (London: Routledge), pp. 88–91.

Eruli, B. (2012) 'The Use of Puppetry and The Theatre of Objects in the Performing Arts of Today', in P. Francis (ed.) *Puppetry: A Reader in Theatre Practice* (Basingstoke: Palgrave Macmillan), pp. 141–144.

Erven, E. (1988) *Radical People's Theatre* (Bloomington, IA: Indiana University Press).

Evans, G. & Tilley, J. (2015) 'The New Class War: Excluding the Working Class in 21st-Century Britain', in *Juncture*, 21 (4), pp. 298–304.

Fabre, G. (1983) 'The Free Southern Theatre, 1963–1979', in *Black American Literature Forum*, 17 (2), pp. 55–59.

Farrell, J. (1989) 'Dario Fo - Zanni and Guillare', in C. Cairns (ed.), *The Commedia Dell'Arte: from the Renaissance to Dario Fo* (Lewiston, NY: Edwin Mellon Press), pp. 315–328.

Fiske, J. (1989) *Understanding Popular Culture* (Boston, MA: Unwin Hyman).

Forgács, E. (1995) *The Bauhaus Idea and Bauhaus Politics*, trans. J. Batki (London: Central European University Press).

Fox, J. (2002) *Eyes on Stalks* (London: Methuen).

_____ (2005) *Whose Culture?*, http://www.welfare-state.org/pages/resources/resources.htm, accessed 3 March 2012.

Francis, P. (2012) *Puppetry: A Reader in Theatre Practice* (Basingstoke: Palgrave Macmillan).

Frank, T. (2004) *What's the Matter with Kansas?* (New York: Henry Holt and Co.).

Gamble, B. (2014) 'Meet the Family: An Interview with Ali', http://www.nofitstate.org/blog/admin/meet-the-family-interview-ali, accessed 5 May 2015.

Gardner, L. (2001) 'First Night', *The Guardian*, http://www.theguardian.com/stage/2001/oct/02/theatre.artsfeatures, accessed 24 September 2014.

Gay Liberation Front (1973) 'What is Action?' in *Gay Pride Week Programme of Events*, photocopied leaflet, Gay Liberation Front Papers, The Keep, Brighton.

Geldern, J. (1993) *Bolshevik Festivals, 1917–1920* (Berkeley, CA: University of California Press).

Germani, I. (2006) 'Staging Battles: Representations of the War in the Theatre and Festivals of the French Revolution', in *European Review of History*, 12 (3), pp. 203–227.

Goldberg, R. (2001) *Performance Art: From Futurism to the Present* (London: Thames and Hudson).

Goldstein, R.J. (2010) 'Labor History Symposium: Political Repression of the American Labor Movement During its Formative Years – A Comparative Perspective', in *Labor History*, 51 (2), pp. 271–293.

Gorchakov, N. (1957) *The Theatre in Soviet Russia*, trans. E. Lehrman (New York: Columbia University Press).

Gordon, M. (1974) 'Meyerhold's Biomechanics', in *The Drama Review*, 18 (3), pp. 73–88.

Gorelik, M. (1932) 'Scenery: The Visual Attack', in *Workers' Theatre*, March, n.p..

Gramsci, A. (1971) *Selections from Prison Notebooks*, trans. Q. Hoare & G. Nowell-Smith (London: Lawrence and Wishart).

Gropius, W. (1919) *Manifesto of the Staatliches Bauhaus in Weimar*, http://bauhaus-online.de/en/atlas/das-bauhaus/idee/manifest, accessed 23 April 2014.

_____ (1961) *The Theatre of the Bauhaus*, trans. A.S. Wensinger (Middletown, CT: Wesleyan University Press).

Hall, S. (2009) 'Notes on Deconstructing the Popular', in J. Storey (ed.) *Cultural Theory and Popular Culture: A Reader*, 4th edn (Harlow, UK: Pearson Longman), pp. 508–518.

Hall, S. & Whannel, P. (1964) *The Popular Arts* (London: Hutchinson).

Heynen, R. (2015) *Degeneration and Revolution: Radical Cultural Politics in the Body in Weimar Germany* (Leiden, Netherlands: Brill Publishers).

Himelstein, M. (1963) *Drama Was a Weapon: The Left-Wing Theatre In New York 1929–1941* (New Brunswick, NJ: Rutgers University Press).

Holdsworth, N. (1997) 'Good Nights Out: Activating the Audience with 7:84 (England)', in *New Theatre Quarterly*, 13 (49), pp. 29–40.

Hood, S. (1987) 'Introduction: The Theatre of Dario Fo and Franca Rame', in D. Fo, *Can't Pay? Won't Pay!* (London: Methuen).

Houchen, J. (2003) 'The Origins of the Cabaret Artistique' in J. Schechter (ed.), *Popular Theatre: A Sourcebook* (London: Routledge), pp. 180–188.

Hutcheon, L. (1989) *The Politics of Postmodernism* (London: Routledge).

Hutchinson, Y. (1994) 'Masks Today: Mediators of a Complex Reality', in *South African Theatre Journal*, 8 (1), pp. 45–62.

Innes, C. (1972) *Erwin Piscator's Political Theatre: The Development of Modern German Drama* (Cambridge: Cambridge University Press).

Jameson, F. (1984) 'Postmodernism, or The Cultural Logic of Late Capitalism', in *New Left Review*, July–August, pp. 53–92.

Jaspers, A. (2011) 'Brown Council: Critical Comedy', in *Runway* (18), pp. 14–17.

Johnstone, R. & Meecham, T. (2013) 'Tristan Meecham: An Interview', *Time Out Melbourne*, http://www.au.timeout.com/melbourne/art/features/3184/tristan-meecham-interview, accessed 12 July 2014.

Jones, O. (2011) *Chavs: The Demonization of the Working Class* (London: Verso).

Kantor, T. (1993) *A Journey Through Other Spaces: Essays and Manifestos, 1944–1990*, M. Kobialka (ed.) (Berkeley, CA: University of California Press).

Kershaw, B. (1992) *The Politics of Performance: Radical Theatre as Cultural Intervention* (London: Routledge).

_____ (1999) *The Radical in Performance: Between Brecht and Baudrillard* (London: Routledge).

Klee, A. (2006) 'Felix Klee and the Puppet Theatre', in Z.P. Klee (ed.) *Paul Klee: Hand Puppets* (Berlin: Hatje Cantz), pp. 39–42.

Kleiman, G. & Makishi S. (2011) 'Stacy Makishi: Real and Fake', http://www.bellyflopmag.com/interviews/stacy-makishi-real-and-fake, accessed 4 July 2014.

Kleist, H. (2012) 'On the Marionette Theatre', in P. Francis (ed.) *Puppetry: A Reader in Theatre Practice* (Basingstoke: Palgrave Macmillan), pp. 121–125.

Koss, J. (2003) 'Bauhaus Theater of Human Dolls', in *The Art Bulletin*, 85 (4), pp. 724–745.

_____ (2014) 'Facing Design', in M. Sundell (ed.) *Xanti Schawinsky: Head Drawings and Faces of War* (New York: The Drawing Centre), pp. 10–43.

Kourilsky, F. (1974) 'Peter Schumann's Bread and Puppet Theatre', in *The Drama Review*, 18 (1), pp. 104–109.

Kurlansky, M. (2005) *1968: The Year That Rocked the World* (London: Vintage).

Leach, R. (1994) *Revolutionary Theatre* (London and New York: Routledge).

Leavis, F. (2006 [1933]) 'Mass Civilisation and Minority Culture', in J. Store y (ed.), *Cultural Theory and Popular Culture: A Reader*, 4th edn (Harlow, UK: Pearson Longman).

Lenin, V. (1919) 'First Congress of the Communist International', http://www.marxists.org/archive/Lenin/works/1919/mar/comintern.htm, accessed 29 October 2013.

_____ (2008) 'On Proletarian Culture', in *Lenin on Literature and Art* (Rockville, MD: Wildside Press), pp. 141–142.

Loffe, D. & White, F. H. (2012) *The Russian Avant-Garde and Radical Modernism* (Boston, MA: Academic Studies Press).

Lo Teatre de la Carriera (1975) *La Pastorale de Fos* (Paris: Pierre Jean Oswald).

_____ (1980) *L'ecrit des Femmes: Paroles de Femmes de Pays d'Orc* (Paris: Solin Editions).

Lynd, S. (1969) 'The New Left', in *Annals of the American Academy of Political and Social Science*, 382, pp. 64–72.

Lyotard, J. (1984 [1979]) *The Postmodern Condition: A Report on Knowledge* (Manchester: Manchester University Press).

MacColl, E. (1985) 'Some origins of Theatre Workshop: Narrative', in R. Samuel, E. MacColl & S. Crosgrove (eds.), *Theatres of the Left 1880–1935: Workers' Theatre Movements in Britain and American* (London: Routledge & Kegan Paul), pp. 205–255.

Macdonald, D. (1953) 'A Theory of Mass Culture', in *Diogenes*, 1 (1), pp. 1–17.

MacLennan, E. (1990) *The Moon Belongs to Everyone: Making Theatre with 7:84* (London: Methuen).

Maeterlinck, M. (1909) *The Tragical in Daily Life*, http://www.unz.org/Pub/MaeterlinckMaurice-1909v03-00095, accessed 3 August 2014.

Mally, L. (1990) *Culture of the Future: The Proletkult Movement in Revolutionary Russia* (Berkeley, CA: University of California Press).

_____ (2003) 'Exporting Soviet Culture: The Case of Agitprop Theatre', in *Slavic Review*, 62 (2), pp. 324–342.

Mandel, E. (1979) *Late Capitalism* (London: Humanities Press).

Mann, C. (1985 [1933]) 'How to produce Meerut', in R. Samuel, E. MacColl & S. Cosgrove (eds.) *Theatres of the Left 1880–1935: Workers' Theatre in Britain and America* (London: Routledge & Kegan Paul), pp. 106–108.

Mannucci, E.J. (2004) 'Revolution and the Last Judgement', in *Quaderni Online*, http://www.library.vanderbilt.edu/Quaderno/Quaderno2/Q2.C13.mannucci.pdf, accessed 3 August 2014.

Marcuse, H. (1964) *One Dimensional Man* (London: Sphere).

Marinetti, F.T. (1971a) 'Dynamic and Synoptic Declamation', in R. Flint (ed.) *Marinetti: Selected Writings*, trans. R. Flint & A.A. Coppotelli (London: Secker & Warburg), pp. 142–147.

_____ (1971b) 'The Founding Manifesto of Futurism', in R. Flint (ed.) *Marinetti: Selected Writings*, trans. R. Flint & A.A. Coppotelli (London: Secker & Warburg), pp. 39–44.

_____ (1971c) 'The Pleasure of Being Booed', in R. Flint (ed.) *Marinetti: Selected Writings*, trans. R. Flint & A.A. Coppotelli (London: Secker & Warburg), pp. 113–115.

_____ (1971d) 'The Variety Theatre', in R. Flint (ed.) *Marinetti: Selected Writings*, trans. R. Flint & A.A. Coppotelli (London: Secker & Warburg), pp. 116–122.

Martin, B.D. (2004) *The Theatre Is in the Street: Politics and Performance in Sixties America* (Amherst and Boston, MA: University of Massachusetts Press).

Mason, L. (2013) 'Red Ladder', in *Unfinished Histories*, http://www.unfinishedhistories.com/history/companies/red-ladder-3, accessed 31 August 2014.

Mason, S.V. (2005) *The San Francisco Mime Troupe Reader* (Ann Arbor, MI: University of Michigan Press).

Marx, K.A. (2000) 'The Communist Manifesto', in D. McLellan (ed.) *Karl Marx: Selected Writings*, 2nd edn (Oxford: Oxford University Press), pp. 245–272.

Matsuda, M.K. (2001) 'Plays Without People', in L. Jessup (ed.) *Antimodernism and Artistic Experience: Policing the boundaries of modernity* (London: University of Toronto Press), pp. 192–205.

Mayer, D. (1977) 'Towards a Definition of the Popular', in D. Mayer & K. Richards (eds.) *Western Popular Theatre* (London: Methuen), pp. 257–277.

McDermott, D. (1965) 'The Theatre Nobody Knows: Workers' Theatre in America, 1926–1942', in *Theatre Survey*, 6 (1), pp. 65–82.

McDermott, D. (1966) 'Agitprop: Production Practice in the Workers' Theatre, 1932–42', in *Theatre Survey*, 7 (2), pp. 115–124.

McGrath, J. (1981) *A Good Night Out* (London: Methuen).

_____ (1990) *The Bone Won't Break: On Theatre and Hope in Hard Times* (London: Methuen).

McVeigh, T. & Gibson, O. (2012) 'London 2012: Danny Boyle Thrills Audiences with Inventive Olympics Opening Ceremony', *The Guardian*, http://www.theguardian.com/sport/2012/July/28/London-2012-boyle-olympics-opening-ceremony, accessed 13 August 2013.

Meecham, T. (2014) 'Tristan Meecham interviewed by J. Price', London, 31 July 2014.

_____ (2015) 'Fun Run in Ansan', personal email correspondence, 11 May 2015.

Merkin, R. (1994) *Popular Theatres? Papers from the Popular Theatre Conference* (Liverpool: John Moores University).

Meyerhold, V. (1988a) 'On the Contemporary Theatre', in E. Braun (ed.) *Meyerhold on Theatre* (London: Methuen Drama), pp. 167–169.

_____ (1988b) 'The Fairground Booth', in E. Braun (ed.), *Meyerhold on Theatre* (London: Methuen), pp. 119–142.

Montaigne, M. (1967) *The Essays of Michael Lord of Montaigne*, Vol. III, trans. J. Florio (New York: AMS Press).

Moody, C. (1978) 'Vsevolod Meyerhold and the "Commedia dell'Arte"', in *The Modern Language Review*, 73 (4), pp. 859–869.

Moss, J. (1987) 'Women's Theatre in France', in *Signs*, 12 (3), pp. 548–567.

Moss, T. (2010) 'The Making of Faulty Optic's Dead Wedding: Inertia, Chaos and Adaptation', in A. Mermikides & J. Smart (eds.) *Devising in Process* (Basingstoke: Palgrave Macmillan), pp. 74–91.

Mueller, R. (1994) 'Learning for a New Society: The *Lehrstück*', in P. Thomson & G. Sacks (eds.) *The Cambridge Companion to Brecht* (Cambridge: Cambridge University Press), pp. 79–95.

Muñoz, J. (1999) *Disidentifications: Queers of Color and the Performance of Politics* (Minneapolis, MN: University of Minnesota Press).

Mumford, M. (2009) *Bertolt Brecht* (London and New York: Routledge).

National Workers' Theatre Conference (1985 [1932]) 'First National Workers Theatre Conference', in R. Samuel, E. MacColl & S. Cosgrove (eds.) *Theatres of the Left 1880–1935: Workers' Theatre in Britain and America* (London: Routledge & Kegan Paul), pp. 280–285.

Nye, E. (2014) 'Jean-Gaspard Deburau: Romantic Pierrot', in *New Theatre Quarterly*, 30 (2), pp. 107–119.

O'Dell, K. (1998) *Contact with the Skin: Masochism, Performance Art and the 1970s* (Minneapolis, MN: University of Minneapolis Press).

O'Neal, J. (1968) 'Motion in the Ocean: Some Political Dimensions of the Free Southern Theatre', in *The Drama Review*, 12 (4), pp. 70–77.

Odets, C. (1985 [1935]) 'Waiting for Lefty', in R. Samuel, E. MacColl & S. Cosgrove (eds.) *Theatres of the Left 1880–1935: Workers' Theatre in Britain and America* (London: Routledge & Kegan Paul), pp. 323–352.

Orenstein, C. (1998) *Festive Revolutions: The Politics of Popular Theatre and the San Francisco Mime Troupe* (Jackson, MS: University of Mississippi Press).

Oxford English Dictionary (n.d.) 'Popular', http://www.oed.com/view/Entry/1 47908?redirectedFrom=Popular#eid, accessed 13 August 2013.

Ozouf, M. (1988) *Festivals and the French Revolution* (Cambridge, MA: Harvard University Press).

Pal, S. (2010) 'Theatre and Activism: The Agitprop Theatre Way', in *Music and Art in Action*, 3 (1), pp. 48–64.

Papa, L. (2009) *Staged Action: Six Plays from the American Workers' Theatre* (Ithaca, NY: ILR Press).

Peacock, L. (2009) *Serious Play: Modern Clown Performance* (Bristol, UK: Intellect Books).

Piscator, E. (1980 [1963]) *The Political Theatre* (London: Eyre Methuen).

Posener, J. (1987) 'Any Woman Can', in J. Davis (ed.) *Lesbian Plays* (London: Metheun), pp. 13–25.

Priestland, D. (2009) *The Red Flag: A History of Communism* (New York: Grove Press).

Prolet-Buehne (1980 [1930]) 'Tempo, Tempo', in D. Bradby, L. James & B. Sharratt (eds.) *Performance and Politics in Popular Drama*, trans. B. Stern (Cambridge: Cambridge University Press), pp. 315–318.

Richter, H. (1965) *Dada: Art and Anti-Art* (London: Thames and Hudson).

Robinson, L. (2007) *Gay Men and the Left in Britain: How the Personal Got Political* (Manchester: Manchester University Press).

Rolland, R. (1918) *The People's Theatre*, trans. B.H. Clark (New York: Henry Holt and Company).

Rorrison, H. (1980) 'Introduction to Chapter 3', in E. Piscator, *The Political Theatre* (London: Eyre London), pp. 37–41.

Rousseau, J. (1960 [1758]) *Politics and the Arts: Letter to M. D'Alembert on the Theatre*, trans. A. Bloom (Ithaca, NY: Cornell University Press).

Samuel, R. (1980) 'Workers' Theatre 1926–36', in D. Bradby, L. James, and B. Sharratt (eds.), *Performance and Politics in Popular Drama* (Cambridge: Cambridge University Press), pp. 213–230.

_____ (1985) 'Theatre and Socialism in Britain' in R. Samuel, E. MacColl & S. Cosgrove (eds.) *Theatres of the Left 1880–1935: Workers' Theatre in Britain and America* (London: Routledge & Kegan Paul), pp. 3–73.

Samuel, R. and Thomas, T. (1977) 'Documents and Texts from the Workers' Theatre Movement (1928–1936)', in *History Workshop*, 1 (4), pp. 102–142.

Sandle, M. (2012) *Communism* (Harlow, UK: Pearson Education Limited).

San Francisco Mime Troupe (1966) 'A Minstrel Show, Or: Civil Rights in a Cracker Barrel', performance programme, personal collection.

Saville, I. (1990) *Ideas, Forms and Developments in the British Workers' Theatre, 1925–1935*, PhD Thesis (London: The City University).

Saxe, A. (1985 [1934]) 'Newsboy: from Script to Performance', in R. Samuel, E. MacColl & S. Cosgrove (eds.), *Theatres of the Left 1880–1935: Workers' Theatre Movements in Britain and America* (London: Routledge & Kegan Paul), pp. 289–296.

Sayler, O.M. (1922) *The Russian Theatre* (New York: Brentano's Publishers).

Schawinsky, X. (1971a) 'From the Bauhaus to Black Mountain College', in *The Drama Review*, 15 (3), pp. 30–44.

_____ (1971b) 'Spectodrama: Play, Life, Illusion', in *The Drama Review*, 15 (3), pp. 45–59.

Schechter, J. (1985) *Durov's Pig: Clowns, Politics and Theatre* (New York: Theatre Communications Group).

_____ (2003) *Popular Theatre: A Sourcebook* (London: Routledge), pp. 35–39.

Schlemmer, O. (1961) 'Man and Art Figure', in W. Gropius (ed.) *The Theatre of the Bauhaus*, trans. A.S. Wensinger (Middletown, CT: Wesleyan University Press), pp. 17–46.

Schopenhauer, A. (1969) *The World as Will and Representation*, trans. E.F.J. Payne (Mineola, NY: Courier Dover Publications).

Scuderi, A. (1988) *Dario Fo and Popular Performance* (Toronto: Legas).

Segal, H.B. (1987) *Turn-of-the-century Cabaret* (New York: Columbia University Press).

Selwood, S., Muir, A. & Moody, D. (1995) 'Developing New Circus in the UK', in *Cultural Trends*, 7 (28), pp. 49–62.

Shiach, M. (1989) *Discourse on Popular Culture* (Cambridge: Polity Press).

Sibley, K. (1998) *The Cold War* (Santa Barbara, CA: Greenwood Press).

Sinfield, A. (1999) *Out on Stage: Lesbian and Gay Theatre in the Twentieth Century* (New Haven, CT: Yale University Press).

Skeat, W.W. (1911) *A Concise Etymological Dictionary of the English Language* (Oxford: The Clarendon Press).

Sontag, S. (2009 [1965]) 'One Culture and the New Sensibility', in *Against Interpretation* (London: Penguin Books), pp. 293–304.

Spigel, L. (1993) *Make Room for TV: Television and the Family Ideal in Postwar Britain* (Chicago: Chicago University Press).

Stiglitz, J.E. (2011) 'Of the 1%, by the 1%, for the 1%', *Vanity Fair*, http://www.vanityfair.com/news/2011/05/top-one-percent-201105, accessed 7 August 2015.

Storey, J. (2006) *Cultural Theory and Popular Culture: An Introduction*, 4th edn (Athens, GA: The University of Georgia Press).

Stourac, R. & McCreery, K. (1986) *Theatre as a Weapon: Workers' Theatre in the Soviet Union, Germany and Britain 1917–1934* (London: Routledge and Kegan Paul).

Sweeney, R.M. (2001) *Singing Our Way To Victory: French Cultural Politics and Music During the Great War* (Middletown, CT: Wesleyan University Press).

Tait, A. (1974) 'Lunacharsky, the "Poet-Commissar"', in *The Slavonic and East European Review*, 52 (127), pp. 234–251.

Tatchell, P. (2009) 'Celebrating 40 Years of Gay Liberation', *Polari Magazine*, http://www.polarimagazine.com/opinion/celebrating-40-years-of-gay-liberation/, accessed 17 November 2014.

Thomas, T. (1985a) 'A Propertyless Theatre for a Propertyless Class', in R. Samuel, E. MacColl & S. Cosgrove (eds.) *Theatres of the Left 1880–1935: Workers' Theatre in Britain and America* (London: Routledge & Kegan Paul), pp. 77–98.

_____ (1985b) 'The New Stage Group', in R. Samuel, E. MacColl & S. Cosgrove (eds.) *Theatres of the Left 1880–1935: Workers' Theatre in Britain and America* (London: Routledge & Kegan Paul), pp. 171–173.

_____ (1934) 'The Workers' Theatre in Britain', in *The International Theatre*, 1 (1), pp. 22–24.

Thomas, W. (1721 [1550]) 'Whether it be better for a Commonwealth that the power be in Nobility or in the Commonality', in J. Strype *Ecclesiastical Memorials*, Vol. II, pt. 2 (Oxford: Clarendon Press), pp. 372–377.

Thompson, E.P. (2009) 'Preface from The Making of the English Working Class', in J. Storey (ed.) *Cultural Theory and Popular Culture: A Reader* (Harlow, UK: Pearson Longman), pp. 41–44.

Toller, E. (1935) 'Transfiguration', in *Seven Plays by Ernest Toller* (London: John Lane The Bodley Head), pp. 59–106.

Tolstoy, V. (1998) 'Street Art of the Revolution', in J. Cohen-Cruz (ed.), *Radical Street Theatre* (London: Routledge), pp. 15–25.

Trimingham, M. (2007) *The Theatre of the Bauhaus: The Modern and Postmodern Stage of Oskar Schlemmer* (New York: Routledge).

Trueman, M. (2008) 'Exploring Existence: Tim Etchells', http://matttrueman .co.uk/2008/11/one-of-lifes-brighter-days.html, accessed 15 September 2015.

Vincent, A. (2014) 'The Truth Behind Fargo's "True Story"', *The Telegraph*, www.telegraph.co.uk/culture/tvandradio/10792814/The-truth-behind-Fargos-true-story.html, accessed 22 September 2014.

Walker, L., Kerrigan, S., Evans, N. & Wright, S. (2012) *Plucked. A True Fairytale.*, dir. L. Walker & N. Evans, Roundhouse Studio Theatre, London, 18 January 2012.

Whitford, F. (1984) *Bauhaus* (London: Thames and Hudson).

Whitney Museum of American Art (2013) *Rituals of Rented Island: Julia Heyward*, http://www.whitney.org/WatchAndListen/Exhibitions?play_id=894, accessed 9 October 2014.

Willett, J. (1986) *The Theatre of Erwin Piscator: Half a Century of Politics in the Theatre* (London: Methuen Drama).

_____ (1988) *The Theatre of the Weimar Republic* (New York and London: Holmes and Meier).

Williams, J. (2005) '"Circus with Heart": New Circus and NoFit State Circus', *Wales International Arts*, http://www.wai.org.uk/2070.file.dld, accessed 1 January 2014.

Williams, R. (1957) 'Working Class Culture', in *Universities and New Left Review*, 1 (2), pp. 29–32.

Wilson, M.L.J. (2001) 'Portrait of the Artist as a Louis XIII Chair', in G. Weisberg (ed.) *Montmartre and the Making of Mass Culture* (Piscataway, NJ: Rutgers University Press), pp. 180–204.

Workers' Laboratory Theatre (1985 [1934]) 'Newsboy', in R. Samuel, E. MacColl & S. Cosgrove (eds.) *Theatres of the Left 1880–1935: Workers' Theatre Movements in Britain and America* (London: Routledge & Kegan Paul), pp. 316–322.

Zabel, M.D. (1960) *The Art of Ruth Draper: Her Dramas and Characters* (London: Oxford University Press).

Zinn, H. (1968) 'Marxism and the New Left', in A. Young (ed.) *Dissent: Explorations in the History of American Radicalism* (Dekalb, IL: Northern Illinois University Press), pp. 355–372.

Zolotnitsky, D. (1995) 'The Mexican, as visualised by Sergei Eisenstein', in *Contemporary Theatre Review*, 4 (1), pp. 1–9.

Index